Crazy Useful Things

A Dictionary of Natural Resources and Their Products

(from the Past, in the Present, and for the Future)

ISBN 978-1-892619-13-6

Published by Crazy Useful, an imprint of Mutaneers Publishing
1011 University Village
Salt Lake City, UT 84108
www.crazyuseful.com

Printed in the United States of America
by CreateSpace

Cover image: *Passiflora cerulea*, from *Specimens of the plants and
fruits of the island of Cuba* by Anne Kingsbury Wollstonecraft
Courtesy of the Hathi Trust, www.hathitrust.org

TABLE OF CONTENTS

INTRODUCTION

This book began with this question: *what is gum Arabic, and where does it come from?* A quick trip to an online dictionary answered that question for me, but I realized that the real question in my mind was much bigger and would require much more work to answer:

How did people make what they needed and wanted, before synthetics and plastics?

What other kinds of crazy useful stuff is out there in nature?

How can we blend our knowledge of the past and present, to bring us into a more sustainable future?

The first book I found on the subject, which became the inspiration for this book, was *A Dictionary of Natural Resources and Their Principal Uses*, written by Nora Jackson and Philip Penn and published in 1969. In the introduction, the authors expressed confidence that this book (at just under 200 pages and with about 700 listings of animal, vegetable, and mineral) contained information on "every resource of economic importance in the world." When I actually began work on this project, my principal resource for information on plants became *World Economic Plants: A Standard Reference* (2nd Ed.), by John Wiersema and Blanca Leon. This book, published in 2013, has over 1300 pages and listings for over 12,000 plants — and it's still missing some. Many, many sources were consulted in the creation of this book—some huge, some no more than a few pages—and none contained the entire scope of the world of useful things.

I make no claim that this book you're holding is in any way comprehensive. It's not meant to be. My primary goal for this project was twofold: in part, I wanted to create in you, the reader, a sense of connection with the world around you—to look at the plants, animals, and the earth itself, with the knowledge that there was a time, before there were laboratories and factories turning out plastics and synthetics, everything you wanted and needed for your daily life would have come more or less directly from the plants animals and materials around you, made useful by skills and knowledge that were within the reach of pretty much the average person.

Secondly, I wanted to give you the opportunity to discover the interesting patterns that begin to emerge in the world of natural resources. For example: unusual (and mostly unheard-of) plant families that are surprisingly important; how wild-harvested (or hunted) species fare, versus those that are farmed or cultivated; the relatively "high-tech" uses of many minerals, versus other resources. There are many other patterns, and I hope that this book inspires you to explore them.

Because this book is not comprehensive, you will no doubt spot some gaps. You will ask yourself: why is *X* included, but not *Y*? Some explanation for the method of choosing is in order. For the most part, I have tried to include resources that have use and economic importance outside of a strictly local or homegrown setting. In addition, I have mostly excluded plants that are solely known as traditional herbal medicines (there are thousands of them, and they are better treated elsewhere). Finally, I have mostly excluded those things that are used strictly for ornamental purposes, including plants, animals (like the pelt animals), and minerals. Of course, there are some exceptions to all of these rules.

More than anything else, I hope you will find in this book inspiration from the crazy beauty and utility of your fellow inhabitants, sparks of joy that will move you to go deeper, learn more, explore further, and maybe even make things for yourself and others.

Enjoy this work: it was made for you, with love and hope for the future.

Heidi McDonald

Abaca   *Manila hemp*
Musa textilis

A species of plant in the banana (*Musaceae*) family, native to the
Philippines. The plant has been introduced to other tropical areas
such as Indonesia, India, and Central America, but the majority of
cultivation still takes place in the Philippines. It is cultivated for
the fiber (called abaca, or Manila hemp) obtained from the leaf
sheaths and leaf stems. The best abaca, which is classified as a
hard fiber (like coir and sisal), is one of the strongest and hardest
of fibers. Its resistance to salt water makes it valuable in the production of ropes and cables, and especially marine cordage and
hawsers. It is also used for making paper, hats and mats.

Abyssinian cabbage   *Abyssinian mustard, Ethiopian kale*
Brassica carinata

A species of perennial herb in the cabbage (*Brassicaceae*) family,
native to northeastern tropical Africa. Traditionally, it has been
cultivated in Ethiopia as a vegetable crop, a fodder crop, and an
oilseed crop. Currently, it is cultivated mainly as an oilseed crop,
and is being explored as a source of biofuel.

Acacia   *wattles*
Acacia spp.

A genus of thorny trees and shrubs of the *Mimosoideae* subfamily
of the pea (*Fabaceae*) family. This genus consists of many species
which are widely distributed throughout the tropical, subtropical, and warm temperate regions of the world, especially
Africa and Australia. The bark of many species is a rich source of
tannin, especially the Australian and South African wattles. Other
products derived from certain species include **gum arabic**, dye,
essential oils and cabinet woods.

Acai palm   *cabbage palm*
Euterpe oleracea

A species of tree in the palm (*Arecaceae*) family, native to the Amazon region of Brazil. It is cultivated primarily for its edible berry
(acai), which is also a source of oil used for cooking and cosmetics. The tree is also a source of **hearts of palm** (a vegetable). A
closely related species (*E. edulis*) also called the acai palm or jucara, is the primary source of hearts of palm.

Achiote tree
Bixa orellana
lipstick tree, annatto

A shrub or small tree in the *Bixaceae* family, native to the tropical regions of the Americas. It is primarily known and used for the production of **annatto**, an orange-red substance extracted from the arils that coat the seeds; it is used as food coloring and dye.

Ackee
Blighia sapida
ackee-apple

A species of evergreen tree in the soapberry (*Sapindaceae*) family, native to West Central and West Tropical Africa, but now also cultivated in other tropical regions, particularly the Caribbean. It is cultivated for its edible fruit, the ackee or ackee-apple. The ackee figures prominently in Jamaican cuisine, and is the national fruit of that country. Like other members of the soapberry family (including the lychee), the plant contains a compound that is toxic and potentially fatal to humans. The seed arils are the only edible part of the fruit; they can only be eaten when the fruit is fully ripened, and must be cooked prior to eating.

Adzuki bean
Vigna angularis

A species of annual vine in the pea (*Fabaceae*) family, native to the temperate regions of East Asia and the Indian continent. It is also now cultivated elsewhere in the world, notably Brazil and western South America. There are several cultivars; all are cultivated for their edible and highly nutritive bean. The beans are most often red, but some cultivars produce other colors such as black or mottled. The bean is most commonly prepared as a sweetened paste, but they are also eaten sprouted or boiled whole.

What's in a name?

In botanical taxonomy, the specific epithet (the second part of the official Latin name, coming after the genus name) often gives a clue about the plant's uses. For example: *methysticum* means "intoxicating"; *officinalis* means "having medicinal properties"; *esculenta* is "edible"; *oleracerus* are plants "used for a vegetable"; and *tinctoria* signifies a plant used for dyeing.

African oil palm
Elaeis guineensis   *macaw-fat*

A species of tree in the palm (*Arecaceae*) family, native to west and
southwest Africa, but now naturalized to and cultivated in many
countries in the tropical regions throughout the world. The tree
is cultivated for its fruit, which is the primary source of edible
palm oil. Since the mid-twentieth century, cultivation for palm
oil has rapidly expanded: in the early 1960's production was
about half a million tons per year; by 2018 it was at about 72 million tons per year. Palm oil is valued as one of the few supersatu-
rated vegetable oils and is used in a large number of food products. Palm kernel oil is a different product, derived from the seed
of the fruit; it is used as food and in the manufacture of soap. The
closely related American oil palm (*E. oleifera*) also produces palm
oil. Although it is not often commercially planted, it is used to
create hybrids with the African oil palm to improve certain characteristics such as disease resistance and productivity.

Agar-agar
Gracilaria spp.   *red algae*

A genus of red algae known primarily for the production of the
jelly-like substance called **agar**. It is also known as Japanese isin-
glass, Ceylon moss, and Jaffna moss. Agar has many uses, including: as a thickening agent for food and vegetarian substitute
for gelatin; as a solid substrate for culture media for microbiological work; as paper sizing; as a clarifying agent in brewing; and
medicinally as a laxative.

Agate
silicon dioxide

A variety of chalcedony quartz with striped or clouded coloring
which occurs mainly in association with volcanic rocks. Agates
are found in many parts of the world, but most are produced
commercially in India and the Americas. Due to its hardness,
resistance to corrosion, and ability to take and retain a high
polish, it is used to make mortars and pestles, leather burnishing
tools, and in precision balances. It is also widely used as a semi-
precious stone, as a small sculpture medium, and as an ornamental building material.

Agave

Agave spp.

maguey

Agave is a genus of flowering plants in the *Asparagaceae* family, native to the hot, arid regions of Mexico and the southwestern United States. Several species are cultivated for the production of sugar syrup that is used as a base for several types of fermented beverage, notably: the century plant (*A. americana)* and the pulque agave (*A. salmiana*) are used to make pulque, a beverage made from fermenting the sap; mezcal agave (*A. angustifolia*), among others, is used to make mezcal, a beverage made from the cooked hearts; blue agave or tequila agave (*A. tequilana*), is used to make tequila, a type of mezcal. In addition, many species are cultivated for their leaf fiber (see separate entries for sisal and henequen). In addition, the leaves, stems, and flowers have many traditional uses as food, medicine, and in the making of tools.

Ailanthus silkmoth

Samia cynthia ricini

eri silkmoth

A moth whose larvae produce the silk fiber known as eri **silk**. Its primary food source is the leaves of the castor plant (*Ricinus communis*), as well as of the genus *Alianthus* (tree of heaven). It is native to northeast India, parts of China, Japan, and Thailand. Eri silk is more durable than that produced by the mulberry silkworm (*Bombyx mori*), but has a more wooly texture.

Aji

see ***Chili pepper***

Ajowan

Trachyspermum ammi

bishop's weed, kummel, Ethiopian caraway

A species of annual herbaceous plant in the parsley (*Apiaceae*) family, native to the Near East and India. It is cultivated mainly in India and Iran, where its seed-like fruits are used as a culinary herb similar to caraway, cumin, and fennel. Steam-distillation of the fruits yields an essential oil.

Alabaster

A semi-transparent form of gypsum (hydrous sulfate of calcium) or calcite (calcium carbonate) that has an appearance similar to marble, but is softer. For millennia, it has been used for carving statues and ornaments, and as an ornamental building material.

Alexanders   *horse parsley, black lovage*
Smyrnium olusatrum

A species of herbaceous annual plant in the parsley (*Apiaceae*)
family, native to Europe. It was once widely cultivated for its
edible stems, very similar to celery but with a more bitter taste.
Today, it is grown mainly as an ornamental plant.

Alfalfa   *lucerne*
Medicago sativa subsp. sativa

A perennial plant of the pea (*Fabaceae*) family, native to Western
Asia but now widely naturalized to and cultivated in many of the
warmer temperate regions of the world. It is a highly nutritious
and quick-growing fodder crop in the form of pasturage, hay, or
silage. It has been cultivated in Europe since ancient Roman
times. Alfalfa sprouts are common ingredients in human food,
though the unsprouted seeds are toxic. The plant can withstand
heat and cold, and does well in regions susceptible to drought
because it has tap roots up to forty feet long which are able to
find moisture where many other plants could not.

Alkanet   *dyer's bugloss, orchanet*
Alkanna tinctoria

A species of plant in the borage (*Boraginaceae*) family, native to
North Africa, West Asia, Southeast and Southwest Europe, and
the Middle East. Since antiquity, it has been cultivated for the red
pigment (**alkanet**) extracted from its roots. The pigment is used
as a food dye, in varnishes, and in cosmetics.

Alligator pepper   see *Grains of Paradise*

Allspice   *Jamaica pepper, pimenta*
Pimenta dioica

A species of tree in the myrtle (*Myrtaceae*) family, native to the
Greater Antilles, southern Mexico, and Central America, but now
cultivated elsewhere in tropical regions. It is cultivated as the
source of allspice, made from the dried unripe berries. An essential oil is also distilled from the berries, which is used as a food
flavoring, in cosmetics, and soap. Allspice is closely related to the
bay-rum tree (*Pimenta racemosa*).

Almandine

see *Garnet*

Almond
Prunus dulcis

A species of tree in the rose (*Rosaceae*) family, and in the same genus (*Prunus*) as cherries, plums, apricots and peaches; it is most closely related to peaches, being in the same subgenus *Amygdalus*. It originated in western and middle Asia, but is now widely naturalized to and cultivated in many of the temperate regions of the world. It is cultivated for its nuts, which have many food uses. This species name refers to the edible sweet almond; the species variation (*Prunus dulcis* var. *amara*) produces an inedible bitter almond that is used only for its oil. Bitter almonds contain harmful levels of toxic cyanogenic glycosides, a trait shared with the seeds and leaves of many other species within the genus.

Aloe
Aloe spp.

A genus of flowering succulents in the *Asphodelaceae* family, native to southern and tropical Africa, Madagascar, Jordan, and the Arabian peninsula. Aloe has been naturalized to many other parts of the world. The most commonly cultivated species are: *A. vera* (true aloe), whose transparent mucilaginous sap is used in cosmetics as a skin moisturizer; *A. ferox* (bitter aloe) and *A. perryi* (Socotrine aloe), whose yellow latex contains **aloin**, which has been used medicinally as a laxative, though its use is somewhat controversial due to its potential toxicity.

Alpaca
Vicugna pacos

A domesticated camelid native to the high Andean regions of Peru and Chile. It is valued for its fleece, which grows up to two inches in length. It is closely related to the llama, the vicuna (thought to be its wild ancestor), and the guanaco. Alpaca cloth was originally made from alpaca wool, but the name is now also used to refer to cloth made from other fibers such as mohair and wool. Alpaca fiber is long, silky, and does not bear lanolin, which makes it hypoallergenic.

Aluminum

A metallic element, it is the third most common element (after oxygen and silica), and the most common metal, in the earth's crust. Alumina, its oxide, is the most abundant metallic oxide on the planet. The chief advantages of aluminum are its lightness and resistance to corrosion. It is relatively soft, but can be hardened by alloying with other minerals. The most common ore of aluminum is the mineral bauxite.

Alunite
hydrated aluminum potassium sulfate

A naturally-occurring mineral containing **alum**. Alum is a chemical compound that is a double sulfate salt of aluminum and either potassium, aluminum, or sodium. Alum by itself usually refers to potassium alum, which is widely used industrially to give permanency to dyes (a mordant), in tanning, in making paper and baking powders, to purify piped water, and as an astringent.

Amami-gum   *West Indian locust, Brazilian copal*
Hymenaea courbaril

A tree of the pea (*Fabaceae*) family, native to southern Mexico, through Central and South America. It is cultivated for several uses, including: its extremely hard wood; its edible fruit pulp, which was an important food source to the inhabitants of its native region; and its resin (called **anime**, due to the fact that it is usually full of insects), which is used for incense and varnish. The amami-gum is closely related to the Zanzibar copal (*Hymenaea verrucosa*), which produces a similar resin called **copal.**

Amber

A fossilized resin varying in color from yellow to brown, and sometimes containing inclusions of insects and other animal and plant material. It has the property of becoming charged with electricity when rubbed with a soft cloth. When heated above 200 deg. Celsius, amber decomposes to produce amber oil (used in perfumery), and amber pitch, which can be dissolved into turpentine or linseed oil to form amber varnish. Amber has been used as a gemstone since at least the Neolithic era, about 10,000 years ago.

Amboyna wood *Burmese rosewood, Malay padauk, narra*
Pterocarpus indicus

A large deciduous tree in the pea (*Fabaceae*) family, native to
southeastern Asia, northern Australasia, and the western Pacific
Islands. It is highly valued as a multi-use resource: the wood is a
termite-resistant rose-colored and scented hardwood; the tree
also produces a burlwood known as **amboyna wood** that is used
decoratively; the leaves have a history of use as traditional medicine; it also produces a useful resin. The tree is important in agro-
forestry as a nitrogen-fixing plant that helps to stabilize and ferti-
lize soil. In several regions, the tree is endangered due to overexploitation. The closely-related *P. macrocarpus*, native to Burma, is
widely known as rosewood and also produces amboyna wood.

American basswood see *Linden*

Amethyst

A transparent bluish-violet semi-precious stone that is a variety
of quartz. Its color is due to irradiation, iron impurities, and the
presence of trace elements. It is primarily used as a gemstone.

Anchovy
Engraulis spp.

Anchovy refers to a group of species of small forage fish in the
Engraulidae family. The six species that are commercially important are native to various locations around the world. They
are in the same taxonomic order (*Clupiformes*) as sardines and
herrings. They are valued as a food fish, being high in omega-3
fatty acids and vitamin D.

Andiroba *crabwood*
Carapa guianensis

A species of tree in the mahogany (*Meliaceae*) family, native to
South America. It is not cultivated, but is wild harvested, particularly in northern Brazil. It is valued for its wood, a hardwood
that resembles mahogany, and for the oil extracted from its seed,
known as **carap oil** or crab oil. Carap oil is used in soap making,
as an insect repellent, a wood protector, and as an ingredient in
the traditional medicine of the Amazon region.

Angelica   *angelique*
Angelica archangelica

The most commonly known and used species of the *Angelica* genus of herbs, within the parsley (*Apiaceae*) family, native to the temperate and subarctic regions of the Northern Hemisphere. It is used in cooking, with a flavor very different from its close relatives (parsley, fennel, anise, and caraway). It is the most commonly-used flavoring for gin. An essential oil is derived from the fruit and roots, which is used as a scent in perfumes and cosmetics, often as a replacement for animal-sourced musk. The stalks and shoots are eaten as a vegetable. Many other species within the genus have a history of medicinal use within their native regions, which span the temperate zones of the Northern Hemisphere. As a member of the *Apiaceae* family, careful identification is necessary, as it bears a strong resemblance to its highly toxic relatives, such as water hemlock.

Anhydrite
anhydrous calcium sulfate

A mineral found most frequently in evaporite deposits in association with the mineral gypsum, such as the salt mines in Austria (where it was discovered). It is important as a source of calcium, and also in the manufacture of fertilizer and sulfuric acid.

Anil   see *Indigo*

Anise   *sweet cumin, aniseed*
Pimpinella anisum

An herbaceous annual plant in the parsley (*Apiaceae*) family. Its origin is unknown, but is likely the eastern Mediterranean region or Southwest Asia. It is now widely naturalized to and cultivated in many temperate regions around the world. Its fruit (anise, or aniseed) is used as a spice flavoring, and for its essential oil. Its distinctive flavor is an important component in many traditional foods and liquors, such as Greek *ouzo* and Italian *sambuca*. It is similar in flavor to the unrelated star anise (*Illicium verum*). Other members of the genus, notably *P. major* (greater burnet-saxifrage) and *P. saxifraga* (burnet-saxifrage or lesser burnet) have a history of use in traditional medicine in Asia and Europe.

Antimony

A metallic element obtained mainly from the ores stibnite and antimonite. It is obtained as a byproduct of refining other metals. Its chief importance is as a hardening agent in the manufacture of alloys in combination with tin, copper, and especially lead.

Apatite

A group of phosphate minerals, whose primary use is as a source of phosphate in the manufacture of fertilizer. The green and blue varieties can be finely ground and used as dye. It is one of the few minerals that is produced and used by biological systems; for example, the form known as hydroxylapatite, is one of the major components of tooth enamel and bone material.

Apple
Malus pumila

A species of deciduous tree in the rose (*Rosaceae*) family of plants, and the most widely cultivated of the *Malus* genus. Other species of *Malus* are used to create hybrids and cultivars of domesticated apple. The apple tree originated in Central Asia, but is now the most widely cultivated fruit of the temperate zones. Apples have been domesticated and cultivated in Europe and Asia for thousands of years. Apples were introduced to the Americas by Spanish and English colonists in the 16th and 17th centuries. Today, there are at least 7500 known cultivars, most of which can be divided into three main groups: dessert apples, cooking apples, and cider apples. In addition, the hard, densely grained wood is used for tool handles and for general turnery.

Apricot
Prunus armeniaca

Apricots represent a group of about six species within the genus *Prunus*, which also contains peaches, almonds, cherries, and plums. Apricots are most closely related to plums, as both are in the subgenus *Prunus*. The exact region of origin is unknown, but is thought to be China or the Near East. Apricot trees are cultivated for their fruit, with *P. armeniaca* by far the most commonly cultivated species. The kernel (seed) of the apricot fruit contains the poisonous compound amygdalin, a cyanogenic glycoside that can cause cyanide poisoning if consumed.

Aquamarine

Aragonite
calcium carbonate

One of the two most common, naturally-occurring forms of calcium carbonate. It has been demonstrated to be effective in the removal of metals such as cadmium, zinc, cobalt, and lead from contaminated waste water.

Araroba
Vataireopsis araroba

A species of tree in the pea (*Fabaceae*) family, native to Brazil. The resin found in the heartwood of the tree has a history of use as a traditional medicine. The oxidized resin is ground into a powder known as araroba, Goa powder, or Bahia powder. It was used as a treatment for inflammatory skin diseases such as eczema and psoriasis.

Archil
orchella weeds

Roccella tinctoria

The most commonly-used of several species of lichen from which the substance **orcinol** is extracted, which is used to produce a variety of very fast dyes (that is, dyes that can be used without a mordant). These dyes include orcein, archil, orchil, and lacmus. It is also one of the ingredients in litmus dye, which is one of the earliest pH indicators, as it changes color based on the acidity of the solution to which it is exposed.

Argan tree
goat tree

Argania spinosa

A species of evergreen tree in the gutta-percha (*Sapotaceae*) family, native to Morocco. It is cultivated mainly there, and secondarily in Israel. It is grown primarily for the oil (*argan oil*) extracted from the fruit kernels. The oil has traditionally been used as a food, and as an ingredient in cosmetics, with the fruit pulp used as animal fodder. In the early part of the twenty-first century, the oil has rapidly gained in popularity as an ingredient in hair care products and other cosmetics.

Arjuna tree   *kumbuk*
Terminalia arjuna

A species of evergreen tree in the *Combretaceae* family, native to
south and central India. It is commercially important as one of
several species in the genus *Terminalia* whose leaves provide food
for the larvae of *Antheraea* moths, which produce Tassar silk, a
commercially important wild silk.

Arnica   *mountain tobacco*
Arnica spp.

A genus of several species in the sunflower family (*Asteraceae*),
native to the temperate (and more rarely Arctic) regions of North
America and Eurasia. Some species, notably *A. montana* and *A.
chamissonis*, contain the toxic compound helenalin, which has a
history of use as a traditional medicine. Arnica is also the name
of a tincture derived from the roots and leaves of the plants.

Arracacha   *Peruvian carrot, Peruvian parsnip*
Arracacia xanthorrhiza

An annual herbaceous plant in the parsley (*Apiaceae*) family, native to the western Andes, but now cultivated elsewhere in South
America and the Caribbean. It is a root vegetable, and an important commercial crop in South America, with nutritional value
and uses similar to the potato.

Arrowroot   *maranta*
Maranta arundinacea

A species of herbaceous perennial plant in the arrowroot
(*Marantaceae*) family whose exact native range is obscure, but is
likely the tropical regions of northern and southern Mexico and
South America. Archaeological evidence shows cultivation as
early as 8200 - 5600 B.C.E., making it one of the earliest cultivated
food crops in South America. It is now widely cultivated
throughout the tropics. It is cultivated for its rhizome, which is
processed into arrowroot flour, an easily-digestible starch that is
often used to feed infants, and others with dietary issues. Due to
its high viscosity, the starch is also used industrially in the manufacture of items such as cosmetics and glue. The fibrous material
remaining after starch extraction is used as feed for livestock.

Arsenic

A widely distributed element which occurs in metallic form in the ores of lead, silver, and nickel. It is a strong poison, and has been used in the making of weed killers, insecticides, wood preservatives, paint, and medicine. Most of these uses have been discontinued due to its toxicity. Today, it is primarily used in the manufacture of some metal alloys.

Arsenopyrite   *mispickel*
iron arsenic sulfide

A mineral that is the primary ore of arsenic. When heated, it produces poisonous arsenic and sulfur fumes.

Artichoke   *cardoon*
Cynara cardunculus

A species of herbaceous perennial thistle in the sunflower (*Asteraceae*) family, native to the Mediterranean region, but now naturalized to and cultivated in many other temperate regions. There are two main cultivar groups in the species: the artichoke (Scolymus Group), cultivated for the edible flower buds; and the cardoon (Cardoon Group), cultivated for its edible leaf stems.

Arugula   *garden rocket*
Eruca vesicaria subsp. sativa

A species of annual herbaceous plant in the cabbage (*Brassicaceae*) family, native to the Mediterranean region. It has been cultivated as a leafy vegetable at least since Roman times. It is now widely naturalized elsewhere in the world, and is cultivated as a salad green, and as fodder for animals.

Asafoetida   *devil's-dung*
Ferula assa-foetida

A perennial herbaceous plant in the parsley (*Apiaceae*) family, native to Iran and Afghanistan, and now naturalized to the Indian subcontinent. It is mainly cultivated for the latex extracted from its rhizome, which is used to manufacture asafoetida, a gum oleoresin that is used as a food flavoring and has a history of use as a traditional medicine.

Ash tree

The name given to a number of species of deciduous trees, not necessarily closely related, which grow in temperate climates. Some species yield hard, durable timber with a variety of uses.

Asparagus
Asparagus officinalis

A species of herbaceous perennial plant in the asparagus (*Asparagaceae*) family, native to the sandy soils of North Africa, western Asia, and Europe. It is now widely naturalized to and cultivated in many regions of the world. It is cultivated for its edible young shoots, which are eaten as a vegetable. The plant is mildly toxic when raw; cooking removes the toxicity.

Asparagus bean   see *Cowpea*

Aspen   *Quaking aspen*
Populus tremula, Populus tremuloides

Aspens are a variety of species in the genus *Populus* (which also includes the poplars and cottonwoods), within the willow (*Salicaceae*) family. Aspens are widespread, being native to cold climates with cool summers. The best-known species are *P. tremula* (European aspen) and *P. tremuloides* (American aspen). Aspens form large colonies of a single organism, which is enabled by their rhizomatic root structure. The Pando colony in Utah is believed to be the oldest living organism on Earth, with an estimated age of 80,000 years. Aspen is a fast growing and lightweight wood with low flammability and a resistance to rotting and warping. Shredded aspen wood is called **excelsior** (wood wool) and is used as a packing material.

Asphalt   *Bitumen, tar*

Naturally-occurring asphalt is a liquid or semi-solid form of petroleum, which has resulted from the partial evaporation of mineral oil. The best-known source is the pitch lake of Trinidad. Asphalt is used primarily as a sealer and waterproofing for things like roads and roofing material. Asphalt is also manufactured as a byproduct of the distillation of petroleum.

Australian blackwood   see *Acacia*

Autumn crocus
Colchicum autumnale

meadow saffron

A species of perennial herbaceous plant in the *Colchicaceae* family, native to Europe and West Asia. In spite of the common name, the plant is not closely related to the true crocus. Many species within the genus *Colchicum* are popularly grown as ornamentals; all species in the genus are poisonous, containing the toxic compound colchicine. *C. autumnale* is cultivated as a source of this compound, which is used pharmaceutically to treat gout, percarditis, and Familial Mediterranean Fever.

Avocado
Persea americana

Alligator pear

A species of evergreen tree in the laurel (*Lauraceae*) family, native to South Central Mexico and Central America, but now widely cultivated throughout the tropical and subtropical regions. It is cultivated for its edible fruit, the avocado, which is botanically classified as a berry. The leaves, bark, and pit of the fruit are toxic to animals.

Awapuhi
Zingiber zerumbet

Shampoo ginger

A species of perennial plant in the ginger (*Zingiberaceae*) family whose exact origin is unknown, but is now widely cultivated throughout the tropics. It was distributed across Polynesia by early Polynesian settlers, where it became an important crop. The leaves and rhizomes are used as a food flavoring and medicinally. The mucilage present in the mature flower heads is traditionally used directly as a shampoo or hair conditioner. Today, it is commonly used as an ingredient in commercial hair products.

Axlewood
Anogeissus latifolia

buttontree, dindiga-tree, ghattitree

A species of small flowering tree in the *Combretaceae* family, native to the India, Myanmar, Nepal, and Sri Lanka, but also found throughout tropical Asia. It is cultivated as a source of tannin (extracted from the leaves), and dye. The bark is a source of **ghatti gum,** which is used as a substitute for gum arabic. The tree is an important source of hardwood, firewood, charcoal, and cattle fodder in its native region.

Babassu palm
Attalea speciosa

A species of tree in the palm (*Arecaceae*) family, native to the Amazon region of South America. It is cultivated primarily for its seeds, which are pressed to produce babassu oil, used as food, in cosmetics, and as a potential biofuel. The flesh of the nut is dried and ground into flour; the shell is used to make charcoal; the leaves are used for thatch, basketry, and other woven items. Other species of the genus are also cultivated for their oil-rich seeds, including: the cohune palm (*A. cohune*), from southern Mexico and Central America; the piassava palm (*A. funifera*) from Brazil, also cultivated for its leaf fiber; and the maripa palm (*A. maripa*).

Bactrian camel
Camelus bactrianus

One of two domesticated species in the genus *Camelus* (the other being the dromedary), the bactrian camel is native to Central Asia. They have been used for centuries, primarily as extremely hardy pack animals. They are also a source of camel hair fiber, typically producing more fiber than the dromedary.

Baeltree
Bengal quince, golden apple
Aegle marmelos

A thorny tree in the citrus (*Rutaceae*) family, native to tropical south Asia, it is now cultivated in the tropical regions of south and southeast Asia. It is cultivated mainly for its edible fruit, the baelfruit. It is also a source of wood, gum resin, and essential oils. It is considered a sacred tree in the Hindu religion, as the residence of the goddess Lakshmi. Traditionally, unripe fruit has been dried and used for medicinal purposes. The leaves and bark contain compounds that can be toxic to humans.

Balata
Bulletwood, massaranduba
Manilkara bidentata

An evergreen tree in the gutta-percha (*Sapotaceae*) family, native to South and Central America, and the Caribbean. It is cultivated for its latex, which is nearly identical to gutta-percha, in that it is similar to rubber but inelastic. The wood is a durable hardwood known as bulletwood, that is so dense it does not float. Its fruit, like that of its relative the sapodilla (*Manilkara zapote*) is edible.

Balsa tree
Ochroma pyramidale

corkwood, downtree

Ochroma is a genus in the mallow (*Malvaceae*) family that contains a single species, the balsa tree. Balsa is a fast-growing tree native to tropical South America, but which is now naturalized to and cultivated in other tropical regions. The wood, also known as corkwood, is the lightest commercial wood. The soft silky hairs that cover the seeds are used for padding in cushions.

Balsam fir
Abies balsamea

A species of fir tree in the pine (*Pinaceae*) family, native to boreal North America. It is best known for its popularity as a Christmas tree, and for its resin, which is used to make the turpentine known as **Canada balsam**. The essential oil is used as fragrance, and as a rodent repellent. The wood is used in construction, and as pulp for paper manufacture.

Bambara groundnut
Vigna subterranea

Congo goober

A species of annual plant in the pea (*Fabaceae*) family, native to tropical Africa, but now cultivated in many tropical regions; it is particularly important in West Africa. It is closely related to the mung bean, adzuki bean, and cowpea. It is similar to the peanut, in that the flower head buries itself underground and then ripens into an edible seed. The plant can tolerate high temperatures and marginal soils where other legumes can't grow. This, along with its high nutritive value, makes it the third most important grain legume in semi-arid Africa.

Bamboo
Bambusoideae subfamily

A group of 115 genera and 1462 known species of evergreen perennial plants within the subfamily *Bambusoideae* of the grass family (*Poaceae*). Many species of bamboo are extremely fast-growing and are commercially valuable as a source of building material, food, and other uses. As a building material, bamboo has a higher specific compressive strength than wood, brick, or concrete, and a specific tensile strength that rivals steel.

Banana
Musa spp.

A genus of about thirty species of large herbaceous plants that are cultivated primarily for their fruit, a large berry, known as either "banana" (referring to varieties that are eaten raw, or "dessert" bananas) or "plantain" (the varieties used for cooking). Bananas and plantains are widely cultivated in tropical areas all over the world, and are among the world's most important food crops. There are more than a hundred varieties of the plant, with varying amounts of starch versus sugar, size, and color. However, nearly all modern cultivated bananas are the result of various hybrids of two banana species: *M. acuminata* and *M. balbisiana*. Dessert bananas have more genetic material from the former, plantains from the latter.

Banyan tree   *Bengal fig*
Ficus benghalensis

A species of large tree in the mulberry (*Moraceae*) family, native to the Indian subcontinent. The banyan is one of the largest trees in the world when measured by canopy coverage. One specimen in particular, known as Thimmamma Marrimanu, is in fact the largest canopy in the world, at nearly 5 acres in spread. The banyan is important in India, where it is the national tree, as a source of fruit (the banyan fig), wood, and for its religious significance. The tree is considered sacred within the Buddhist religion, as the tree under which the Kassapa Buddha achieved enlightenment.

Baobab tree   *dead rat tree, monkeybread tree*
Adansonia spp.

A genus of about eight species of deciduous trees in the mallow (*Malvaceae*) family, native to Madagascar, Africa, Arabia, and Australia. The edible pulp of the fruit is known as **monkey bread** or sour gourd. An edible oil can be extracted from the seed, and the meal remaining after extraction is used for animal fodder. The fibers of the inner bark of the trunk are used to make cloth, paper, and rope. Some species are a source of tannin, used for tanning leather. The most widespread species is *A. digitata*, native to the African savannah, but other species are also cultivated.

Barberry
Berberis vulgaris

A species of deciduous shrub in the *Berberidaceae* family, native to central and southern Europe, northwest Africa, and central Asia, but widely naturalized to other regions of Europe and North America. In former times, it was widely cultivated for its small, edible (though very sour) fruit, which is high in vitamin C. The plant is still cultivated today, particularly in Iran, but its thorny branches make harvesting on a large scale difficult. In addition, the plant is a host to a serious fungal disease that affects wheat production, so its cultivation is prohibited in some areas of the United States and Canada. The branches, leaves, and roots of the tree are toxic. Barberry is a source of berberine, a compound with a long history of use as a traditional medicine, that is being investigated as an antibiotic and other pharmaceutical uses.

Barley
Hordeum vulgare

Barley is a cereal grain of the grass (*Poaceae*) family, in the top five most important grains produced for human consumption. Native to the Fertile Crescent region of Asia, it was one of the first domesticated grains, with evidence of domestication dating back to at least 8500 BC. It is very similar to wheat, but its use is mostly as animal fodder and as a malted grain for use in the production of alcoholic beverages and various food items. There are at least a hundred common cultivars, each with various characteristics of disease resistance and productivity.

Barwood tree   *African kino, black camwood, madobia*
Pterocarpus erinaceus

A tree in the pea (*Fabaceae*) family, native to the Sahel region of Africa. In that region, it is an important source of firewood, woodworking material, animal fodder, and as a nitrogen-fixer for enriching farmland. It also produces a red gum (**kino**) that is used to make a red dye for leather and textiles. Although it is easily cultivated, it has not been widely cultivated but instead has mainly been wild harvested.

Basil
Ocimum spp.

A genus of annual or perennial aromatic herbs belonging to the mint (*Lamiaceae*) family. Native to tropical regions from central Africa to Southeast Asia, it is now widely cultivated throughout many regions of the world. Basil is mainly cultivated for the leaves, which are used as food flavoring, a vegetable, and as a source of essential oil. Most basils in culinary use are cultivars of *O. basilicum*, but there are a few other species and hybrids of those species also in common use, including: *O. x africanum* (lemon basil); *O. gratissimum* (clove basil); *O. kilimandscharicum* (camphor basil); *O. minimum* (Greek basil); and *O. tenuiflorum* (holy basil). The essential oil extracted from the leaves of several species is used in perfumery, and is reported to have insect-repellent, mosquito toxicity, and anti-fungal properties.

Bay laurel   *sweet bay, true laurel*
Laurus nobilis

A large evergreen shrub in the laurel (*Lauraceae*) family, native to the Mediterranean region, but now widely naturalized to and cultivated in other regions of the world. Its dried leaves are used as a flavoring, while the dried berries and essential oil of the leaves are used as a spice. Laurel oil is the main ingredient and distinguishing characteristic of Aleppo soap. In both ancient Greek and Roman culture, the laurel was the symbol of status, wealth, and victory. In Greece, the laurel wreath was used to crown the winner of the Pythian games (similar to the Olympic games, but for art and dance), and this practice is the source of modern terms "baccalaureate" and "poet laureate."

Bay rum tree   *West Indian bay*
Pimenta racemosa var. racemosa

A species of plant in the myrtle (*Myrtaceae*) family, native to the Caribbean region and still cultivated mainly there, although it has spread to other tropical regions, primarily in Oceania. The bay rum tree is closely related to allspice (*Pimenta dioica*). Its leaves are used as a flavoring in cooking. The distilled essential oil is toxic, but is used in perfumery. In the Caribbean, it is particularly used to produce a cologne called "bay rum," which is a mixture of rum and the essential oil.

Bean
Phaseolus vulgaris

A species of herbaceous annual plant in the pea (*Fabaceae*) family, native to the Americas but now extensively naturalized to and cultivated on every continent except Antarctica, for their edible seed pods and seeds (generally called "beans"). The plant is highly variable, and there are many cultivars that fall into general categories: dry beans (seeds that are harvested at complete maturity), such as navy beans, kidney beans, and pinto beans; snap beans (var. *vulgaris*, tender pods that are harvested before seed development phase), such as green beans. Common beans have high nutritional value for humans, and like most legumes, are nitrogen-fixing plants. They have a long history of cultivation in the Americas and were one of the Big Three food staples, along with maize and squash. Many varieties of the common bean contain a toxin (phytohaemagglutinin) that must be deactivated by proper cooking; it is especially present in kidney beans, which cannot be eaten raw. Minor uses include using the straw for fodder and eating the leaves as vegetables. In addition, bean leaves can be used to trap bedbugs, which will not walk on the leaves because of the presence of tiny hairs on them. Some cultures engage in the practice of favomancy, which is fortune-telling by "throwing the beans." Common beans are closely related to lima beans (*P. lunatus*) and scarlet runner beans (*P. coccineus*), both of which are also widely cultivated as food crops.

Bee
see *Honey Bee*

Beebalm
monarda, bergamot

Monarda spp.

Monarda is a genus of perennial herbaceous plants in the mint (*Lamiaceae*) family, native to North America. Several species have a long tradition of use by Native Americans as a medicinal herb. Crimson beebalm (*M. didyma*) is the natural source of the antiseptic compound **thymol**, which is the active ingredient in most commercial mouthwashes. It is also an important nectar source for honeybees. Lemon beebalm (*M. citriodora*) is cultivated for its essential oil, which contains the compound citronellol (the active ingredient in **citronella oil**), a natural insect repellent.

Beech tree
Fagus spp.

A genus of deciduous trees in the oak and beech family *Fagaceae*, native to temperate Europe, Asia, and North America. The European common beech (*F. sylvatica subsp. sylvatica*) is the most commonly cultivated. The species *F. grandifolia* (American beech) is the only species native to North America. Beech is a multipurpose tree: the wood is used as firewood, in construction, and is pulped to make the textile fiber **modal**; its nuts (**beechmast**) are used in Europe as animal fodder, primarily for pigs. The oil obtained from beechmast is suitable for fuel and cooking; in France it is sometimes used as a substitute for butter. Beechwood ash is used to make **bistre**, a brown pigment used to make ink.

Beet
Beta vulgaris subsp. vulgaris

A species of biennial plant in the amaranth (*Amaranthaceae*) family. It is presumed to have originated in the region around the Mediterranean, but it is now widely naturalized to and cultivated in many regions around the world. There are four main categories of cultivars within the species: the sugar beet, an important source of table sugar; the garden beet, cultivated as a root vegetable; the leaf vegetables chard and spinach beet; and mangel or mangelwurzel, an important fodder crop. In addition to these uses, the beet is being explored as a possible source of biofuel.

Bell pepper   see *Chili pepper*

Belladonna   *Deadly nightshade*
Atropa belladonna

A perennial herbaceous plant in the nightshade (*Solanaceae*) family, native to the temperate regions of Central and Southern Europe, North Africa, and the Fertile Crescent region. It is now naturalized to some parts of North America and is cultivated in many temperate regions. The plant has a long history of use as both a poison and a medicine. All parts of the plant are highly toxic, containing the alkaloids **atropine**, **hyoscine** (scopolamine), and **hyoscyamine** (daturine). All three compounds are important today for their medicinal value; atropine and hyoscine are on the World Health Organization's Model List of Essential Medicines.

Benzoin tree   *gum benjamin*
Styrax spp.

Styrax is a genus of over a hundred species of large shrubs or
small trees in the *Styracaceae* family, mostly native to temperate
and tropical regions of China and Southeast Asia. Several species
native to Java, Sumatra, and Thailand (*S. tonkinensis, S. benzoin,*
and *S. benzoides*) are cultivated for the balsamic resin known as
benzoin, or gum benjamin. Benzoin has been used since antiquity as an incense, perfume, flavoring, and in traditional medicine.

Bergamot orange
Citrus bergamia

A small deciduous tree in the citrus (*Rutaceae*) family whose
origin is obscure, but is probably a hybrid of lemon and bitter
orange. It is now cultivated almost exclusively in the Ionian Sea
coastal regions of Italy. It is cultivated for its fruit, which is used
primarily for its peel and for the essential oil (Bergamot) distilled
from the inside layer of the peel.

Beryl
beryllium aluminum silicate

This mineral is the chief source of the element beryllium. It
comes in a variety of colors and some of these are considered
semi-precious and precious gemstones; most notably, the sea-
green aquamarine and the brilliant green emerald. One of the
largest and most famous cut emeralds is the Mogul Mughal emerald at 218 carats, mined in Columbia in the 17th century, then cut
and sold to a noble of the Mughal Empire in India. Pure beryl is
colorless, and the first magnifying glasses and eyeglass lenses,
invented in the 1200's, were made from beryl and quartz crystals.

Beryllium

A silver-white metallic element that does not occur free in nature,
but only in the form of minerals. Its pure form is derived mainly
from the mineral beryl. It is a very hard, strong metal with a high
melting point. It is used for hardening copper and nickel alloys,
which are desirable in the aerospace industry. Tools made from
beryllium-copper alloys do not create sparks when striking steel.

Betel palm
Areca catechu

areca palm, catechu

This species of palm tree from the *Arecaceae* family is believed to be native to the Philippines, but is now widely naturalized throughout the Pacific Islands, Asia, and Africa. It is mainly cultivated for its fruit, the **betel nut** (also called areca nut). Betel nut is commonly chewed throughout South Asia, India, and Melanesia because of its effect as a stimulant. However, the fruit contains known carcinogens and carries other significant health risks. The fruits and seeds are also a source of tannin, while the leaves and fibers are also used to make items such as bowls and baskets.

Betony
Stachys officinalis

bishop's-wort

A species of herbaceous perennial plant in the mint (*Lamiaceae*) family, native to the temperate regions of North Africa, eastern Europe and Asia. Betony has a long history of cultivation in Europe as a traditional folk medicine. The plant contains organic compounds that give it potential use as an herbicide. A closely related species, *S. affinis* (the Chinese artichoke, knotroot, or crosne), is widely grown in temperate regions as a root vegetable.

Bilberry
Vaccinium myrtillus

whortleberry, blaeberry, whinberry

A low-growing shrub in the heather (*Ericaceae*) family, native to Europe. Its berries are very similar to North American blueberries (*V. corymbosum*), and are commonly wild-gathered and eaten across Great Britain and the Scandinavian countries. It is rarely cultivated, as it is difficult to grow and the proportion of fruit is small. It is a close relative of lingonberry (*V. vitis-idaea*), which is commercially cultivated. It is also an important nectar source for honeybees. In the past it was used as a dark blue to purple dye for wool, and as a source of tannin.

The Father of Modern Taxonomy

Carl von Linné, also known as Carl Linnaeus, was an 18th-century scientist who formalized the system of binomial nomenclature, or how we name living organisms in order to better understand the relationships among them.

Birch tree
Betula spp.

Betula is a genus of many species of deciduous trees in the *Betulaceae* family, which are widespread across the temperate and boreal climates of the Northern Hemisphere. The tree has many uses: it yields a strong hard timber; the bark is easily removed from fallen trees and is a lightweight flexible material. Birch oil can be rendered from the bark. Some species, particularly *B. lenta* (black birch or sweet birch), are a source of **wintergreen oil**. The silver birch (*B. pendula*) is traditionally important in the Northern European countries as a source of wood and fiber, and for its sugary sap and essential oil, which is used in traditional medicine.

Bismuth

A hard, brittle metallic element, almost as dense as lead, which is derived chiefly as a byproduct in the smelting of other metals. It is naturally diamagnetic, meaning that it is repelled by a magnetic field. Surface oxidation of the native metal gives it an iridescent sheen. It is mainly used for making medicines (e.g., bismuth subsalicylate, also known as Pepto-Bismol) and as a pigment in cosmetics. Due to its low melting point, it has also been used to produce alloys with low melting points, and as a substitute for lead in certain products.

Bitter vetch   *ervil*
Vicia ervilia

A species of herbaceous plant in the pea (*Fabaceae*) family, one of the most commonly grown of the ancient, and widely-cultivated genus *Vicia*, commonly known as the vetches. Bitter vetch was one of the earliest domesticated crops, with evidence for cultivation in the Near East dating to 7000 B.C. Its edible grains resemble lentils, to which it is closely related. In modern times, the vetches have largely fallen out of human use, but are commonly used (especially *V. sativa*) as a rich fodder for livestock. Bitter vetch is also closely related to the fava bean or broad bean (*V. faba*), which is also widely grown as a food and forage crop.

Black pepper
Piper nigrum

pepper, white pepper

A species of flowering vine in the pepper (*Piperaceae*) family, native to the Kerala region of India, where it is still intensively cultivated. It is also cultivated elsewhere in the tropics. The plant is grown for its fruit (the **peppercorn**), which is dried and ground for use as a spice. It is one of the oldest known spices, and is still the most widely traded spice in the world. There are three preparations of pepper spice: black pepper (cooked and dried unripe peppercorn), green pepper (dried unripe peppercorn), and white pepper (ripe fruit seeds). The flavor of the spice is attributable to the compound piperine, which is different from capsaicin (the compound found in chili peppers, of the genus *Capsicum*).

Black salsify
Scorzonera hispanica

black oyster plant, viper's grass

A species of herbaceous perennial plant in the sunflower (*Asteraceae*) family, native to Southern Europe and the Near East. It is cultivated mainly in Europe, primarily for its edible taproot, whose flavor is similar to oysters. The name salsify also applies to members of the genus *Tragopogon*, whose most notable species is purple salsify (*T. porrifolius*), which is grown as an ornamental and as a root vegetable.

Blue gum tree
Eucalyptus globulus

A species of evergreen tree in the myrtle (*Myrtaceae*) family, native to Australia and Tasmania, but now naturalized to other parts of Europe, Asia, the United States, and some Pacific and Atlantic islands. It is one of the most widely cultivated trees in Australia. It is the principle source of **eucalyptus oil**, since its essential oil does not contain the compound phellandrene (found in the essential oil of other *Eucalyptus* species), which makes it suitable for internal pharmaceutical use. Blue gum wood is used as pulpwood for papermaking and as fuel wood. Like many *Eucalyptus*, it is a source of gum resin. The tree is also an important nectar source for honeybees.

Blueberry
highbush blueberry

Vaccinium corymbosum

A species of low-growing shrub in the heath (*Ericaceae*) family, native to North America. It has been widely introduced and cultivated in temperate regions of the world. The genus *Vaccinium* contains a number of important fruit-bearing species that include: cranberry, lingonberry, and bilberry. There are several species classified as "blueberry," but V. *corymbosum* is the most widely commercially cultivated, with lowbush blueberry (*V. angustifolium*) and rabbit-eye blueberry (*V. virgatum*) also of some importance. The blueberry is primarily used for food, especially in jams, jellies, and fillings.

Boldo
Peumus boldus

A species of tree in the *Monimiaceae* family, native to the central region of Chile, but naturalized to other parts of North and South America. It is closely related to the laurel (*Lauraceae*) family, and its leaves are used similarly as a food flavoring, and a tea. The leaves also have a history of use in the traditional medicine of its native region. The leaves contain a toxic alkaloid that is removed by cooking, so most culinary purposes are safe; however, the essential oil is highly toxic and the leaves should not be eaten raw.

Bonito

A group of four genera of fish within the mackerel (*Scombridae*) family. The most well known species used as food fish are in the *Sarda* genus, primarily: the type species Atlantic bonito (*S. sarda*); and the Pacific bonito (*S. chiliensis lineolata*).

Borage
beebread, starflower, talewort

Borago officinalis

A species of annual herbaceous plant in the borage (*Boraginaceae*) family. It is native to the Mediterranean region but has been naturalized to many other areas. It is primarily cultivated for its edible leaves, as a nectar source for honeybees, and for the oil extracted from its seeds. This oil has traditional medicinal use, but is also under investigation for use in treating inflammatory disorders. The plant contains potentially toxic pyrrolizidine alkaloids and therefore should not be consumed in large amounts.

Borax
Sodium borate

A white crystalline compound found in volcanic regions, and in arid regions on the bed of evaporated salt lakes. Borax has a wide range of uses, including: glass and enamels manufacturing, metallurgy, water softeners, laundry and other cleaning products, fertilizers, as an anti-fungal compound and fire retardant.

Boxwood
Buxus sempervirens

A species of evergreen shrub or small tree in the boxwood (*Buxaceae*) family, native to North Africa, West Asia, and Eastern Europe. It is now naturalized to and cultivated in other temperate regions. Many species in the genus are popular ornamentals, but *B. sempervirens* is cultivated for its very dense, finely-grained wood, which is one of the few woods that is denser than water. It is popular for use in small carvings and woodblock printing.

Bramble
Rubus spp.

Also referred to as the blackberry or raspberry genus, *Rubus* is a genus of perennial brambles in the rose (*Rosaceae*) family, widespread throughout the temperate zones of the Northern Hemisphere. Many species are cultivated or wild-gathered for their edible berry. The berries are widely used as food, primarily jams, jellies, and fillings. The best-known species and variations include the raspberry, blackberry, salmonberry, and loganberry (boysenberry), though there are many others.

Brazilnut tree   *creamnut, Paranut*
Bertholletia excelsa

A species of large deciduous tree in the *Lecythidaceae* family, native to South America. The tree, which can reach a height of 160 feet, is among the tallest in the rainforest. It is known mainly for its highly nutritious edible seed, called the Brazil nut. Brazil nut oil (extracted from the seeds) is also a food item. The nuts are gathered almost entirely from wild trees, as the tree requires a very specific set of bee pollinators in order to produce fruit, and is therefore very difficult to cultivate. The wood is useful, but the trees are rarely cut down, as the nuts are far more valuable.

Brazilwood

Caesalpinia echinata

Pernambuco wood

A species of tree in the pea (*Fabaceae*) family, native to Brazil and still cultivated mainly in Brazil and the Caribbean. It is known for its rich red heartwood, which is the source of the red dye **brazilin**. The tree was recognized by Portuguese explorers of the 16th century as related to the Asian tree known as sappanwood, or Pau-brasil (*Caesalpinia sappan*) which was already used as a source of the dye. The brazilwood tree became such an important source, that the country of Brazil was named after it. The full name of the country is actually Terro do Brasil, or the "Land of Brazilwood." The red heartwood is also used to make bows and fine stringed instruments. The tree is currently listed as endangered, and trade in the wood is restricted.

Breadfruit

Artocarpus altilis

A species of tree in the mulberry (*Moraceae*) family, with origins in Oceania but now naturalized to many tropical regions. It is cultivated mainly for its fruit, the breadfruit, which is an important staple among many cultures of the South Pacific. The leaves and inedible fruit parts are used as cattle fodder. The tree's lightweight and insect-repellent wood was traditionally used to build canoes and houses. The tree produces a latex that has a history of use as a traditional medicine, among other uses. Breadfruit is closely related to jackfruit (*Artocarpus heterophyllus*), and chempedak (*Artocarpus integer*), also common food sources in the South Pacific and neighboring regions.

Broccoli

see *Cabbage*

Brussel sprouts

see *Cabbage*

The Barnacle Tree

It was a common belief in 16th century Europe that migrating wild barnacle geese coming from the north grew on trees. Though no one had ever seen this "Barnacle tree," its existence was taken for granted by renowned botanists and zoologists, and it was often included in formal herbals, such as John Gerard's *Herball or Generall Historie of Plants* (1597).

Buckthorn
Rhamnus spp.

A genus of over 100 species of shrubs and trees within the *Rhamnaceae* family, which is native to many temperate and subtropical regions in both hemispheres. Although some species have been used medicinally, its potential toxicity has largely negated that use. Several species are used in dye-making: *R. purshianus* (cascara buckthorn), whose bark and fruit yield a yellow dye (or green, when mixed with alum); *R. utilis* (Chinese buckthorn) yields a green dye; *R. saxatilis* (Avignon berry) yields a yellow dye from the fruit. The seed oil of species *R. globosa* (lokao) has been used in soap-making, printing ink, and as lubricating oil.

Buckwheat   *common buckwheat*
Fagopyrum esculentum

A species of pseudocereal in the buckwheat (*Polygonaceae*) family that is related to sorrel, knotweed, and rhubarb. It is native to Central Asia, but has been widely naturalized to and cultivated in Europe and North America. It is cultivated for its seeds, which are most frequently ground into a flour and used similarly to wheat, though buckwheat does not contain gluten. It is also used as a cover crop, a fodder crop, and as green manure to enrich agricultural soil. It is a bee-friendly plant which produces a flavorful honey. The closely related species *F. tataricum* (Tartary buckwheat) is similarly used, but is not as commonly cultivated.

Burrstone

Siliceous or siliceo-calcareous stones whose dressed surfaces provide a sharp cutting texture. In the past, they were widely used as millstones. The best stones were found in the Paris basin.

Cabbage
Brassica oleracea

A species of herbaceous plant in the cabbage (*Brassicaceae*) family, native to the coastal regions of southern and western Europe. Wild cabbage is tolerant of high salt and lime soil conditions. Domesticated cabbage is now widely cultivated throughout the world, with many cultivars of great importance as a food crop. The main cultivar groups include cabbage, kale, broccoli, cauliflower, brussels sprouts, kohlrabi, and collard greens.

Cadmium

A bluish-white metallic element derived mainly as a byproduct in the processing of zinc ores. It is used for plating iron and steel to provide rust-proofing, and as a hardening agent in the manufacture of alloys, particularly copper.

Caimito   see *Mamey sapote*

Cajuput   *paperbark teatree*
Melaleuca cajuputi

A species of tree in the myrtle (*Myrtaceae*) family, native to Australia, Southeast Asia, and New Guinea. It is one of several species in the genus *Melaleuca* that is known by the common names cajaput and paperbark teatree. These species are sources of essential oils, wood, and gum resin, as well as nectar for honeybees. *M. cajaputi* is particularly known for **cajuput oil**, which is extracted from the leaves and is an ingredient in liniments such as Tiger Balm and topical decongestants such as Olbas Oil.

Calabar bean   *ordeal bean*
Physostigma venenosum

A large climbing perennial in the pea (*Fabaceae*) family, native to tropical West and Central Africa. Its beans are highly toxic to humans, but two alkaloids have been identified and refined for medicinal purposes. Calabarine has an atropine-like effect; physostigmine has been used to treat myasthenia gravis, glaucoma, and other illnesses of the nervous system.

Calabash tree
Crescentia cujete

A flowering tree in the *Bignoniaceae* family, whose native origins are obscure, but are likely Central America and Western South America. It is widely naturalized to and cultivated in other tropical regions. It is valued for its large fruit; it is not only edible, but the hard rind is also used to make eating utensils such as bowls. The calabash vine or bottle gourd, which is in the gourd (*Cucurbitaceae*) family and is native to southern tropical Africa, is cultivated and used for similar purposes.

Calamine
Zinc carbonate

Calamine is the historical name of a zinc ore that is a carbonate of zinc. Refined, pharmaceutical-grade zinc carbonate is an astringent and is used in the preparation of ointments, lotions, and cosmetics. It is a primary ingredient in **Calamine** lotion, which is a topical anti-itch medication. Calamine lotion has been used as far back as 1500 BC, and is on the World Health Organization's Model List of Essential Medicines.

Calcite
Calcium carbonate

An important constituent mineral of chalk, limestone and marble. It occurs in various forms, such as Iceland spar and aragonite.

Calcium

A silvery metallic element, the compounds of which are widely distributed, primarily as calcium carbonate or calcite, which comes in many forms (e.g., chalk, limestone, gypsum, and many others). It is the fifth most abundant element, but must be extracted from its compounds by electrolysis. Among its uses are the making of alloys, bleaches, pottery, paints, medicines, and fertilizer. Calcium is an essential nutrient, and is the fifth most abundant element in the human body.

Calendula   see *Marigold*

Camel   see *Bactrian camel, Dromedary*

Camellia
Camellia spp.

A genus of evergreen shrubs or trees in the tea (*Theaceae*) family, native to East Asia, India, and Southeast Asia. The genus has several notable species: *C. sinensis* (the tea plant, see separate entry); *C. oleifera* (tea-oil-plant), whose seeds are the main source of **tea oil**, an important cooking oil in South Asia; *C. japonica* (common camellia), which is the source of the fragrant **tsubaki oil**, used as a hair care product. In addition, several species are used locally to make tea and oil, though they are not produced commercially.

Camphortree
Cinnamomum camphora   *Camphor laurel*

A large evergreen tree in the laurel (*Lauraceae*) family, native to southern China, Japan, Korea, and Taiwan. It is now naturalized to and cultivated in a number of temperate zone countries. It is cultivated primarily for its wood and leaves, which contain several essential oils, most notably **camphor**, which is used medicinally and as an insect repellent.

Cananga tree   *ylang-ylang, Macassar oiltree, wooley pine*
Cananga odorata

A species of fast-growing tree in the custard apple (*Annonaceae*) family, native to Indonesia, Malaysia, and the Philippines, but now cultivated elsewhere in tropical regions. It is cultivated almost exclusively for the essential oil called **ylang-ylang**, derived from its flowers, which is used in perfumery. The climbing ylang-ylang (*Artabotrys hexapetalus*) is a perennial vine in the same family that yields a similar aromatic oil.

Candlenut tree   *lumbangtree, kukui nut tree, varnish tree*
Aleurites moluccanus

A species of tree in the spurge (*Euphorbiaceae*) family, whose exact native distribution is unknown due to its early dispersion by humans. It is presumed to have originated in East Asia, and Southeast Asia down to Australia. It is now naturalized throughout the Old and New World tropical regions. In modern times, the tree is grown on plantations mostly for the edible seed oil. However, in the Pacific regions, other parts of the tree have many uses. It was one of the items brought to Hawaii by the first Polynesian colonizers. The wood is used to make many parts of the traditional outrigger canoes. The raw seeds are mildly toxic, but prepared seeds are an important food item. The seeds, which have a very high oil content, were also burned as a light source. A varnish and preservative for cordage was also made from the seed oil. The charred nuts were used to make ink for tattoos, and the inner bark was used to make a red-brown dye for tapa cloth.

Canella tree
Canella winterana   *barbasco, wild cinnamon*

A single-species genus of tree within the *Canellaceae* family, native
to the southeastern United States, the Caribbean, and northern
South America. It is cultivated in those regions for its extremely
hard and dense wood, and for a spice obtained from the inner
bark that is similar to cinnamon.

Canistel
Pouteria campechiana   *egg fruit*

A species of evergreen tree in the gutta-percha (*Sapotaceae*) family,
native to southern Mexico and Central America, but now also
cultivated in the United States and South America, and Southeast
Asia. It is cultivated for its edible fruit, the canistel or egg fruit.
The tree also produces a latex which has been used as an adulterant of chicle. The canistel is closely related to several other species of fruit-bearing trees in the *Pouteria* genus, all of which are
native to South and Central America or the Caribbean. These
include: the mamey sapote (*P. sapota*), the caimito (*P. caimito*), and
the lucuma (*P. lucuma* and *P. macrophylla*).

Caper bush
Capparis spinosa   *Flinders rose*

A flowering shrub in the caper (*Capparaceae*) family, native to the
Mediterranean region, but now widely naturalized to and cultivated in various parts of the world, particularly Asia and the
eastern Pacific regions. It is cultivated primarily for the edible
flower buds (called capers) and the fruit (called caper berries).
Both are eaten pickled.

Caraway
Carum carvi   *carum*

A biennial herbaceous plant in the parsley (*Apiaceae*) family, native to North Africa, temperate Asia and the Indian subcontinent,
but now widely cultivated in the temperate regions of the world.
It is cultivated almost exclusively for its fruit, commonly and er-
roneously referred to as a "seed," which is used as a spice.

Carbon

A nonmetallic element that is the fourth most abundant element in the universe by mass. It is widely distributed in many forms in animals, vegetation, and minerals. Its abundance, diversity of organic compounds, and unusual ability to form polymers at temperatures commonly found on Earth has led to its becoming the common element of all known life on Earth. Diamond and graphite are carbon in its purest form.

Cardamom (false)
Amomum spp.

Amomum is a genus of herbaceous plants in the ginger (*Zingiberaceae*) family, with several species native to various regions in Asia. Several of the species are cultivated, primarily for their seeds, which yield a spice called cardamom, although true cardamom comes from the *Elettaria cardamomum*.

Cardamom (true)
Elettaria cardamomum

An herbaceous perennial plant in the ginger (*Zingiberaceae*) family, native to a region from India to Malaysia, but now widely cultivated elsewhere. It is cultivated primarily for its seeds, which produce cardamom spice. True cardamom is the third most expensive spice by weight, behind saffron and vanilla.

Cardoon   see *Artichoke*

Carnauba palm   *wax palm*
Copernicia prunifera

A species of tree in the palm (*Arecaceae*) family, native to and cultivated only in northeastern Brazil. It is cultivated mainly for the wax (**carnauba wax**) extracted from its leaves, which is highly valued as a polish for floors, leather, cars, and shoes; the wax is also used in the manufacture of a variety of items such as candles, paper, soap, and wood finishes. The biomass remaining after wax extraction is known as "bagana" and is used as fuel and fertilizer. The tree also produces edible fruit and leaf fibers that can be woven into useful items.

Carnelian   see *Chalcedony*

Carob tree   *St. John's bread, locust bean*
Ceratonia siliqua

A species of tree in the pea (*Fabaceae*) family. It is presumed native to the Mediterranean region, but its exact native range is unknown. It is widely naturalized to and cultivated in a number of temperate regions around the world. It is cultivated for its edible seeds and seed pods. These are dried and ground into a powder, which is used as a food flavoring, a substitute for cocoa powder, and animal fodder. A syrup is made from sugar extracted from the pods which is used as a sweetener and as a beverage base.

Carp

The name "carp" refers to a variety of species of oily freshwater fish within the *Cyprinidae* family, native to Europe and Asia. The bighead carp (*Hypophthalmichthys nobilis*) is a popular food item in Europe, and is one of the most intensively farmed fishes in the world.

Carrageen   *Irish moss*
Chondrus crispus

A species of red algae that grows abundantly along the rocky Atlantic coast of North America and Europe. It derives its name from a town in southeast Ireland. The algae is mainly composed of **carrageenan**, a polysaccharide that is used commercially in the food industry as a thickening agent.

Carrot
Daucus carota subsp. sativus

A species of herbaceous annual plant within the parsley (*Apiaceae*) family, presumed to be native to Europe and Southwestern Asia, but now widely cultivated throughout the world. Carrots are one of the ten most important food crops in the world, cultivated mainly for their edible taproot. There are two main varieties of the species: *sativus* (the standard orange carrots), and *atrorubens* (black carrot, purple carrot, or eastern carrot). There are many cultivars within these varieties. **Carrot seed oil**, both pressed and distilled from the seed, are used in cosmetics, perfumery, and traditional medicine.

Cascara buckthorn   *chittambark*
Frangula purshiana

A species of shrub within the buckthorn (*Rhamnaceae*) family,
native to North America from British Columbia to south central
California, and eastward to Montana. It is known primarily for
its bark, which has been used for centuries as a powerful laxative.
It was the principle ingredient in commercial laxatives until the
early twenty-first century. It remains one of the most important
native pharmacological crops in North America.

Cashew
Anacardium occidentale

A tropical evergreen tree in the sumac (*Anacardiaceae*) family,
native to northern and western South America and Brazil, but
now widely cultivated in tropical areas around the world. It is
cultivated mainly for its edible seed (the cashew "nut"), as well as
a resin obtained from the nutshell called cashew shell oil, and its
fruit, the cashew apple. The resin is allergenic and can cause a
rash; likewise, the waxy coating on the fruit contains the irritant
urushiol (like other members of the sumac family), and may
cause contact dermatitis in people allergic to the substance. If the
substance is ingested or inhaled, it can cause a severe allergic
reaction. These compounds pose a health risk to people involved
in the manual processing of cashew products.

Cassava   *manioc, Brazilian arrowroot, tapioca*
Manihot esculenta

A species of shrub in the spurge (*Euphorbiaceae*) family, native to
South America but widely cultivated in the tropical and subtropical regions. It is cultivated for its starchy, tuberous root and is the
third largest source of carbohydrates in the tropics, behind rice
and maize. The two main varieties are bitter and sweet, with
bitter containing more antinutritional factors and toxins. Cassava
must be properly prepared before consumption, due to the risk of
toxicity. When the root is dried to a granular powdery extract, it
is called tapioca. The closely-related Ceara rubber tree (*M. cartha-
genensis subsp. glaziovii*) is also native to Brazil and is cultivated
there for its edible root, and for its rubber latex (**caoutchouc**).

Castor bean
Castor oil plant

Ricinus communis

A species of shrub in the spurge (*Euphorbiaceae*) family, presumed native to the southeastern Mediterranean basin and East Africa and India, but whose origin is obscure due to a long history of intensive cultivation. It is widely cultivated in the tropical regions, primarily for its seed, called the castor bean (though it is not a true bean). **Castor oil** is extracted from the bean, which has a variety of uses, including medicinal and as a motor lubricant.

Catechu
black cutch

Senegalia catechu

A species of deciduous thorny acacia tree in the pea (*Fabaceae*) family, native to parts of Asia. The tree is cultivated for its edible seeds, its wood, and as a host for lac insects. However, it is best known for the extract of its heartwood, known as **catechu**. Catechu is used for dying and tanning, as well as medicinally. A concentrated version of the extract, known as khayer gum or cutch, is used medicinally. The tree is closely related to the gum-arabic tree (*Senegalia senegal*).

Catjang
see *Cowpea*

Catnip
catmint, catswort

Nepeta cataria

A species of perennial herbaceous plant in the mint (*Lamiaceae*) family, native to Southern and Eastern Europe, the Middle East, Central Asia, and China. It is widely cultivated and naturalized to many regions around the world. The essential oil obtained by steam distillation of the leaves contains the chemical compound nepetalactone, which (besides being a cat attractant) also acts as an insect repellent, particularly for cockroaches and mosquitoes.

What Do We See as Useful?

In this dictionary, there are listed 66 animals, 162 minerals, and 572 plants. There are two fungi (though one of those is the broad category of "mushrooms"), and one bacterium. Of the animals, only five species listed are insects, though there are an estimated 6 to 10 million species of insect in the world.

Cattle
Bos taurus

The most widespread species in the genus *Bos*, and the most common domesticated ungulates. Cattle are raised for their milk, meat (beef), and hides. They also serve as draft animals (in this capacity, they are known as oxen) pulling carts, plows, and other vehicles. Their manure is used as fertilizer, and as fuel, both directly (when it is dried and burned) and indirectly (when methane gas produced by the dung is collected). Cattle were domesticated about 10,000 years ago in the area of the Fertile Crescent. Since then, cattle have become enormously important in many regions of the world, both economically and culturally.

Cauliflower
see *Cabbage*

Cayenne pepper
see *Chili pepper*

Cedar
true cedar

Cedrus spp.

A genus of evergreen conifers in the pine (*Pinaceae*) family, native to the mountains of the western Himalayas and the Mediterranean region. They are cultivated primarily for the wood, which is rich in a scented oil that is an effective insect repellent. The use of true cedar has been greatly reduced due to the overexploitation and almost complete eradication of, in particular, the Lebanon cedar (*Cedrus liberii*). Cedar has been replaced in many of its uses by other species of tree with similar characteristics, which are traded as "cedar" but are not true cedar.

Celeriac
see *Celery*

Celery
Apium graveolens

A marshland plant in the parsley (*Apiaceae*) family that has been cultivated as food since ancient times. The part of the plant that is eaten depends on the cultivar; most are cultivated for the edible stems and leaves; celeriac (*A. graveolens var. rapaceum*) is grown for the edible stem, hypocotyl (stem of the germinating seedling), and shoots. Celery seeds are also used as a spice, or for their essential oil, which is used in perfumery.

Cesium

A silvery-gold alkali metallic element whose low melting point makes it one of five metals that are liquid at or near room temperature. It is the most reactive metal, and is pyrophoric, meaning that it reacts explosively on contact with water. Some isotopes of cesium are radioactive and therefore toxic; however, many compounds of cesium are only mildly toxic. The metal and its compounds have many uses in industry; most famously, the isotope cesium-133 is widely used in highly accurate atomic clocks.

Chalcedony
Silicon dioxide

A mineral found in volcanic rocks that is chemically identical to quartz, but with a different crystalline structure. Its colored varieties are agate, carnelian, onyx, sardonyx, mtorolite, heliotrope (bloodstone), and chrysoprase. In most forms (with the exception of agate), it is used primarily as a semiprecious gemstone.

Chalcopyrite
Copper iron sulfide

A brassy yellow mineral known mainly as the most important copper ore.

Chalk
Calcium carbonate

A soft, white, porous sedimentary carbonate rock. It forms as the result of deep-water deposition of the shells of minute marine life. Chalk contains a very high percentage of calcium carbonate in the form of calcite. It is used in making putty, writing chalk, Portland cement, lime, and fertilizer.

Chamois
Rupicapra rupicapra

A small goat antelope in the *Bovidae* family, native to mountains of Europe but also naturalized to New Zealand. It is best known for the leather (called chamois) made from its hide, which is very smooth and absorbent and is most commonly used for cleaning, buffing and polishing.

Chamomile
Matricaria chamomilla

scented mayweed

An annual plant in the daisy (*Asteraceae*) family, native to North Africa, Europe and India, but widely naturalized to and cultivated in many other parts of the world. The dried flowers have a long history of use in herbal medicine, and are used to make a popular herbal tea. The essential oil rendered from the flowers is being investigated for potential medicinal uses. Another species popularly known as chamomile is *Chamaemelum nobilis* (Roman chamomile), which is in the same taxonomic family and has a similar geographic distribution and use.

Champak
Magnolia champaca

A large evergreen tree in the magnolia (*Magnoliaceae*) family, native to South Asia, Southeast Asia, and southern China. It is known primarily for its strongly scented flowers, from which is extracted an essential oil widely used in incense, perfume, and scented oils, including massage and hair oils. The word shampoo derives from the Hindi *champo*, which means "to massage," and is in turn derived from the *champa*, the Sanskrit name for the tree. The wood is also highly valued for its fine grain and color, and is used in making furniture and cabinetry. The tree is protected in some areas due to its religious significance in the Buddhist and Hindu faiths.

Chard

see *Beet*

Chempedak

see *Breadfruit*

Cherimoya
Annona cherimola

custard apple

A species of deciduous tree in the custard apple (*Annonaceae*) family, native to western South America, but now widely cultivated in tropical areas throughout the world. It is cultivated for its large edible fruit, which can sometimes grow up to five pounds in size. It shares the name "custard apple" with several other species in the *Annona* genus, also cultivated for their fruit.

Cherry tree
Prunus avium, Prunus cerasus

The name "cherry" refers to several species of deciduous trees in the *Prunus* genus, within the rose (*Rosaceae*) family. The cherry tree is presumed native to Asia, but is now widely cultivated in temperate zones throughout the world. Archaeological evidence suggests that cherries were actively being cultivated in Asia Minor by about 800 BCE. Today, the two main species of cherry tree cultivated for their fruit are the sweet cherry (*Prunus avium*), which is the ancestral species, and the sour cherry or pie cherry (*Prunus cerasus*). There are many cultivars within each of these species, and several hybrids with other species in the genus. Cherry wood is also prized for its rich color and straight grain, and us used to make furniture. Cherry trees are in the same genus as plums, apricots, peaches, and almonds.

Chervil   *French parsley*
Anthriscus cerefolium

A species of herb in the parsley (*Apiaceae*) family, native to the Caucasus region of Eastern Europe but naturalized to the rest of Europe since Roman times. It is particularly cultivated in France for its parsley-like leaves, which are used as a culinary herb.

Chestnut tree
Castanea spp.

A genus of about nine species within the oak and beech (*Fagaceae*) family, native to temperate regions of the Northern Hemisphere. The primary cultivated species are the European sweet chestnut (*C. sativa*) and the Japanese chestnut (*C. crenata*). The American chestnut (*C. dentata*) used to be a very important food and wood source, but a blight in the early 20th century devastated the species and it is still in the process of recovering. In addition to its edible seed, the tree is also valued for its fine hardwood.

Chica   *cricket vine*
Arrabidaea chica

A species of climbing plant in the *Bignoniaceae* family native to South America, known primarily for the orange-red dye (chica) produced from its leaves. It also has a history of use in traditional medicine in its native region.

Chicken
Gallus gallus domesticus

Most of the fowl we know as chickens are the domesticated relative of the red junglefowl (*Gallus gallus*), native to Southeast Asia. The exact origins and time of domestication is debated, but chickens were likely domesticated first in Southern China or Southeast Asia, probably about 8,000 years ago. From there, they have spread all over the world, and today, chickens are the most commonly-kept poultry in the world. About 50 billion chickens are raised every year, primarily for their meat and eggs.

Chickpea
Cicer arietinum   *garbanzo, gram*

A domesticated species of annual plant within the pea (*Fabaceae*) family. It is one of the earliest cultivated legumes, with evidence for its cultivation dating back to the Neolithic era in the Near East. It is widely cultivated throughout the world for its highly nutritious, protein-rich seed, which is food for humans and animals. The leaves are also edible and are a significant source of minerals and other micronutrients.

Chicory
Cichorium intybus

A perennial herbaceous plant in the dandelion (*Asteraceae*) family, native to Europe but now widely naturalized to North America, China, and Australia. It is closely related to and often confused with endive (*Cichorium endivia*). Many varieties are cultivated for their edible leaves, chicons (blanched flower buds), or roots. The latter are baked, ground, and used as a coffee substitute. Chicory is the most common source of **inulin**, a polysaccharide used as a sweetener and a dietary fiber.

The Bo Tree: Value Beyond Measure

The bo tree (*Ficus religiosa*), native to India and Sri Lanka, is revered by Buddhists of India. It was under a bo tree that Gatauma Buddha sat for seven weeks until he gained perfect knowledge and enlightenment of Nirvana. Today a bo tree grows in every Indian village near the temple and serves as a center for meetings and meditation.

Chilean hazelnut
Gevuina avellana

avellana

A species of evergreen tree in the genus *Gevuina*, in the *Proteaceae* family. It is native to southern Chile and Argentina, and has been introduced to temperate oceanic climates in Europe and in the Pacific Northwest of the United States. It is cultivated for several purposes. The tree's edible nut is rich in nutrients; the oil from the nut is used in cosmetics, and is high in omega-7 fatty acids. The seed shells contain tannin, and the wood is used for musical instruments and cabinetry. The flowers are an important source of nectar for honeybees.

Chili pepper
Capsicum spp.

Capsicum is a genus of plants within the nightshade (*Solanaceae*) family, native to the Americas but now widely cultivated elsewhere. *Capsicum* have been cultivated for thousands of years, and there are currently five domesticated species: *C. annuum* is the most widely cultivated, and includes among its many cultivars, bell peppers, jalapenos, and cayenne peppers; *C. baccatum* includes the aji pepper; *C. chinense*, or the habanero pepper, whose cultivars include the hottest peppers in the world; *C. frutescens*, the Tabasco pepper; and *C. pubescens*, which includes most notably the rocoto pepper of Peru and Ecuador.

Chinese cassia
Cinnamomum cassia

Chinese cinnamon

A species of evergreen tree in the laurel (*Lauraceae*) family native to southern China but now cultivated in southern and eastern Asia. It is grown for its bark, which is a source of the spice **cinnamon**. It is closely related to four other species within the genus that also produce cinnamon, including Ceylon or true cinnamon (*C. verum*). Most cinnamon sold in the U.S. is Chinese cinnamon.

Chinese indigo
Persicaria tinctoria

Dyer's knotweed

A species of herbaceous plant in the buckwheat (*Polygonaceae*) family, native to Eastern Europe and Asia. It was an important source of the blue dye **indigo**, before the introduction of Indian indigo (*Indigofera tinctoria*).

Chinese quince
Pseudocydonia sinensis

A species of deciduous or semi-evergreen tree that is the sole member of its genus, within the rose (*Rosaceae*) family. It is native to eastern Asia and China. It is related to the true (European) quince (*Cydonia oblonga*). It is cultivated as an ornamental and for its edible fruit, which is usually eaten in jams and preserves, as it is very astringent when raw. It has a long tradition of use in Chinese medicine to treat arthritis, and is being investigated for use as an antiviral and antioxidant.

Chinese tallowtree   *candleberry tree*
Triadica sebifera

A species of deciduous tree in the spurge (*Euphoribiaceae*) family, native to southeast China, Japan, and Taiwan. In these regions, the waxy coating of the seeds is used in candle making and soap making. It is being explored as a potential source of biodiesel. Its leaves and sap are toxic, and the leaf litter inhibits the growth of other plants, due to its toxicity. It is considered an invasive and noxious plant in the United States.

Chives   *giant garlic*
Allium schoenoprasum

A species of herbaceous perennial plant in the amaryllis (*Amaryllidaceae*) family. It is the only species in the *Allium* genus that is native to both the Old and New Worlds. It is a close relative of garlic, shallots, leeks, and Chinese onion. It is widely cultivated for its edible stems and unopened immature flower buds, which are used as an herb. The mature flowers are also edible. It is a very pollinator-friendly plant, as one of the highest nectar producers. Its essential oil has insect repellent properties.

Chromium

A very hard, whitish metallic element. It is mostly used in steel manufacturing as a hardening agent and for producing stainless steels, but is also used for electroplating nickel to provide a hard, shining, non-tarnishing coating. It is also used in dyeing and tanning, and in the manufacture of green, red and yellow paints.

Cicely   *garden myrrh, sweet chervil*
Myrrhis odorata

A species of herbaceous perennial plant in the parsley (*Apiaceae*)
family, native to southern and central Europe. Its roots, seeds,
and leaves are all edible, and are used as a food flavoring similar
to anise.

Cider gum tree
Eucalyptus gunnii

A species of evergreen eucalyptus tree in the myrtle (*Myrtaceae*)
family, native to Tasmania. It is known for the sweet sap, similar
to maple syrup, which can be extracted by making holes in the
bark. The sap can be fermented to make a drink similar to apple
cider. Like other eucalyptus trees, it is also a source of tannin.

Cilantro   see *Coriander*

Cinchona   *yellowbark, quinine*
Cinchona calisaya

A species of evergreen shrub or tree in the madder (*Rubiaceae*)
family, native to the tropical Andean forests of western South
America. It is best known and utilized for the medicinal properties of compounds found in the bark; these include the antimalarial drug **quinine** (on the World Health Organization's Model List
of Essential Medicines), and the antiarrhythmic drug quinidine.

Citron tree
Citrus medica

A species of tree in the citrus (*Rutaceae*) family. Its native origins
are obscure due to a long history of cultivation, but it is believed
to be native to India, in the eastern Himalayas. It is one of the
original citrus fruits; most cultivated citrus fruits arose by hybridization of the ancestral species, one of which is the citron, which
gave rise to lemons and most limes. It is cultivated for its edible
fruit, and for the essential oil that is extracted from the outermost
pigmented layer of its thick rind. This oil is used in perfumery,
and medicinally for its antibiotic properties. The Buddha's hand
(*C. medica var. sarcodactylis*) is one of the more dramatic varieties.

Clay   *Argil*

Clay is a finely-grained rock or soil that combines one or more
clay minerals, often with traces of quartz, metal oxides, and organic matter. Clays are notable for their plasticity and their ten-
dency to become hard and brittle upon drying or firing. These
qualities that have made clay valuable since antiquity in the manufacture of eating utensils, storage vessels, and ornamental items.
Clay is also used as a building material, as in adobe or terra cotta.

Clementine
Citrus clementina

The clementine is a hybrid between a willowleaf mandarin (*C. x
deliciosa*) and a sweet orange (*C. x sinensis*). The hybrid arose
spontaneously in Algeria at the turn of the twentieth century.
Shortly after, it was introduced to other citrus-growing regions
and has become one of the more intensively cultivated citrus
fruits. The essential oil extracted from the rind of the fruit is also
used as a scent; the oil is phototoxic, meaning that it reacts with
sunlight and can cause skin irritation.

Climbing ylang-ylang   see *Cananga tree*

Clove
Syzygium aromaticum

A species of tree within the myrtle (*Myrtaceae*) family, native to
the Moluccas in Indonesia, but today most clove trees are cultivated on the East African islands of Zanzibar and Pemba, and
Madagascar. They are cultivated for the spice produced from the
dried, unopened flower buds. The spice is used mostly as food
flavoring, but it also has insect repellent properties.

Clover
Trifolium spp.

Trifolium is a genus of about 300 species of plants within the pea
(*Fabaceae*) family. The most widely cultivated are white clover (*T.
repens*) and red clover (*T. pratense*). It is extensively cultivated in
the cool temperate regions of the world, mainly as fodder and for
soil improvement, as it is a nitrogen-fixing plant. Several species
provide nectar for honey bees, such as Kura clover (*T. ambiguum*),
and small hop clover (*T. dubium*). A few species are grown as
food, like large hop clover (*T. aureum*), or flavoring (red clover).

Coal

Coal is a sedimentary rock formed primarily of vegetable matter, usually wood. For that reason, it is composed mainly of carbon. Coal comes in three main types: anthracite, which has the highest pure carbon content and thus is the most highly valued for energy production; bituminous, whose carbon content ranges from 50 -80%, it is used for fuel, but also supplies a range of useful products when it is carbonized (including gas, coke, and most notably coal tar, which can be further refined into many other products); lignite or brown coal is the lowest quality in terms of carbon content, and is used almost exclusively as fuel for steam-driven electric power generation.

Coast redwood   *California redwood*
Sequoia sempervirens

The sole living species in the genus *Sequoia*, coast redwood trees are giant evergreens in the cypress (*Cupressaceae*) family, native to and found only on the north coast of California and southern coast of Oregon. Redwood trees are the tallest on Earth, reaching heights of up to 379 feet, with a diameter of up to 29 feet at chest height. They are extremely long-lived, with the oldest known specimens dating over two thousand years. After their discovery by European settlers in the early 19th century, they were extensively logged for their timber, which is a rich red color, lightweight, and pest-resistant and fire-resistant. Today, old-growth redwood is no longer logged, as it is an endangered species. However, cultivated redwood is still being grown and harvested.

Cobalt

A metallic element found only in small quantities, it is used mainly in the production of hard, rust-resistant steels; these are used in high-speed tools, permanent magnets, and high-temperature and stress engine parts. Cobalt is also used as a pigment that imparts its distinctive blue color in glass-making, pottery, and paint. The mineral is the basis of an important group of vitamins (such as B12), which are essential for human life; in its natural form, it is an important micronutrient for bacteria, algae, and fungi.

Cobaltite

A silvery white mineral with a brilliant luster, it is mined mostly in Scandinavia, where it is used to make jewelry. It is also found in India, where it is called sehta (or saita) by jewelers and used to give a blue color to gold jewelry. It is also one of the ores of the mineral cobalt.

Coca
Erythroxylum spp.

The common name "coca" generally refers to the two commercially cultivated species of shrubs in the *Erythroxylum* genus, within the coca (*Erythroxylacea*) family, both native to western South America. Each of the two species has two primary cultivars: *E. coca var. coca* (Bolivian coca), *E. coca var. ipadu* (Amazonian coca), *E. novogranatense var. novogranatense* (Colombian coca), and *E. novogranatense var. truxillense* (Trujillo coca). Of these, only Bolivian coca is cultivated in tropical regions outside of South America. Coca plants are cultivated almost exclusively as the source of the psychoactive alkaloid cocaine, extracted from the leaves, which acts as a narcotic and a stimulant. The chewing of coca leaves has been part of the cultural traditions of certain parts of South America, especially Peru, since ancient times. In the United States, the extract of coca leaves was the key medicinal ingredient in the original formulation of the soft drink "Coca-cola," which, like many other soft drinks of the time, was marketed as a health tonic. Currently, cocaine is an illegal drug in most parts of the world.

Cochineal
Dactylopius coccus

A scale insect, native to the southwestern United States, Mexico, and South America. They are parasitic insects that live on cacti in the genus *Opuntia* (prickly pear). The red pigment called **carmine** is produced from these insects. The insects contain carminic acid, which is harvested from their dried bodies, then mixed with aluminum and calcium salts to make the dye. Carmine is used as a food colorant and in cosmetics.

Coco de mer
Lodoicea maldivica

sea coconut, double coconut

Lodoicea is a single-species genus in the palm (*Arecaceae*) family. It is native to the Seychelles, and is in danger of extinction as a species. The edible nut is the largest seed in the plant kingdom; it has an extremely hard outer shell and takes six to seven years to mature, with another two years to germinate. Before the Seychelles became inhabited in the 18th century, the nuts were known only because they drifted ashore to other inhabited islands, such as the Maldives. The nuts have the shape of a woman's buttocks, and the combination of this and their mysterious origin gave rise to many myths surrounding their origin and properties. Many believed that the tree grew on the bottom of the ocean. The fruit was valued in both Ayurvedic and Chinese traditional medicine and cuisine; the mystery and rarity of the shells, combined with their beauty when polished, made them valuable collectors' items. Today, the trees are grown mainly as ornamentals in tropical regions; trade is highly restricted due to their protected status.

Cocoa tree
Theobroma cacao

Cacao tree

A small evergreen tree in the mallow (*Malvaceae*) family, native to the Amazon basin, but now cultivated in other equatorial tropical regions, mainly in South America and Africa. The trees are cultivated for their seeds, called cocoa beans. The beans are dried and ground to a powder which is used to make a variety of food items, most famously chocolate. The seeds also produce the cocoa butter, used for food and for cosmetics. The seeds contain the alkaloid theobromine, which acts as a mild stimulant. Cocoa has a long history of cultural and religious significance for particularly the Aztec and Maya; it was introduced to Europeans by the Spanish explorers of the 16th century. Today, there are three main cultivar groups: Forastero, Criollo, and Trinitario, with Criollo (the original Mayan cultivar) as the rarest and most prized as being the least bitter and most aromatic. Several other species within the genus are locally cultivated in their native region of South and Central America, primarily for their fruit (as opposed to the seed) including the patashte (*T. bicolor*), and the cupuassu (*T. grandiflorum*), which is the national fruit of Brazil.

Coconut palm
Cocos nucifera

The coconut tree is the single species in the genus *Cocos*, which is in the palm (*Arecaceae*) family. Its place of origin is debated, but is generally accepted to be in the region of India-Indonesia. Now, it is widely distributed and cultivated along coastal margins throughout the tropics. Almost every part of the tree is useful, but it is best known for its seed (the coconut), which is the source of many useful materials. These include: **coir** fiber, which is taken from the thick outer layer of the fruit; the hard outer shell is used for fuel, charcoal, and to make bowls; the flesh within the seed is edible, and is also dried to make **copra**, from which **coconut oil** is extracted; the liquid in the center of the seed, **coconut milk**, is a nutritious beverage. The wood of the tree is used for building, the leaves are used for thatch, and for weaving mats and baskets. The roots provide a medicinal latex, and the sap of the flower buds is fermented into palm wine, also called **toddy**.

Cod
Gadus spp.

A genus of three species of fish in the *Gadidae* family. They are the Atlantic cod (*G. morhua*), the Pacific cod (*G. macrocephalus*), and the Greenland cod (*G. ogac*). Of these, the Atlantic cod is by far the most intensively commercially fished. It is valued for its meat, which contains important vitamins and fatty acids. In addition, the liver is processed to produce **cod liver oil**, a popular dietary supplement.

Coffee tree
Coffea spp.

A genus of shrubs or small trees in the madder (*Rubiaceae*) family. There are many species, but the three main cultivated species are: *C. arabica* (arabica coffee), native to Yemen and Ethiopia; and *C. liberica* (liberica or excelsa coffee) and *C. canephora* (robusta coffee), both native to Western and Central Africa. These species are now widely cultivated at middle elevations (1200 to 6000 feet) in many tropical regions of the world. Coffee trees are cultivated for their seeds (coffee beans); the beans contain the alkaloid caffeine, which acts as a stimulant. Coffee beans are most often consumed as a beverage made from the dried and ground seeds.

Collard greens

see *Cabbage*

Colocynth
Citrullus colocynthis

bitter apple, bitter cucumber

A species of perennial ground vine in the gourd (*Cucurbitaceae*) family, native to the arid, sandy soils of Mediterranean Basin and the Near East. The plant is cultivated primarily for its fruit pulp, which is used medicinally as a laxative, diuretic, and emetic. The seeds are edible and nutritious, though bitter; they produce an edible seed oil and are sometimes ground to make flour. The plant is also used to breed pest resistance into watermelons.

Commiphora
Commiphora spp.

The genus *Commiphora*, in the torchwood (*Bursuraceae*) family, is native mostly to Northeast Africa, India, and the Arabian peninsula. It contains many species of small trees and shrubs known for their aromatic resins. The better-known species include *C. myrrha* (the myrrh tree, see separate entry); *C. wightii* (Indian bdellium tree), which produces the resin **bdellium**, used in perfumery and incense; *C. mukul* (guggel), which is the source of the dietary supplement **guggelsterone**; *C. erythraea* and *C. kataf,* which produce **opopanax** or bisabol, a gum resin believed to have medicinal properties and used as pest control for livestock; and *C. gileadensis*, which produces the resin **Balm of Gilead**, valued since antiquity as a perfume with medicinal qualities.

Copaiba
Copaifera officinalis

The best-known of several species of tree in the pea (*Fabaceae*) family, native mainly to Brazil, but also other parts of northern and western South America. The species are known mainly as a source of the resin called copaiba balsam. Copaiba has a long history of use as a traditional medicine, as well as an ingredient in varnishes, and as a fixative in the perfume industry. The resin is also being explored as a source of biodiesel.

Copal tree
Protium copal

A species of tree in the torchwood (*Burseraceae*) family, native to Mexico and Central America. It is known primarily for its resin, called **copal**, which is used as an incense similar to frankincense. Copal incense has a long history of importance in the religious traditions of the Maya and Aztec people of Central America and Mexico. The word "copal" is derived from the Nahuatl (the language of the Aztecs) word *copalli*, which means "incense."

Copper

A reddish metallic element very widely distributed in the Earth's surface rocks. It is believed to have been the first metal worked by man, as it is comparatively easily separated from the ore. The oldest archaeological evidence for copper smelting comes from Eastern Europe and dates to about 7000 years ago. Copper is the most important non-ferrous metal. It is a relatively soft metal, but is hardened by alloying with other metals. It is a good conductor of electricity, and is therefore used extensively in all branches of the electrical industry. About 80% of the world's copper is used for this purpose.

Corals

A class of marine invertebrates known as *Anthozoa* that live in colonies of thousands to millions of individual polyps. Corals include the reef builders, which have skeletons of calcium carbonate; these live in warm, shallow waters of the world. Coral reefs comprise entire complex ecosystems that include many species of marine plants and animals. The material we call "coral," which is the calcium carbonate skeleton of the polyp, is an important source of lime. Precious coral is a red coral (made red by the presence of carotenoid pigments incorporated into the exoskeleton) produced by the genus *Corallium*, and is used to make jewelry. Many coral reefs are protected to avoid or repair overexploitation.

Corchorus
Corchorus spp.

A genus of mostly annual plants in the mallow (*Malvaceae*) family whose native range is obscure due to a long and extensive history of cultivation. It is now widely naturalized to many tropical and subtropical regions of the world. Two main species are cultivated for their fiber (**jute**), which is the second most commonly used vegetable fiber after cotton. These are: *C. capsularis* (white jute), and *C. olitorius* (tossa jute). Jute fiber is used to make the textiles known as burlap, hessian, or gunny cloth, among other uses. Both species are also cultivated for the edible leaves, called molo-khia or mallow-leaves.

Coriander   *cilantro, Chinese parsley*
Coriandrum sativum

A species of annual herb in the parsley (*Apiaceae*) family. It is likely native to the Mediterranean region, but is widely natural-ized to and cultivated throughout many parts of the world. All parts of the plant are edible, but the most commonly used parts are the fresh leaves, known commercially as cilantro or Chinese parsley, and the dried seeds, known as the spice coriander. The essential oil of coriander is currently being investigated for use as an anti-bacterial medicine. In addition, the plant is experimental-ly being intercropped with lettuce as a natural means of aphid control, as it attracts beneficial insects that are aphid predators.

Cork oak
Quercus suber

An evergreen tree in the oak and beech (*Fagaceae*) family, native to the Mediterranean region, particularly Spain. It is an ancient species, with fossil remains dating back at least 2.5 million years. It is cultivated primarily as the source of natural cork, which is harvested from the very light, thick outer bark of the tree. The bark is stripped from the living tree every eight to ten years; the trees live for about 150 years on average. Cork is put to a variety of uses, including wine bottle stoppers, flooring, among others.

Corundum
Aluminum oxide

A mineral that is the crystalline form of aluminum oxide (alumina), which is second in hardness only to diamond. It is used as an abrasive and for polishing. The precious gemstones sapphire and ruby are transparent colored varieties of corundum. It is also used as watch crystals and bearings in electrical appliances. The abrasive **emery** is a dark, granular rock comprised mostly of corundum, mixed with other minerals and oxides such as spinel, magnetite, and rutile. Long-term exposure to breathing in of the finely granulated powder can pose a health hazard.

Cotton
Gossypium spp.

A genus of about fifty species of perennial flowering shrubs in the mallow (*Malvaceae*) family. The name of the genus derives from the Arabic word *goz*, which means silk. The genus is native to arid and semi-arid tropical regions of both the Old and New World. Four species of the genus are widely cultivated, with one species (*G. hirsutum*, a species native to Mesoamerica) accounting for 90% of the world's production. *G. barbadense* (Pima cotton), native to South America, is also widely cultivated. *G. herbaceum* (Arabian cotton), is native to tropical Africa and is cultivated widely in Asia. The plant is cultivated primarily for the fibrous boll surrounding the seed, from which cotton fiber is spun. It is the primary natural fiber used by man, and it is also a major oilseed crop. The pulp remaining after extraction of oil from the seeds is used to make a high-protein cattle cake.

Cowpea   *Black-eyed pea*
Vigna unguiculata subsp. unguiculata

A species of annual plant in the pea (*Fabaceae*) family, believed to have originated in West Africa, but now widely cultivated throughout the tropical regions of the world. It is one of the oldest cultivated crops. It is still an important food source today due to its high tolerance for drought and sandy soil. It is cultivated mainly for its edible bean, although the leaves, green peas and pea pods can be eaten. It is also used as cattle fodder. Other cultivated subspecies of *V. unguiculata* include: *sesquipedalis* (asparagus bean, or yardlong bean), and *cylindrica* (catjang).

Crab
Brachyura infraorder

A infraorder of crustaceans found in all of the world's oceans, in fresh water, and on land. Some species are popular food items in many parts of the world.

Crambe   *colewort, Abyssinian kale*
Crambe hispanica subsp. abyssinica

A species of herbaceous plant in the cabbage (*Brassicaceae*) family, native to western and eastern tropical Africa. It first came into cultivation in the early 20th century in Europe and then the United States, primarily as an oilseed crop similar to rapeseed. **Crambe oil** is inedible, but is useful for industrial purposes, such as a lubricant and fuel. The plant material remaining after oil extraction is used as animal fodder.

Cranberry   *large cranberry, American cranberry*
Vaccinium macrocarpon

A species of evergreen dwarf shrubs or trailing vines in the heather (*Ericaceae*) family, native to the cooler, marshy regions of the North America. It is cultivated in North America and Europe for its edible fruit, the cranberry. A species of cranberry native to western Asia and Europe (*V. oxycoccus*, the small cranberry) is also cultivated in central and northern Europe. The plant is closely related to other berries, including the bilberry, lingonberry, and blueberry.

Cricket   *common house cricket*
Acheta domesticus

A species of insect in the *Gryllidae* family, most likely native to Southwestern Asia. Since the mid-twentieth-century, these crickets have become the standard feeder insects for the pet and research industry. They are also coming into wider use in the United States as a source of nutritional protein for humans, usually in the form of "cricket powder" or "cricket flour."

Crosne
artichoke betony

Stachys affinis

A species of herbaceous perennial plant in the mint (*Lamiaceae*) family, native to China, but now widely cultivated in temperate regions as a root vegetable. Its common name "artichoke betony" indicates its relationship to the medicinal plant betony (*Stachys officinalis*). A closely related plant, the Hubei-artichoke (*Stachys adulterina*) is also grown in China as a root vegetable.

Croton

Croton spp.

A genus of small trees and shrubs in the spurge (*Euphorbiaceae*) family, widely distributed in the Old World and New World. Several species are of medicinal importance, including: *Croton lechleri* (sangre de drago or dragon's blood), the source of **crofelemer** (a treatment for diarrhea) and **taspine** (a neurotoxin with several industrial and medicinal uses); and *C. stellatopilosus*, the source of **plaunotol** (an anti-ulcer medication). Purging croton (*C. tiglium*) has a history of use in traditional medicine, and is currently used as an herbicide. *C. laccifer* is important as a host for lac insects (see separate entry). *C. megalocarpus* is a fast-growing tree native to Sub-Saharan Africa, where it is cultivated for its seeds, which produce a non-edible oil used to make biodiesel fuel. The pulp residue left after oil extraction is used to make high-protein feed cake for animals, and the husks are used as fertilizer.

Cubeb
Java pepper

Piper cubeba

A species of herbaceous plant in the pepper (*Piperaceae*) family, native to and cultivated mostly in Java and Sumatra. It is cultivated for the berries, which are picked unripe, dried, and used as a spice and for medicinal purposes. An essential oil is also extracted from the berries. The berries were at one time used to make medicinal cigarettes for the treatment of catarrh (inflammation of a mucous membrane).

Cucumber
Cucumis sativus var. sativus

A species of annual creeping vine in the gourd (*Cucurbitaceae*) family, native to South Asia, but now widely cultivated, especially in the U.S. and Europe. It is cultivated for its fruit, which is eaten as a vegetable. The cucumber has been cultivated for at least 3000 years, and is mentioned in the ancient text the *Epic of Gilgamesh*. The many cultivars fall into three general categories: slicing (those intended to be eaten fresh); pickling (smaller fruits, also called gherkins or cornichons); and burpless, which are cultivated to be seedless and with thinner skins. The cucumber's popularity is in spite of its lack of nutritional value; it is mostly water, with few calories or essential nutrients, with the exception of vitamin K. Cucumbers are closely related to melons (*Cucumis melo*).

Cumaru   *tonka-bean*
Dipteryx odorata

A species of tree in the pea (*Fabaceae*) family, native to Central and South America, and now cultivated mainly in South America and central Africa. It is known for its seeds, called tonka beans, which are used as a spice similar to vanilla. Its essential oil is used in perfume. The seeds contain coumarin, from which is derived the chemical compound that forms the basis of anticoagulant drugs such as warfarin and coumadin. Coumarin itself, however, is not an anticoagulant. The wood of the cumaru tree is also coming into use as a hardwood flooring material.

Cumin
Cuminum cyminum

A species of annual plant in the parsley (*Apiaceae*) family, whose exact native range is unknown, but is presumed to be the Middle East and eastward to India. It is now widely cultivated for its seeds, which are dried, ground, and used as a spice. Archaeological evidence suggests that cumin has been cultivated in Egypt since at least 1600 BC, and was used as a spice and in the preservation of mummies.

Currant bush
Ribes spp.

Ribes is a genus of about 150 species of plants in the gooseberry (*Grossulariaceae*) family, native to the temperate regions of the Northern Hemisphere. The genus includes the widely cultivated species that produce the edible berries called currants and gooseberries, for example: black currant (*R. nigrum*); redcurrant (*R. rubrum*); English gooseberry (*R. uva-crispa*); as well as other species, and several hybrid cultivated species such as jostaberry and the garden currant.

Cuttlefish
Sepia spp.

Sepia is a genus of cuttlefish, which is a type of cephalopod similar to a squid. The most commonly known and fished species is the common cuttlefish, *S. officinalis*, which is native to the Mediterranean, North Atlantic, and Baltic seas. The genus is best known as the source of **sepia**, a rich brown ink obtained from its ink sac. Sepia has been an important painting, drawing, and writing ink since the Greco-Roman era. In modern times, the ink is more commonly used as a food dye and flavoring. Potential uses in cosmetics and medicine are being explored. The cuttlefish is also fished for its edible meat. The genus is unique for its interior shell, called the cuttlebone, which is composed of aragonite (a form of calcium carbonate). In the past, this bone served a variety of purposes, mostly in powdered form as an abrasive. In modern times, it is mostly used as a calcium-rich dietary supplement for pet animals such as birds and reptiles.

Cypress pine
Callitris spp.

Callitris is a genus of about fifteen species of evergreen trees in the cypress (*Cupressaceae*) family, native to Australia and New Caledonia. It is harvested for its softwood, which is resistant to decay and termites. At least two of the species, *C. endlicheri* and *C. collumelaris*, also produce the resin known as **sandarac**, which is used to make varnish.

Dandelion
Taraxacum officinale

A species of annual plant in the sunflower (*Asteraceae*) family, native to Europe but now widely naturalized to the temperate regions. In North America, dandelions are considered a weed, but they were brought to the New World by European settlers as food and for use in traditional medicine. Dandelions are entirely edible, including the flowers, leaves, stems, and roots, and are rich in vitamins. Dandelion wine, made by fermenting the flower petals in sugar, is still a common use of the plant. The closely-related species *T. kok-sagbyz* (Russian dandelion) is cultivated as a source of latex similar to that of the rubber tree.

Date palm
Phoenix dactylifera

A domesticated species of tree in the palm (*Arecaceae*) family, most likely descended from the wild ancestor *P. sylvestris* (the silver date palm). It is by far the most common source of the date fruit. Fossil records show that the date palm is an extremely ancient plant, at least 50 million years old. Archaeological evidence suggests cultivation as early as the 6th millennium BCE, in the Fertile Crescent region. The date palm was one of the most ancient symbolic forms of the Tree of Life in the Near East, and was the sacred emblem of Judea after the Exodus from Egypt. In the first century BC, the Romans took the palm leaf as the symbol of their victory over Judea and the destruction of Jerusalem. The palm leaf was then adopted as the symbol of Christ's triumphant entry into Jerusalem in defiance of Roman rule and the Hebrew hierarchy. The date palm is now widely cultivated and naturalized to hot arid regions around the world. In addition to producing edible fruit, seeds of the date fruit can be ground for animal fodder, and the leaves are used to make baskets and other items.

Deodar cedar   *Himalayan cedar*
Cedrus deodara

A species of cedar in the pine (*Pinaceae*) family, native to the western Himalayas. It is prized for its fine-grained and rot-resistant hardwood. An essential oil is also extracted from the inner wood, which is used for incense, as an insect repellent, and as an antifungal agent.

Diamond
carbon

A solid form of carbon with a diamond cubic crystal structure, formed under conditions of intense heat and pressure. At room temperature and pressure, diamond is technically unstable, with graphite being its stable form. However, diamond almost never reverts to graphite. It has the highest hardness and thermal conductivity of any bulk material, which gives it great value as an industrial material. It is also a highly valued gemstone. The first diamonds were found in alluvial deposits in India, roughly 3000 years ago. Diamonds can be colorless, or come in a variety of colors due to the presence of impurities in the matrix. The famous Hope Diamond is blue due to the presence of boron atoms. **Bort** is shards of small, impure diamonds that is utilized mainly as abrasives. **Carbonado** or black diamond is a dark, impure form that is used as an abrasive and for diamond set drills.

Diatomaceous earth   *Kieselguhr, diatomite*

A naturally-occurring, hydrous form of silica, it is a sedimentary rock made up of the microscopic shells of diatoms, a type of algae. It resembles chalk but is very porous and easily crumbles into powder. Unlike chalk, it is chemically inert. It has many uses, including: water filtration (most notably, it was used to successfully filter water during a cholera epidemic in Hamburg in 1892); filtration of other liquids such as crude sugar, fruit juices, mineral oil, perfumes, and others. In brick or powder form it is used for the insulation of furnaces and refrigerators, and for soundproofing. It is used as a mild abrasive (as in metal polishes, toothpaste and facial scrubs), and is an ingredient in some kinds of concrete. It is also used as an insecticide, due to its abrasive and moisture-absorbing properties.

Dika   *bush mango*
Irvingia gabonensis

A species of tree in the *Irvingiaceae* family, native to the humid tropical forest zone of Africa. They are valued for their edible mango-like fruit, and the fat and protein rich seed, called the dika nut. These can be eaten raw or roasted, or pressed for an edible oil. The pulp remaining after oil extraction is used as animal fodder. Until recently, the fruits were only wild-gathered. Cultivation has been only moderately successful.

Dill
Anethum graveolens

An annual herb in the parsley (*Apiaceae*) family, native to and cultivated in many parts of the world. It is widely cultivated for its carminative (digestive gas-inhibiting) fruits (commonly called "seeds"), and its essential oil, both of which are used for a food flavoring. The leaves are also used, though not as commonly.

Dividivi   *cascalote, guatapana, nacascolote*
Caesalpinia coriaria

A tree in the pea (*Fabaceae*) family, native to Mexico and South America, and now widely cultivated in the tropics. The seed pods contain tannin, which is extracted for use in tanning leather.

Dock   see *Sorrel*

Dogbane   *hemp dogbane*
Apocynum cannabinum

A species of perennial herbaceous plant in the dogbane (*Apocynaceae*) family, native to much of North America and East Asia. All parts of the plant are toxic to humans and livestock. Nevertheless, it is the source of strong fibers that do not shrink and retain their strength in water. It was used extensively by Native Americans for cordage. It has traditionally been used as a medicinal plant, but contains compounds that can be deadly even in moderate doses. North American dogbane is closely related to swordleaf dogbane (*A. venetum*), which is native to western Asia, Eastern Europe, and India. In those regions, it is an important source of nectar for bees, fiber, resin, and traditional medicine.

Dogwood tree
Cornus spp.

Cornus is a genus of about fifty species of small deciduous trees in the *Cornaceae* family, known generally as the dogwoods. They are native to and widely distributed throughout the temperate and boreal zones of Eurasia and North America, and naturalized elsewhere. The wood is valued for its hardness and fine grain. The fruit (cornelian-cherries) of the species *Cornus mas* are cultivated for use in syrups and preserves. The bark of most species in the genus is rich in tannins.

Dolomite
Calcium magnesium carbonate

A mineral, or a sedimentary carbonate rock composed mainly of the mineral. Dolomite and dolomitic limestone are used in horticulture, commonly added to potting mixes as a pH buffer and source of magnesium. It has uses in glass manufacture, and the gasification of biomass. It is also used as a concrete aggregate.

Donkey   *Ass*
Equus africanus asinus

A domesticated species of the horse (*Equidae*) family, whose ancestor is the wild donkey (*Equus africanus*). Donkeys have been domesticated for at least 5000 years. Their primary use is as pack animals, though their meat, milk, and hide have been used and continue to be used to a limited extent.

Douglas fir
Pseudotsuga menziesii

A species of evergreen conifer in the pine (*Pinaceae*) family, native to western North America. It is widely cultivated elsewhere as a valuable source of timber, and as a source of pine resin. Despite the common name, the tree is not a true fir. There are two main varieties: *P. menziesii var. glauca* (Rocky Mountain Douglas fir); and *P. menziesii var. menziesii* (coastal Douglas fir). The coast variety can grow up to 100 meters tall.

Dromedary   *Arabian camel*
Camelus dromedarius

One of two domesticated species in the genus *Camelus* (the other being the bactrian camel), the dromedary inhabits the Horn of Africa and the Middle East. It is widely used there as a source of milk, meat, fiber, and as an extremely hardy pack animal.

Dulse   *sea lettuce flakes, creathnach*
Palmaria spp.

The name dulse refers to two species of red algae (*Rhodophyta*) that grow on the northern coasts of the Pacific (*Palmaria mollis*) and Atlantic (*Palmaria palmata*) oceans. It has been a traditional food source in northern Europe and Great Britain for centuries, and is high in vitamins, minerals, protein, and fiber.

Durian
Durio zibethinus

A species of tree in the mallow (*Malvaceae*) family, it is one of several species in the genus *Durio* that produces the edible fruit called durian. However, this is the only species currently available on the international market. Other species and varieties are primarily sold only within the local markets. The trees are native to Thailand, Indonesia, and Malaysia, and are cultivated almost exclusively in those regions. The fruit is known for its powerful (and for some people, very unpleasant) scent, and for that reason is banned from certain public areas in the countries where it is commonly grown.

East Indian arrowroot   *narrow-leaved turmeric*
Curcuma angustifolia

A species of perennial herbaceous plant in the ginger (*Zingiberaceae*) family, native to the Indian Subcontinent and Indo -China. It is cultivated for its rhizome, which is used to make an easily-digestible starch flour with uses similar to true arrowroot.

Ebony tree
Diospyros spp.

Ebony is a term that refers to several species within the genus *Diospyros*, in the *Ebenaceae* family, native to tropical regions of the Northern Hemisphere. Several species have been harvested for their dark, sometimes black heartwood: especially *D. ebenum* (Ceylon ebony); *D. crassiflora* (Benin ebony); and *D. celebica* (black ebony). The trees are very slow-growing and have not historically been cultivated, but were wild-harvested. Most of the species are now endangered, and in some of the native countries it is illegal to harvest and export them. Ebony trees are closely related to the species that produce the edible fruit known as persimmon.

Eel   *European eel*
Anguilla anguilla

A now critically-endangered species of snake-like fish that is an important food source in Europe. Since the 1950's wild-fishing of the European eel has largely been replaced by farmed fish.

Eelgrass
Zostera spp.

grass wrack

Zostera is a small genus of seagrasses found off the coasts of temperate zones around the world. It has long, narrow grass-like leaves. Its roots and leaf bases have been used as food by Native Americans from the coast of Sonora, Mexico; the leaves have been used as thatching material by the residents of the Danish island of Laeso; in Europe, it has been used as packing material and as stuffing for mattresses and cushions; it can also be used to produce biomass energy.

Eggplant
Solanum melongena

aubergine, brinjal

A species of herbaceous perennial plant in the nightshade (*Solanaceae*) family, likely native to Africa and then naturalized to Asia. It is now widely cultivated in many regions of the world. Eggplant is a domesticated version of the thornapple (*S. incanum*). Its fruit is a commercially important food vegetable.

Eider duck
Somateria spp.

A genus of three species of sea duck in the *Anatidae* family, native to the higher latitudes of the Northern Hemisphere. They are known for their fine down feathers, called eiderdown. Eider ducks are not domesticated; the down is collected from human-protected nesting areas, mainly in Iceland and Scandinavia. The down is used as insulation material in clothing and bedding.

Einkorn

see **Wheat**

Elbaite
sodium, lithium, aluminum borosilicate

A mineral in the tourmaline group used as a gemstone and prized for its variety and depth of color, and the quality of the crystals. The color depends on the relative presence of sodium, lithium, and aluminum, and also on the presence of trace impurities. The crystals can exhibit multicolor zonation.

Elder
elderberry

Sambucus spp.

A genus of shrubs or small trees in the moschatel (*Adoxaceae*) family. It is found in the temperate to subtropical regions of the world, though it is more common in the Northern Hemisphere. It is used and cultivated mainly for its berries (elderberries) and flowers. All parts of the plant are toxic, but cooking the berries and flowers renders them edible without harm. The berries are used in pies and jams and to make wine; the flowers are used to make sugar syrup and flavor essences. The berries contain anthocyanins which are used as food coloring, and as a fabric dye. The most commonly cultivated species are the American elder (*S. canadensis*), the blue elderberry (*S. cerulea*), and the European elder or black elder (*S. nigra*). The black elder has a long tradition of use as a traditional medicine, and a recent *in vitro* study aiming to explore the efficacy of a plethora of Austrian herbal medicines has demonstrated significant anti-inflammatory effect of the extracts of *S. nigra* fruits and flowers.

Elemi

Canarium luzonicum

A species of tree in the torchwood (*Bursuraceae*) family, native to the Philippines. It is one of several trees in the genus cultivated for the aromatic oleoresin, also called elemi. The term "elemi" in previous times has referred to the resin of the *Boswellia* genus, which is also the source of the resin called frankincense. Elemi is used as an ingredient in varnish and printing ink. An essential oil which is steam-distilled from the resin is used as a fragrance.

Elephant yam
telinga potato

Amorphophallus paeoniifolius

A species of herbaceous plant in the arum (*Araceae*) family, cultivated primarily in Africa, South Asia, Southeast Asia, and the Pacific Islands, where it is an important food source in some regions. Like taro, to which it is related, it is grown for its edible corm (underground stem), which is high in starch. The closely-related species *A. konjac*, also known as the elephant yam or konjac, has a similar geographic distribution and purpose.

Elm
Ulmus spp.

A genus of deciduous trees in the elm (*Ulmaceae*) family, comprised of about forty species, and many cultivars within these species. The genus originated in Central Asia roughly 20 million years ago, but is now widespread throughout the temperate regions of both hemispheres. The trees are highly valued for many purposes, including wood, medicine, fodder, biomass, and food. In recent decades, the North American and European populations of older trees have been virtually wiped out by Dutch elm disease, which has spurred the development of disease-resistant cultivars. The genus has produced many famous trees, such as the tree named "Herbie" in Yarmouth, Maine. It was planted in 1793 and became the oldest and tallest elm in New England, until it died of Dutch elm disease in 2010.

Emerald   see *Beryl*

Emery   see *Corundum*

Endive   *escarole*
Cichorium endivia

A domesticated perennial herbaceous species within the dandelion (*Asteraceae*) family, native to temperate Europe but now widely cultivated elsewhere. It is closely related to and often confused with chicory (*Cichorium intybus*). Endive is cultivated for its somewhat bitter edible leaves, which are eaten raw as a salad vegetable.

Epazote   *wormseed, Jerusalem tea, paico*
Dysphania ambrosioides

A species of perennial herbaceous plant in the amaranth (*Amaranthaceae*) family, native to southern Mexico and Central and South America. It has a long history of use as a medicinal plant and as a leaf vegetable and food flavoring. Its essential oil contains a high percentage of the compound ascaridole, which is toxic to humans. It is also used as a natural pesticide. Its chemical composition can be detrimental to other plants, giving it the potential to become an invasive weed when introduced to areas outside its natural range.

Epsom salt
magnesium sulfate

A white crystalline mineral found in sea water, and in some mineral deposits on land. It was originally found in Epsom in England, for which it is named. Epsom salt is on the World Health Organization's Model List of Essential Medicines. It is used both internally and externally. Externally, it is made into a paste used to treat skin inflammations, or as bath salts. Internally, it is used (among other things) to treat asthma, certain types of heart arrhythmias, and prevention of pre-eclampsia progressing to eclampsia during pregnancy. It also has uses outside of medicine, such as: a soil amendment to increase the magnesium content, and as a coagulant in the production of tofu.

Esparto grass
Stipa tenacissima, Lygeum spartum

The name esparto grass refers to two species of perennial herbaceous plant in the grass (*Poaceae*) family, both native to the Western Mediterranean, primarily North Africa and the southern Iberian Peninsula. It is cultivated for the leaf fiber, called **esparto**, which is used to make items such as sandals, baskets, mats, and ropes. There is a long cultural tradition in Spain surrounding esparto craft. Due to its high tolerance for saline soils, the grass is also used to stabilize sand dunes and for soil rehabilitation.

Eucalyptus   *Gum tree*
Eucalyptus spp.

A diverse genus of about 700 species of trees in the myrtle (*Myrtaceae*) family. Only nine species are not native to Australia, and only fifteen species are naturally found outside of Australia. The genus dominates the tree flora in Australia. The species *E. regnans* (swamp gum) is the tallest flowering plant on Earth, regularly growing to a height of 85 meters. Eucalyptus have been widely introduced to other regions. They are fast-growing and are often grown on plantations to provide wood for charcoal and especially pulp; a medicinal essential oil can be steam distilled from the leaves of many species; all parts of the tree can be used to make a dye for animal fibers. Several species are important nectar sources for honeybees. They are called gum trees because they exude large amounts of **kino** when the bark is damaged.

Fava bean
broad bean

Vicia faba subsp. faba var. faba

A domesticated species of annual plant in the pea (*Fabaceae*) family, widely cultivated for its edible bean. Along with its close relative bitter vetch (*V. ervilia*), it was one of the earliest cultivated crops, with evidence for its domestication dating back to about 5000 B.C. in the Near East. It is toxic to people to who suffer from favism, a genetic disorder that predisposes the person the red blood cell breakdown. Like the vetches, many subspecies and varieties of *V. faba* are cultivated as fodder plants.

Feijoa
pineapple guava, guavasteen

Acca sellowiana

A species of small evergreen tree in the myrtle (*Myrtaceae*) family, native to the highlands of southern Brazil, eastern Paraguay, Uruguay, northern Argentina, and Colombia. It is widely cultivated in South America for local consumption of its edible fruit, which (despite the name) is not a true guava. The flower petals are also edible and are eaten fresh, often in salads.

Feldspar
aluminum silicates of potassium, sodium, and calcium

Feldspar is a group of rock-forming silicate minerals that make up 41% of the Earth's continental crust by weight. They are important in the manufacture of glass and ceramics, with almost 70% of mined feldspar being used for that purpose. Feldspar is also used as an ingredient in paint, plastics, and rubber to improve durability, hardness, and resistance to corrosion. Moonstone (water opal) is a translucent bluish-white variety that can be polished into a cabochon and used as a semiprecious gemstone.

Fennel
Foeniculum vulgare

A species of herbaceous perennial plant in the parsley (*Apiaceae*) family, native to the shores of the Mediterranean. It is now widely cultivated and naturalized elsewhere, especially to dry soil coastlines and riverbanks. Its dried seeds are used as a spice, and also yield an aromatic oil used medicinally and for flavoring. Florence fennel or finocchio (*F. vulgare subsp. vulgare var. azoricum*), has a bulb-like stem that is eaten as a vegetable.

Fenugreek   *Greek clover*
Trigonella foenum-graecum

A species of annual plant in the pea (*Fabaceae*) family, native to
Middle Asia and Eastern Europe, but now naturalized to and
cultivated in other temperate regions. The seeds, pods, and
leaves are all used as culinary spices. The essential oil is used as a
flavoring. The leaves are often eaten raw as a salad. The plant is
also grown as fodder. Blue fenugreek (*T. caerulea*) is the flavoring
ingredient in the traditional Swiss schabziger cheese.

Fescue grass
Festuca spp.

A genus of evergreen perennial plants in the grass (*Poaceae*) family, native to and widespread in Europe. *F. arundinacea* (tall fescue) has served as an important forage crop in Europe for centuries. *F. ovina* (sheep fescue) has been an important hay and pasturage crop in the United States since it was introduced in the
1940's. Several other species are also used as fodder, or lawn and
park grasses. In the U.S., it has quickly become a dominant and
in some places invasive plant.

Fig   *common fig*
Ficus carica

A species of evergreen tree in the mulberry (*Moraceae*) family,
native to the Middle East and western Asia. It has been cultivated since ancient times for its edible fruit, the fig. The fig is one of
the first plants cultivated by humans; subfossilized fruit of a non-
reproductive variety (which indicates cultivation) have been
found in a Neolithic village in the Jordan Valley, dating to about
9200-9400 B.C. It has since been introduced to and is now widely
cultivated throughout the world. The fig has a symbiotic relationship with the fig wasp, and some varieties of fig (for example,
Smyrna-type figs) do not produce fruit without cross pollination
by fig wasps. The common fig tree is one of the most widely
revered sacred trees: among the ancient Hebrews, it was the symbol of peace and abundance; in Islam it is referred to as the Tree
of Heaven, and was considered to be the most intelligent tree,
only one step removed from the animal kingdom.

Finocchio   see *Fennel*

Fir tree
Abies spp.

A genus of about 50 species of coniferous trees in the pine (*Pinaceae*) family, native to the cooler mountainous regions of much of North and Central America, Asia, Europe, and North Africa. They are a fast-growing tree whose timber, considered inferior to pine, is most commonly used for pulp. Because the wood has little resistance to rot or insects once it has been cut, it is used only for interior construction. Several species are popularly used as Christmas trees, especially the silver fir (*A. alba*), Fraser fir (*A. fraseri*), balsam fir (*A. balsamea*), and noble fir (*A. procera*). The sacred fir (*A. religiosa*) serves as the nesting tree for migrating Monarch butterflies. The balsam fir also contains a resin that is used to produce the turpentine known as **Canada balsam.**

Fire clay   *refractory clay*

Fire clay is the name given to a variety of clays that are capable of withstanding heat to at least 1515 deg. Celsius (2759 deg. Fahrenheit). High grade clays can withstand up to 1775 deg. C (3227 deg. F). Fire clays consist of natural argillaceous materials, mostly Kaolinite group clays, as well as fine-grained mica and quartz. They are used to make fire brick for lining furnaces, as well as utensils (such as retorts, crucibles, and saggars) used in the metalworking, glass, and ceramic industries.

Flame of the Forest tree   *Bastard teak, Bengal kino, palash*
Butea monosperma

A deciduous tree in the pea (*Fabaceae*) family, native to tropical and sub-tropical regions of India and South Asia. It is best known for its flowers, which are spectacular and are used as a fabric dye. The dried, powdered flowers are used to make the orange or red *gulal,* the colored powders that are thrown during the Holi festival (the festival of spring) celebrated in India and Nepal. Traditionally, the powders are thrown because they have medicinal value according to the Ayurvedic system, and the various colors are made from sources such as turmeric, bael, indigo, tea, and beetroot. The gum of the tree is a **kino** known as Bengal kino or kamarkas; it is used medicinally, as a dye, and as a food. The tree is also a host for lac insects.

Flax

linseed

Linum usitatissimum

A species of annual plant in the *Linaceae* family. It is believed to have been domesticated from wild flax (*L. bienne*) in the Fertile Crescent region roughly 9000 years ago, though evidence of its use by humans dates back 30,000 years. It now only exists in domesticated form, and is widely cultivated in the cooler temperate zones of the world. It has many uses: the stem fibers are called flax, which are woven into the textile called **linen**; flax seeds are used as food, and the seed oil is known as **linseed oil**. Linseed meal, left after the oil has been expressed from the seeds, is used as feed for ruminants, rabbits, and fish.

Flint

Silicon dioxide

Flint is a sedimentary form of quartz, found as nodules embedded in chalks and limestones; it is categorized as a kind of chert. Due to its cryptocrystalline structure, it is extremely hard and, like obsidian, can be knapped (chipped into flakes) to create very sharp cutting edges. In previous times it was used to create sharp -edged tools and weapons. In modern times it has also occasionally been used as a building material. When struck against steel, it produces a spark, and so has been used as a source of ignition in weapons (e.g., as part of the "flintlock" mechanism), and in fire starting (e.g., the "flint and steel" method).

Fluorite

Fluorspar

Calcium fluoride

A mineral that has several uses: as a flux in smelting and in the production of certain glasses and enamels; in the manufacture of hydrofluoric acid, which is the intermediary source of most fluorine-containing chemicals; transparent crystalline fluorine is used to make lenses for microscopes and telescopes, being particularly useful for optics that are used in the ultraviolet range. It is relatively soft, and can be deeply colored, and has some use in ornamental carvings. Fluorite typically exhibits fluorescence under ultraviolet light (from which the property takes its name), and is thermoluminescent.

Foxglove
Digitalis spp.

Digitalis

Digitalis is a genus of about thirty species of herbaceous perennials, shrubs, and biennials in the plantain (*Plantanginacaea*) family, commonly called foxgloves. They are native to western and southwestern Europe but are widely naturalized to the temperate zones. The best-known species is *D. purpurea*, or common foxglove, which is the source of the heart medication **digoxin**, which is included in the World Health Organization's Model List of Essential Medicines. The species *D. lanata* (woolly foxglove) is a source of digoxin, deslanoside and the lanatosides (also heart medications). The compounds that form the basis of these medications make the plant highly toxic to humans.

Frangipani
Plumeria spp.

plumeria, pagoda tree

A genus of about twelve species of small flowering tree or shrub in the dogbane (*Apocynaceae*) family, native to Mexico, Central America, and northern South America. It is now widespread throughout the tropical, subtropical, and warm temperate zones. The common name for the plant varies widely, depending on the region. They are cultivated mainly as ornamentals, with some species cultivated for their scented flowers (particularly *P. rubra*), from which is produced an essential oil used in perfumes and incense. Like all members of the dogbane family, the tree contains toxic compounds, particularly in its milky latex. In many parts of the world, frangipani has symbolic significance. For instance, it is used in Hawaiian leis (flower garlands) to symbolize positivity. In Southeast Asia the flowers have a strong connection to cemeteries and the dead, and the scent is associated with a particular evil spirit. The flower has a complex symbolic significance in both Mayan and Aztec culture which evolved over centuries, with strong associations with nobility and divinity.

Frankincense tree
Boswellia spp.

A genus of trees within the torchwood (*Burseraceae*) family, native to tropical regions of Asia and Africa. Frankincense has been cultivated for several millennia in these regions. Four species of the genus are cultivated to produce true frankincense, a gum resin used in perfume, incense, and medicinally. The four species are: *B. sacra* (frankincense, or olibanum-tree); *B. frereana* (elemi, or yigaartree); *B. papyrifera* (elephant tree); and *B. serrata* (boswellia, or Indian frankincense). In the Christian tradition, frankincense was one of the three gifts given (along with myrrh and gold) by the Magi to the newborn Christ child.

Freesia
Freesia spp.

A genus of herbaceous perennial flowering plants in the iris (*Iridaceae*) family, native to southeastern Africa but widely cultivated elsewhere. Most cultivated plants are a man-made hybrid between the two wild species *F. refracta* and *F. leichtinii*. There are numerous cultivars, grown mainly as ornamentals for their showy and fragrant flowers. The essential oil is used to scent perfumes, soaps, candles, and other cosmetics.

Fujian cypress
Fokienia hodginsii

A species of coniferous tree in the cypress (*Cupressaceae*) family, native to southeastern China and northern Vietnam. It is valued for its fine-grained, aromatic wood, and for the essential oil called **pemou oil**, which is distilled mainly from the roots. The tree is listed as ecologically vulnerable in Vietnam.

Fuller's earth   *whitening clay*

A clay composed mainly of hydrous aluminum silicates, primarily attapulgite or bentonite, but also kaolinite and montmorillonite. It has the ability to decolorize oil without changing the chemical composition. The name comes from its use in the wool industry ("Fullers" process wool to prepare it for spinning and weaving) to remove lanolin and other greasy impurities from the wool before processing. Currently, it is used in the cosmetics industry, as a decontamination agent, and to clean marble surfaces.

Galena
lead glance
lead sulfide

A mineral that is the chief ore of lead, that also often contains a small percentage of silver. Galena is a semi-conductor, and was at one time used as the crystal in crystal radio receivers; building such radios was at one time a popular home hobby. Because galena contains lead, prolonged exposure to the dust can have harmful health effects.

Gallium

Gallium is a metallic element that does not occur in free form in nature, but only as compounds found in trace amounts in zinc ores and in bauxite. It is used to make alloys with low melting points, and to harden copper. Gallium alloys have been used to make thermometers as a non-toxic alternative to mercury. It also has uses in electronics as a semiconductor.

Galls
cecidia

With regard to plants, galls are abnormal growths of plant tissue that occur in response to infection of the plant by various parasites, such as fungi, mites, insects, or bacteria. Galls are often rich in resins and tannic acid, and various types of galls from specific plants have a long history of use in manufacturing ink (such as **iron gall ink**), dye, in tanning, and as medicine. Galls often represent a very specific relationship between the plant and the invader, and take very specific recognizable forms, sometimes looking very much like a natural part of the plant.

Gambier
pale catechu
Uncaria gambir

A species of shrub in the madder (*Rubiaceae*) family, native to Southeast Asia, mostly Malaysia and Indonesia. It is cultivated for the extract produced from its leaves, called **gambier** or pale catechu. Gambier extract is used as a brown dye, a tanning agent, and a food flavoring. Despite the common name, it is not closely related to the catechu tree (*Senegalia catechu*), though their extracts serve similar purposes.

Gamboge tree
Garcinia spp.

The common name is used to refer primarily to two species of evergreen tree in the *Clusiaceae* family, *Garcinia hanburyi* and *Garcinia morella*, both native to India. These species, among a few others in the *Garcinia* genus, produce a resin that is used to make the saffron-yellow pigment known as **gamboge**; it is the pigment traditionally used to dye the robes of Buddhist monks. The gamboge tree is closely related to the mangosteen (*G. mangostana*), popularly cultivated for its edible fruit.

Gandaria
Bouea macrophylla

A species of evergreen tree in the cashew (*Anacardiaceae*) family, native to Southeast Asia, and widely cultivated there for its edible fruit, the gandaria. The entire fruit is edible, as are the young leaves of the tree.

Ganister   *crowstone*

A hard, fine-grained quartzose sandstone or orthoquartzite cemented with secondary silica, found underlying coal seams; it is physically and chemically inert. The rock is ground down and used to make silica bricks for lining furnaces.

Garbanzo   see *Chickpea*

Garden cress   *pepperwort*
Lepidium sativum

The best-known of several species in the genus *Lepidium* (pepperwort), within the cabbage (*Brassicaceae*) family. It is native to North Africa, the Arabian Peninsula, and India, but is now widely naturalized to and cultivated in other regions of the world. It is grown for its edible leaves and stems, which have a peppery flavor. It is closely related to other members of the cabbage family also known for their pungency, such as watercress, mustard, radish, and wasabi.

Garlic
Allium sativum

A domesticated species of small annual plant in the amaryllis (*Amaryllidaceae*) family, thought to be native to Central Asia and northeastern Iran. It has been domesticated for thousands of years, and is widely cultivated around the world, primarily for its edible bulbous stem, which is used as a food flavoring, and for its medicinal properties as an antibiotic. It is in the same genus as the common onion, shallot, leek, chives, and Chinese onion.

Garlic mustard   *Jack-by-the-hedge, hedge garlic*
Alliaria petiolata

A species of biennial plant in the cabbage (*Brassicaceae*) family, native to Europe, the British Isles, west and central Asia, north Africa, and Scandinavia. Garlic mustard is the oldest known cultivated spice in Europe, with earliest evidence for use coming from archaeological remains in the Baltic dating back to 4100 - 3750 BCE. It was imported to the Americas for use as a food plant and for medicinal use (as a diuretic). It has since become widely naturalized and in some regions invasive.

Garnet

Garnet refers to a group of silicate minerals that contain varying amounts of aluminum and calcium, and magnesium and iron. There are several minerals in the garnet group, with names and properties depending on the relative amounts of each of the four elements above. These are: almandine (carbuncle), pyrope, spessartine, andradite, grossular, and uvarovite. Garnets have a history of use since the Bronze Age, particularly as gemstones and as abrasives. Almandine is used as the jewels watches. Garnet sand is used as a water filtration medium.

Genip   *honeyberry, Spanish lime*
Melicoccus bijugatus

A species of evergreen tree in the soapberry (*Sapindaceae*) family, native to northern and western South America and Brazil, but now widely cultivated in tropical regions, particularly the Caribbean. It is cultivated for its edible fruit, which goes by many names, depending on the region of cultivation.

Gentian
Gentiana spp.

Gentiana is a large genus containing about 400 species of small herbaceous plants within the gentian (*Gentianaceae*) family. They are found mostly in the alpine habitats in the temperate regions of Europe, Asia, and the Americas, but some species are also found in northwestern Africa, eastern Australia, and New Zealand. They are best known for their deep blue flowers. However, the great yellow gentian (*G. lutea*) is the species most commonly cultivated in Europe for its root, which is used as a bitter flavoring and for its medicinal properties; many other species share similar characteristics. The glycoside compounds amarogentin and gentiopicrin are what give gentian its famously bitter taste. Amarogentin is the most bitter substance known, and is used as a standard against which bitterness is measured.

Giant kelp
Macrocystis pyrifera

A species of kelp that is the largest of all algae, and the fastest growing plant in the world. It is found along the coastline of the eastern Pacific, as well as in South America, South Africa, Australia and New Zealand. Its primary use is to produce **alginate**, though it is also a food source rich in iodine and potassium. When burned, it is a source of soda ash, which is important for glass-making and other uses.

Giant sequoia   *giant redwood, Wellingtonia*
Sequoiadendron giganteum

The sole living species in the genus *Sequoiadendron*, giant sequoia are one of three species of giant evergreens in the *Sequoioidae* subfamily of the cypress (*Cupressaceae*) family, which are known collectively as "redwoods." Giant sequoia are native to and found naturally only on the western slopes of the Sierra Nevada mountains of California. Due to the brittle nature of the wood of mature trees, giant sequoia have not historically been successfully commercially harvested. However, the wood of immature trees shares many of the desirable characteristics of coast redwoods (*Sequoia sempervirens*), and for that reason, cultivation of giant sequoia has recently gained in popularity.

Ginger
Zingiber officinale

A species of herbaceous plant in the ginger (*Zingiberaceae*) family, native to the tropical forests of the Indian subcontinent and Southern Asia, but now widely cultivated elsewhere in the world. It is cultivated primarily for its root and its essential oil, which is used medicinally and as a spice. Other species within the genus are also cultivated to a lesser extent, including *Z. minga* (Japanese ginger), and *Z. zerumbet* (shampoo ginger or awapuhi).

Ginkgo tree
Ginkgo biloba

maidenhair tree

The single living species from an ancient phylum of trees that dates back to the Permian era (about 270 million years ago). All other species in the phylum are extinct, and the relationship of the ginkgo to other plants is not well understood. The ginkgo is found growing wild only in China, but it is widely cultivated in the temperate zones of the world. In East Asian countries, the edible seeds are considered a delicacy; however, they contain small amounts of a neurotoxin that can be harmful if eaten regularly over a long period of time. The toxin cannot be neutralized by cooking. Leaf extracts have also long been considered to have medicinal qualities, and are also sold as dietary supplements, but its efficacy has not been supported by systematic research.

Ginseng
Panax spp.

The genus *Panax* consists of several species of herbaceous plants that are known as true ginseng. The best-known species (*P. ginseng*) is native to Asia. Also well-known and cultivated is American ginseng (*P. quinquefolius*), native to North America. Ginseng is wild-gathered and cultivated mostly for its root, which is used as food, flavoring, and also has a long tradition of use in Chinese herbal medicine, although its efficacy has not been supported by systematic clinical research.

Glasswort
Salicornia spp.

Salicornia is a genus of annual succulent halophyte (salt-loving) plants in the amaranth (*Amaranthaceae*) family, native to western Asia, North America, North Africa and Europe. In the past, common glasswort (*S. europaea*) was burned to get soda (sodium carbonate) from the ashes which was used in glass manufacture and soapmaking. The North American species, *S. bigelovii* (dwarf glasswort) is high in unsaturated fats and protein, and can be grown in saltwater to provide fodder for stock animals. It has also been explored as a potential source of biofuel.

Goat
Caprus aegagrus hircus

The domestic goat, a member of the *Bovidae* family, is one of the oldest domesticated animals. They are descended from the wild goats of the Fertile Crescent region of Iran and Iraq. The earliest evidence of domesticated goats dates back 10,000 years. Goats are raised worldwide for their meat, milk, hide, and fleece. Two breeds in particular are raised for their fleece: the cashmere goat (**cashmere wool**), and the angora goat (**mohair** fiber).

Gold

Gold is a relatively rare metallic element, categorized as one of the precious metals. It is notable for being one of the least chemically reactive elements, as well as for its malleability, ductility, and that it conducts electricity. It has a long and continuous history of use, across many cultures, as adornment and coinage. The earliest gold artifacts come from the Levant and from the Balkans, and date to about 6000 years ago. Today, about half of all gold mined is used to make jewelry. It also has a small but important use in industry, such as in the production of corrosion-free electrical connectors. Gold makes few compounds, but these have some use: for example, in making deep-red cranberry glass, and in photography. Several gold "salts" (actually metal thiolate complexes), such as Auranofin and sodium aurothiosulfate, are still in use as treatments for rheumatoid arthritis, though their use is becoming less common due to alternatives that are more effective, or with fewer harmful side effects.

Goose
Anser anser domesticus, Anser cygnoides domesticus

Modern domesticated geese, of the *Anatidae* family, are descend-
ants of either the Greylag goose (native to Western Asia) or the
Swan goose (native to eastern Asia). They have been kept by
humans for their eggs, meat and feathers for at least 4000 years.

Gooseberry   see *Currant*

Gorse   *furze, whin*
Ulex europaeus

A species of small flowering shrub in the pea (*Fabaceae*) family,
native to western Europe, but now widespread due to its use as
an ornamental plant. In some regions it is considered invasive.
Traditionally, gorse was planted and used as fuel, as the wood is
highly flammable, and the ash is a valuable fertilizer. It was also
used as animal fodder.

Grains of paradise   *melegueta pepper, alligator pepper*
Aframomum melegueta

An herbaceous perennial plant in the ginger (*Zingiberaceae*) family, native to the swampy habitats of West Africa. It is cultivated
in the tropical and temperate zones of Africa, North America, and
the Caribbean. It is a particularly important cash crop in tropical
Africa. Its small seeds (Grains of Paradise) are dried and ground
into a spice. Several other species in the *Aframomum* genus are
cultivated in West Africa for the same purpose, notably: *A. corrorima* (Ethiopian cardamom); *A. danielli, A. exscapum,* and *A.
citratum* (mbongo spice or alligator pepper).

Grains of Selim   *Guinea pepper, Ethiopian pepper*
Xylopia aethiopica

A species of small evergreen shrub in the custard apple
(*Annonaceae*) family, native to tropical Africa. It is widely cultivated there, especially for its seed pods, which are dried and
ground as a spice that is used both as a flavoring and medicinally.
In Senegal is it known as *djar*, and is a flavoring in the coffee
known as café Touba.

Granite

An igneous rock composed mainly of the minerals feldspar, mica, and quartz, along with other silicate minerals. It can be found in a variety of colors, including gray, white, pink, red, green, or yellow. It is a very dense, hard rock that has a long history of use as a building material.

Grape   *wine grape*
Vitis vinifera subsp. vinifera

A domesticated species of liana (vine) in the grapevine (*Vitaceae*) family, native to the Mediterranean region, central Europe, and southwestern Asia. It is now widely cultivated worldwide for its edible fruit, the grape. There are between 5000-10,000 cultivars, but only a few are of commercial importance. Several other species within the *Vitis* genus are used as graft stock and to breed desirable characteristics such as disease resistance into the wine grape. The fruits are eaten either fresh or dried (as raisins), but the vast majority of grapes from this species are made into wine. Winemaking dates back to roughly 5000 B.C. In the Near East, and about the 2nd century A.D. In China. In some cultures, grape leaves are eaten, and the stems and leaves are cattle fodder.

Graphite   *black lead, plumbago*
carbon

Graphite is pure carbon that has been subjected to intense heat and pressure. It is a very soft black mineral that has been used for making crucibles, paints, steel manufacture, metal polish, brushes for electric motors, dry storage batteries, and as the lead in pencils (for which it is mixed with fine clay).

Grass pea   *chickling-vetch, khesari*
Lathyrus sativus

A species of climbing perennial plant in the pea (*Fabaceae*) family, native to parts of Africa, Europe and China. It is cultivated for its edible, protein-rich seed which is used for human consumption and animal fodder. The seeds contain a toxic amino acid which is harmless in small amounts, but overconsumption can lead to adverse effects in humans. The closely-related species *L. tuberosus* (tuberous vetch or groundnut pea vine) is also cultivated on a more limited scale for its edible tuberous root.

Guar

cluster-bean

Cyamopsis tetragonoloba

A species of annual plant in the pea (*Fabaceae*) family, whose exact origin is unknown, but is thought to be India. It is cultivated mainly in India and Pakistan, but its cultivation is expanding due to increased demand for use in the natural gas industry. It is cultivated for the **guar gum** extracted from its beans, which is used as a thickener in the food, feed, and cosmetic industry, as well as other industrial applications.

Guarana

Paullinia cupana

A species of tropical evergreen tree in the soapberry (*Sapindaceae*) family, native to northern and western South America and Brazil. It is cultivated in those regions for the seed of the fruit, which is dried, powdered, and used as a beverage base for soft drinks and hot drinks. Guarana seeds contain about twice the concentration of caffeine as coffee beans. Like other members of the soapberry family, the fruit is a translucent fleshy pulp surrounding a black lacquer-like seed, which gives it the appearance of an eyeball. This has given the fruit its name, which is derived from the native word meaning "fruit like the eyes of the people." According to the local myth, the fruit originated when a deity, to atone for the killing of a local child, planted the eyes of the child, which grew into the wild and domesticated forms of the guarana tree.

Guava tree

Psidium guajava

A species of small evergreen tree in the myrtle (*Myrtaceae*) family, native to Mexico, Central America, and northern South America. It is now widely cultivated in many tropical and subtropical regions, particularly India. There are several species in the *Psidium* genus that produce edible fruit, but *P. guajava* (the apple guava) is by far the most widely cultivated. The fruit is most often eaten raw or made into juice. Guava seed oil is used in cosmetics. The wood is popularly used in the United States in barbecuing. The leaves have a history of use in the traditional medicine of Brazil.

Guayule
Mexican rubber

Parthenium argentatum

A flowering shrub in the daisy (*Asteraceae*) family, native to the southwestern United States and northern Mexico, and cultivated in those regions. It is cultivated primarily for its latex, which can be processed to a natural rubber that is hypoallergenic, unlike the latex taken from the rubber tree (*Hevea brasiliensis*).

Gum arabic tree
babul, thorn mimosa, Egyptian acacia

Vachellia nilotica

A species of thorny tree in the *Mimosoideae* subfamily within the pea (*Fabaceae*) family, native to Africa, the Middle East, and the Indian subcontinent. It has become naturalized to other regions, including Australia, where it is considered an invasive weed. The tree was previously the type species for the genus *Acacia*, though the genus has since been divided. *V. nilotica* is the original source of **gum arabic**, and is still cultivated in the Middle East for this purpose. The closely related shittah-tree or red acacia (*V. seyal*) is used in modern times for similar purposes; however, in ancient times, this tree was considered sacred by the ancient Hebrews, who used it to craft the Tabernacle and the Ark of the Covenant. Because of the tree's status, its wood could not be used for any secular purpose. According to legend, the Romans used the thorny branches of the shittah-tree to make the crown placed on Jesus Christ prior to his crucifixion.

Gutta-percha tree
Palaquium gutta

A species of evergreen tree in the sapodilla (*Sapotaceae*) family, native to Sumatra, Malaysia, Singapore, and Borneo. It is cultivated there mainly for its latex, called **gutta-percha**, which when dried is like rubber, but less elastic. Gutta-percha can be dried to a hardened form that (unlike rubber) is not brittle. For a time in the mid-19th century, it was used to make utensils and even furniture. *P. gutta* is one of several species in the genus that is a source of gutta-percha, and is the best known. The tree is also cultivated for its edible oil-rich nut.

Gypsum
calcium sulfate dihydrate

A sulfate mineral widely mined and used as a fluxing agent, a fertilizer, and in the paper industry. When heated, it becomes a white powder known as plaster of Paris which is used in pottery, cement, paints, surgical splints, and molds. It is the primary ingredient in the building material known as drywall. It also has uses as a food additive, such as a coagulant or conditioner, and in that form is a source of dietary calcium. It has also been used to remove pollutants, such as lead and arsenic, from water. A fine-grained form of gypsum known as alabaster has a long history of use as an ornamental carving and building material.

Habanero   see *Chili pepper*

Hackberry   *nettletree, sugarberry*
Celtis spp.

A genus of deciduous trees in the cannabis (*Cannabaceae*) family, native to the warm temperate regions of the Northern Hemisphere. Three species in particular are cultivated for their wood: *C. australis* (European hackberry), *C. occidentalis* (American hackberry), and *C. laevigata* (sugarberry, southern hackberry). The wood is not suitable for building as it rots easily, but is used to make fencing and inexpensive furniture. The pea-sized fruit is edible, and is unusually high in fat, carbohydrates, and protein.

Haddock
Melanogrammus aeglefinus

A species of fish in the single-species genus *Melanogrammus*, within the *Gadidae* family (the true cods). It is an important food fish, especially in the North Atlantic countries.

Hake
Merluccius spp.

A genus of several species of fish in the *Merlucciidae* family. They are in the same taxonomic order (*Gadiformes*) and are similar to cod and haddock. The most important food species are the European hake (*M. merluccius*), the North Pacific hake (*M. productus*) and the Argentine hake (*M. hubbsi*). Most commercial hake species have been depleted due to overfishing.

Halibut
Hippoglossus spp.

A genus of two very large species of bottom-swelling flatfish in the *Pleuronectidae* (righteye flounder) family, highly valued as food fish. The two species are the Atlantic halibut (*Hippoglossus hippoglossus*), which is native to the North Atlantic and has been so overfished that it is on the verge of being declared endangered; and the Pacific halibut (*Hippoglossus stenolepsis*), native to the northern Pacific Ocean.

Halmaddi
White bean, ferntop ash

Ailanthus triphysa

An evergreen tree in the *Simaroubaceae* family, native to India, Southeast Asia and Australia. It is known mainly for its fragrant resin, known as **halmaddi,** which is used in India to make incense. Currently, extraction of the resin is highly restricted in an effort to protect the trees.

Hausa potato
Madagascar potato

Plectranthus rotundifolius

An herbaceous perennial plant in the mint (*Lamiaceae*) family, mostly likely native to tropical Africa, but now cultivated in the tropics of Africa, India, Madagascar, and Malesia. It is cultivated for its edible tuberous root, which is similar to the true potato. Other closely related plants in the genus are also cultivated as a root vegetable, including the forskohlii (*P. barbatus*), the Livingstone-potato (*P. esculentus*), and the Gala-Kartoffel (*P. punctatus*).

Hawksbill sea turtle
Eretmochylus imbricata

A critically endangered species of sea turtle in the *Cheloniidae* family. It is found worldwide, with two main subspecies, one in the Atlantic (*E. i. imbricata*), and one in the Indo-Pacific (*E.i. bissa*). Since antiquity, the hawksbill has been hunted for its shell, which can be cut and highly polished into the material known as **tortoiseshell,** which is used for ornamentation. It is now illegal in many countries to hunt this turtle.

Hawthorn
Crataegus monogyna

English hawthorn

A species of shrub within the rose (*Rosaceae*) family, native to
Europe, western Asia, and northwest Africa. There are many
shrubs within the large genus *Crataegus* that are known as hawthorn, but this is the species that spawned the name. It is mostly
cultivated now as an ornamental or hedge, but in the past, it was
more important as a food source and as a traditional medicine.
The berries (actually botanically a pome), called haws, are edible,
as are the flowers and young leaves. Hawthorn has an important
place in traditional herbal medicine of Europe, as well as in folklore. In Ireland, the hawthorn is associated with the Faerie, and is
traditionally left undisturbed. The wood is used for tool handles,
and the wood of the root was used for making tobacco pipes. The
Hethel Old Thorn, the smallest nature preserve in Great Britain, is
the home to a single tree: a hawthorn that dates back to the 13th
century and is possibly the oldest tree in the UK. Some species of
hawthorn are native to North America and Mesoamerica, and
also have a long history there of use as food and medicine.

Hazel
Corylus spp.

filbert

A genus of deciduous trees and shrubs in the birch (*Betulaceae*)
family, native to the temperate Northern Hemisphere. In the
past, hazel was coppiced, and was an important source of wood
for the making of wattle, withy fencing, baskets, and the frames
of coracle boats. In modern times, they are widely cultivated
almost exclusively for their edible nuts, called virtually inter-
changeably hazelnut or filbert. The nuts of all hazel species are
edible, but only one species is currently commercially important:
the European (or common) hazel (*C. avellana*), native to Northern
Europe but now widely cultivated in temperate zones around the
world. Hazel figures in much European folklore, including the
story of legendary Celtic hero Finn McCool, who ate the Salmon
of Knowledge and acquired its wisdom, which it had gained by
eating the nuts fallen into its pool from a sacred hazel tree.

Heather
Calluna vulgaris

This single species in the genus *Calluna* is a low-growing shrub in the heather (*Ericaceae*) family. It is native to northern Europe, but is now widely cultivated in other temperate regions around the world. In modern times it is grown mainly as an ornamental plant, but it has a long history of use in Europe for making brooms (known as besoms). Heather can be used as sheep pasture, and before the widespread use of hops, it was an ingredient in beer as a bittering agent; its use in beer is highly regulated now, due to the potential presence of the ergot fungus on the leaves. The flowers make a distinctive and highly valued honey.

Helium

A gaseous element, the second lightest and most abundant element in the known universe, after hydrogen. It is colorless, odorless, tasteless, non-toxic, and chemically inert. These properties make it a valuable lifting agent, such as in radiosonde balloons (and formerly, airships), as well as for other industrial uses. It is relatively rare on Earth, and is found mostly as a byproduct of natural gas production.

Hematite
iron oxide

A mineral that is one of several forms of iron oxide, it is the oldest iron oxide mineral formed on Earth. It is colored black, steel to silver gray, brown to reddish brown, and red, which is the form that gives it its name. It is an important iron ore. Red ochre is a mineral clay that is colored with hematite, and is one of the oldest pigments. Hematite is also used as a gemstone in jewelry.

Hemlock tree
Tsuga spp.

A genus of about ten species of coniferous trees in the pine (*Pinaceae*) family, native to North America and East Asia. The common name comes from a perceived resemblance of the smell of the crushed leaves to the highly poisonous species in the *Apiaceae* family, also known as hemlock (*Conium maculatum*). Hemlock trees are valued for their wood, which is mainly used to make pulp, and for their bark, which contains tannin.

Hemp
Cannabis sativa subsp. sativa

A species of annual plant in the cannabis (*Cannabaceae*) family, which also includes hops and hackberries. There are two main subspecies of *C. sativa*: *indica* and *sativa*. The name "hemp" generally represents the subspecies *sativa* and cultivars thereof, that have been selectively bred for the food (seeds) and fiber (hemp) uses of the plant. Plants bred for this purpose contain much less of the psychoactive compounds (such as THC), but still may contain the non-psychoactive compound **cannabidiol** (CBD), which is used medicinally. The name "marijuana" generally refers to the subspecies *indica* (see separate entry).

Henbane
Hyoscyamus spp.

A genus of highly toxic herbaceous plants in the nightshade (*Solanaceae*) family, native to North Africa, the Mediterranean region, Eurasia, India, and the Arabian Peninsula. There are three species widely cultivated as a source of the medications **atropine**, **hyoscine**, and **hyoscyamine**: henbane or Egyptian henbane (*H. muticus*), white henbane (*H. albus*), and black henbane (*H. niger*).

Henequen   *Mexican sisal*
Agave fourcroydes

A species of succulent in the asparagus (*Asparagaceae*) family, native to Mexico and Guatemala, but now naturalized to Italy and some Caribbean Islands. Henequen is cultivated for its leaf fibers (called **henequen**), which are used to make rope and twine but are not as of high quality as the related sisal plant. Like sisal, henequen is a sterile hybrid and must be propagated by humans.

Henna tree   *mignonette tree, Egyptian privet*
Lawsonia inermis

A shrub or small tree in the monospecific genus *Lawsonia*, within the loosestrife (*Lythraceae*) family. Its is presumed native to South Asia. It is widely naturalized and cultivated, especially in the semi-arid regions of tropical Africa and India. It is cultivated as the source of the dye **henna**, which has been used since antiquity as a cosmetic dye for the skin, hair, and fingernails, as well as a dye for silk, wool, and leather. Henna dye is used in the form of body art known as mehndi, which has its origins in ancient India.

Herring
Clupea spp.

A genus of three species of fish in the *Clupeidae* family. They are the Atlantic herring (*C. harengus*), the north Pacific herring (*C. pallasii*), and the Araucanian herring (*C. bentincki*), which is found off the coast of Chile. Of these, the Atlantic herring is by far the most important commercially. Herring has been a staple food in Europe since at least 3000 B.C. Herring fishery laid the foundation for the cities of Great Yarmouth, Amsterdam, and Copenhagen. The fish is valued for its meat, which is high in the omega-3 fatty acids EPA and DHA, and vitamin D.

Hickory tree
Carya spp.

A genus of about twenty species of trees and shrubs, within the walnut (*Juglandaceae*) family. Most are native to North America, with a few species native to China. Hickory wood is noted for its strength and durability, though not for its rot resistance. It has long been used for tool handles, wheels, spokes, carts, skis, cabinetry, flooring, and other uses. All species produce nuts, but not all are edible by humans. In North America, the pecan (*C. illinoinensis*) and shagbark hickory (*C. ovata*) are the species most commonly cultivated for nuts. The shagbark hickory also produces an edible sugary sap that is made into a syrup similar to maple syrup. In China, the Cathay hickory or mountain walnut (*C. cathayensis*) is also cultivated for its edible nuts and seed oil.

Holly   *English holly, Christmas holly*
Ilex aquifolium

The type species for the genus *Ilex* (holly), which is the sole living genus within the *Aquifoliaceae* family. It is an evergreen shrub or tree native to southern and western Europe, northern Africa, and southwest Asia. It has been introduced to other temperate regions, mostly as an ornamental plant. Its bright green leaves and bright red berries have long been associated with Christmas (and previously, with the Roman Saturnalia). In the past, holly leaves from the less prickly cultivars have been used as winter fodder. The white wood, which is hard and stains particularly well, was the preferred wood for Scottish bagpipes, and was also used to make furniture. The berries are toxic to humans, dogs and cats.

Honey bee
Apis mellifera

European honey bee

The most common of the several species of honey bees found worldwide, and only one of over 20,000 known species of bee. Honey bees are raised for their **beeswax, honey, royal jelly**, and **propolis**. In addition, honey bees (among many other species of bees) are important pollinators for very many species of plants, both wild and cultivated. As the bees visit male plants to collect nectar, they also collect pollen on their bodies, which they then carry to and deposit on female plants, completing the process of fertilization. Some species of plants are so dependent on bees, and sometimes on very specific bees (for example, the Brazilnut tree), that without them, the plant will not reproduce at all.

Hop plant
Humulus lupulus

A perennial climbing plant in the cannabis (*Cannabaceae*) family, native to Europe, western Asia, and North America. It is widely cultivated for its flowers (hops), which are used as flavorings, preservatives, and stabilizers in beer. The bitter flavoring agent is a resin produced by glands in the flower cones. The use of hops in brewing is believed to have originated in eighth-century Germany. Prior to hops, brewers used *gruit*, a mixture of a variety of bitter herbs, which could include henbane, ivy, dandelion, burdock root, marigold, horehound, and heather. Hops are edible, can be used to make tea, and are a traditional herbal medicine.

Hornbeam
Carpinus spp.

ironwood, musclewood

A genus of several species of deciduous trees in the birch (*Betulaceae*) family, native to the temperate regions of the Northern Hemisphere. The trees are notable for their very hard wood, which is rarely used in general carpentry due to the difficulty of working it. It is used where hardness and durability is a priority, such as piano actions, as gear pegs in simple machines, and coach wheels. It can be coppiced, and is used to produce hardwood poles. The inner bark produces a yellow dye, and the leaves can be used as animal fodder. The most commercially important species are the European hornbeam (*C. betulus*), the American hornbeam (*C. caroliniana*), and the Asian hornbeam (*C. turczaninovii*).

Horse
Equus ferus caballus

The domesticated subspecies of *Equus ferus*, and one of only two living subspecies; the other is the only true undomesticated horse, Przewalski's horse (*Equus ferus przewalskii*). Horses were domesticated beginning around 4000 BC in Central Asia. The Spanish introduced horses to the Americas in the 16th century, profoundly affecting the economy and culture of many Native American groups. Today, there are more than 300 breeds of horse, with characteristics depending on their intended use, from transportation to racing to pack-and-draft. In some cultures, they are also used for food.

Horse chestnut   *buckeye*
Aesculus hippocastanum

Aescalus is a genus of about 13-19 species of deciduous trees in the lychee (*Sapindaceae*) family, with various species native to Europe, Asia, and North America. The best-known species is *A. hippocastanum*, or the common horse chestnut, which is native to Europe but widely cultivated in North America. This species is the source of the compound aescin, which is used in pharmaceuticals as an anti-inflammatory and a vasoconstrictor. All parts of the tree are mildly toxic, but the nuts have been used for human food and animal fodder, after leaching. Ohio is called the Buckeye state, after Presidential candidate William Henry Harrison, who was a political representative of Ohio, portrayed himself sitting in a cabin made of buckeye logs and drinking hard cider.

Horseradish   *western wasabi*
Armoracia rusticana

A perennial herbaceous plant in the cabbage (*Brassicaceae*) family, presumed to be native to southeastern Europe and western Asia. It is now widely naturalized elsewhere and cultivated worldwide for its tuberous root. When grated, the root produces the compound allyl isothiocyanate (the same compound present in mustard oil and true wasabi), which is an irritant to the mucous membranes and is responsible for the pungent flavor. The root is ground into a paste and combined with vinegar, which is used as a condiment and a traditional herbal medicine.

Huckleberry
Gaylussacia baccata

A species of low-growing shrub in the heather (*Ericaceae*) family, native to North America and cultivated primarily in that region. It is cultivated for its edible fruit, the huckleberry. The berries are used primarily to make jams, jellies, and fillings. Due to its close resemblance to other fruit-bearing members of the *Ericaceae* family, the common name of huckleberry is sometimes used to refer to other species, especially in genus *Vaccinium*, which contains the blueberries and cranberries.

Legacy of the Gods

Like many flowers (heliotrope, narcissus, ivy — to name a few) the hyacinth claims a divine origin in Greek mythology. In this case, it came from the blood of Hyacinthus, lover of the sun-god Apollo, who was slain by the jealous Zephyrus (the west wind).

Hyacinth bean   *lablab bean, bonavist bean*
Lablab purpureus subsp. purpureus

A species of herbaceous annual or perennial plant in the pea (*Fabaceae*) family, native to Africa but now widely cultivated in the tropics all over the world. It is cultivated for its edible bean, leaves, and roots. One cultivar is also grown as cattle fodder. Due to extensive breeding, the plant is widely variable, but in all varieties the raw beans are toxic due to the presence of cyanogenic glycosides. They must be cooked with several changes of water before they are edible. Like many legumes, the plant is cultivated for its nitrogen-fixing abilities, to improve soil quality.

Hyssop
Hyssopus officinalis

A species of shrub or subshrub native to North Africa, western Asia, and Eastern Europe, now also naturalized to other parts of Europe and North America. It has a long history of use as a traditional medicine. Currently, fresh herb hyssop is used in cooking as a food flavoring, and to flavor liqueur; the essential oil is claimed to have medicinal properties, especially as an antiseptic when used externally, but it is toxic even in moderate doses when taken internally. The flowers are a nectar source for honeybees.

Ibope
algarrobo blanco
Prosopis alba

A species of tree in the genus commonly known as mesquite, within the pea (*Fabaceae*) family. It is native to western and southern South America. It is an extremely drought-tolerant tree that is often planted as a windbreak or for soil improvement. Its seeds are edible, containing a sweet nutritious paste known as patay; they are used as animal fodder, or dried and ground into flour for human consumption. The wood is very hard and difficult to work; it is used to make items such as doors, floors, and wine casks. It is very closely related to and often confused with the algarrobo negro (*P. nigra*), as well as the Chilean algarrobo (*P. chilensis*) which are both used for similar purposes.

Iceland moss
Cetraria islandica

A lichen that grows readily in the mountainous regions of the northern temperate zone of the Northern Hemisphere, but particularly Iceland. In Iceland and Norway, in the past it was traditionally used as a food, being ground into an easily-digested flour which was used as a thickener for porridge and soup, or added to milk to form a jelly. It has also been claimed to have some medicinal value. A brown dye can be extracted from it.

Iceland spar
Viking sunstone
calcium carbonate

A transparent variety of calcite (calcium carbonate), that occurs in large, readily cleavable crystals. It is remarkable for its birefrigence, meaning that its refractive index is different for different polarizations of light. It is believed that Iceland spar is the "sunstone" mentioned in the Icelandic texts, which was used as a navigational aid. It is thought that the Vikings used this property to be able to detect the position of the sun in the sky, when the sun was obstructed by clouds. This works because polarized light produces a yellow entopic pattern on the fovea of the human eye, which we can consciously see. Therefore, it is possible to detect the position of the sun by moving the crystal across the field of vision and looking for the entopic pattern, which gives the position of the sun.

Ilmenite
Iron titanium oxide

Manaccanite

Ilmenite is the most important ore of titanium, and the primary source of titanium dioxide, which is used as a pigment in paints, plastics, fabric, paper, sunscreen, food, and cosmetics. Ilmenite itself is used as a flux by steelmakers, and as a sandblasting agent. It is most often found in basic igneous rocks.

Incense cedar
Calocedrus decurrens

A species of large coniferous tree in the cypress (*Cupressaceae*) family, native to a narrow range within western North America. It has had many traditional uses for Native Americans of the region as a building material, medicinally, and for fibers for basket weaving. Now it is grown as an ornamental, and as the primary wood used to make pencils, as it is soft and tends not to splinter.

Indian senna
Senna alexandrina

A species of perennial subshrub in the pea (*Fabaceae*) family, native to Egypt, North Africa, the Arabian Peninsula, West Asia, and India. It is has a long history of medicinal use, and today is cultivated as the source of the medication **senna** (senna glycoside), which is on the World Health Organization's Model List of Essential Medicines and is the key ingredient in many over-the-counter laxatives, such as Senokot and Ex-Lax.

Indigo
Indigofera tinctoria

true indigo, Indian indigo

A species of shrub in the pea (*Fabaceae*) family, of unknown origin. It has become widely naturalized to tropical and temperate Asia, as well as parts of Africa. It has a long history of cultivation, and was the original source of the blue dye called **indigo**. Other species within the *Indigofera* genus have also become widely naturalized outside of their native regions, and are cultivated to produce both tannin and indigo. Notable examples are anil indigo (*I. suffruticosa*, native to the Americas), and Natal indigo (*I. arrecta*). As a legume (a nitrogen-fixing plant), it is often used in crop rotations to improve the soil.

101

Indium

A relatively rare metallic element found as a minor component in zinc sulfide ores and produced as a byproduct of zinc refinement. In the past, it was used to coat bearings to protect against corrosion, but its main application in modern times is as a transparent thin-film coating on glass (in the form of indium tin oxide).

Iodine

A non-metallic element that is not found in native form in nature, but is widely distributed as a compound. Iodine is an essential mineral nutrient for humans, being necessary for the synthesis of thyroid hormones. It has many varied uses, among them: tincture of iodine and povidone iodine, both of which are important antiseptics widely used in medicine; as a nutritional supplement for humans and livestock; as a catalyst in the production of acetic acid and polymers.

Ipe   *guayacan, pui*
Handroanthus spp.

A genus of several species of flowering trees in the *Bignonaceae* family, native to Central and South America. It has been widely naturalized elsewhere, mostly as an ornamental, because of its large, showy flowers. Several species are important timber trees and are cultivated as such. They produce a dense, hard, durable wood that is resistant to rot; the wood is often used for outdoor applications, such as boardwalks and decking.

Ipecac   *ipecacuanha*
Carapichea ipecacuanha

An herbaceous plant in the madder (*Rubiaceae*) family, native to Central America and northern South America. It is best known for the white powder produced from its roots and rhizomes, which contains the medicinal compound emetine. The powder is made into syrup of ipecac, a powerful emetic that was once used as an emergency treatment for the ingestion of poisons. Syrup of ipecac is no longer commonly used, having been replaced by safer, more effective treatments, such as activated charcoal.

Iridium

A white, hard and brittle metallic element, it is one of the rarest elements found in the Earth's crust, and is usually obtained as a byproduct of refining nickel and copper. It is the second most dense element, and the most corrosion-resistant. It is used as an alloy with precious metals to make fine bearings and standard weights and measures, as well as such items as high-performance spark plugs and crucibles. Iridium is found in much higher concentrations in meteorites, and the discovery of an iridium-rich layer in sedimentary rocks around the world gave rise to the meteorite-impact theory of the extinction of the dinosaurs.

Iron

A metallic element that is the most common element by mass on Earth, and the fourth most common element in the Earth's crust. Iron has been extremely useful to humans since ancient times, with earliest artifacts of worked iron dating back to 3500 BC, and smelted iron to about 3000 BC. The utility of iron increased exponentially with the discovery, around 1000 BC, of combining iron with carbon to form **steel**, which is much harder than iron. Steel is now by far the most commonly used metal, with a large number of applications. There are many types of steel, made by adding small amounts of other metals to achieve the desired properties. Iron is strongly magnetic; it is very reactive and forms many chemical compounds, with a variety of uses. Iron is crucial to the functioning of the human body and many other living things: as part of hemoglobin and myoglobin, it enables oxygen transportation; it also plays a role in the metabolism of many proteins and enzymes, among other functions.

Ivory palm   *tagua palm*
Phytelephas spp.

A genus of trees in the palm (*Arecaceae*) family, native to the western regions of Central and South America. They are cultivated or wild harvested mainly for their seeds, whose extremely hard endosperm resembles ivory and is used for similar purposes, such as making buttons or beads, figurines or jewelry. This material is called vegetable ivory, marfim-vegetal, corozo, tagua, or jarina. The primary cultivated species are: *P. macrocarpa* from Brazil; *P. aequatorialis* from Ecuador; and *P. schottii* from Columbia.

Jabilla
Fevillea cordifolia

Antidote vine

A climbing vine in the gourd (*Curcurbitaceae*) family, native to
South and Central America. Its seeds produce a butter-like fat
that was at one time investigated for use as a biofuel. The seeds
have a long history of use in South and Central America as a traditional medicine.

Jaborandi
Pilocarpus spp.

A small genus of plants in the citrus (*Rutaceae*) family, native to
the tropical regions of South America. Several species, especially
P. microphyllus (Pernambuco jaborandi), contain the alkaloid pilocarpine. The compound is extracted from the leaves to make the
glaucoma medication **Pilocarpine**, which is on the World Health
Organization's Model List of Essential Medicines.

Jackfruit
Artocarpus heterophyllus

A species of tree in the mulberry (*Moraceae*) family, in the same
genus as the breadfruit tree (*A. altilis*). It is native to southwest
India, where it has been cultivated for at least 3000 years, and
possibly twice as long. It is now widely cultivated throughout
the tropical regions of the world, mainly for its edible fruit and
seeds. It is the largest tree-borne fruit, and can reach up to 120
pounds. A single tree is capable of producing 100 to 200 fruits a
year. The wood of the tree is a termite-resistant hardwood used
to make furniture, doors and windows, roofing material, and
musical instruments.

Jade
jadeite, nephrite

The name applies to two different minerals, both valued and with
a long history of use as a hard stone for carving figurines, jewelry,
buttons and beads, especially in China. In ancient times, utilitari-
an items such as adze heads and arrow points were made from
jade. In the Maori culture of New Zealand, nephrite jade is called
pounamu, and is considered a *taonga* (a treasure). Its mining and
use are closely protected. Pounamu was used to make tools,
weapons, and jewelry; these items are believed to increase in
power as they pass from generation to generation.

Jalap
Ipomoea purga

A species of herbaceous perennial vine in the morning glory (*Convolvulaceae*) family, native to the eastern side of the Sierra Madre in Mexico, but now naturalized to other tropical areas. In the past, it was cultivated for the resin produced by its tuberous root, which is the source of the cathartic drug called jalap. It is in the same genus as the sweet potato (*I. batatas*), which is also native to the Americas.

Jambolan   *Java plum, rose-apple*
Syzygium cumini

A species of evergreen tree in the myrtle (*Myrtaceae*) family, native to the Indian subcontinent, some parts of Southeast Asia and China, and eastern tropical Africa. It has been introduced and naturalized to tropical areas in Africa and the Caribbean, and Hawaii (where it is considered invasive). It is grown for its edible fruit, a large berry that resembles a plum. The fruit is eaten fresh, or made into wine and vinegar. It is closely related to the clove spice (*S. aromaticum*), and the water rose-apple (*S. aqueum*), which is cultivated in Asia for its edible fruit.

Jandi   *khejri, ghaf*
Prosopis cineraria

A species of small tree in the genus commonly known as mesquite, within the pea (*Fabaceae*) family. It is native to the Arabian peninsula, West Asia, and the Indian subcontinent. Like other members of the genus, it is extremely drought tolerant, and can grow in alkaline or saline soils. It is mainly grown as erosion control, animal fodder, and fuel (as charcoal). Its flowers are an important nectar source for honeybees. The tree is of great cultural significance in its native regions: it is the national tree of the United Arab Emirates, and the state trees of Rajasthan and Telangana in India. It is considered sacred in the Hindu religion, and has a long history of use as a traditional medicine. In the 1970's, the tree was the center of one of the first non-violent environmental protection movements, the Chipko Andolan. The movement began when large stands of trees, an important source of livelihood for the local people, were auctioned by the government to outside corporate interests.

Japanese red cedar

sugi

Cryptomeria japonica

A species of tree in the cypress (*Cupressaceae*) family, native to Japan and cultivated there as an ornamental tree, and for timber. The wood is highly scented, and is weather and insect resistant. As a softwood, it is used mainly for indoor purposes such as furniture, paneling, boxes, veneers, and plywood. When buried, it takes on a green color that is highly valued. The sugi is the national tree of Japan, and is often planted around shrines and temples. The Jomon sugi of Yakushima is the largest and oldest tree in Japan, estimated to be between 2000 and 7000 years old.

Jarrah

Eucalyptus marginata

A large tree in the *Eucalyptus* genus within the myrtle (*Myrtaceae*) family, native to Western Australia. It is a very tall, straight tree that produces extremely hard, dense, and rot-resistant wood. It is logged for use in building furniture, railway sleepers, telephone poles, fencing and other uses. As larger trees are now rare, use for smaller items is more common, with larger items being made from reclaimed wood. Like many other members of the genus, the jarrah is an important source of nectar for honeybees.

Jasmine

Jasminum spp.

A genus of about 200 species of shrubs and vines in the olive (*Oleaceae*) family, native to tropical and warm temperate regions of Eurasia, Australasia, and Oceania. It is widely cultivated and naturalized in many countries of the world. Jasmine has been cultivated for hundreds of years, mainly for the highly scented essential oil extracted from its flowers. The oil is used in cosmetics and perfumery. Jasmine tea is made by mixing fresh flowers with dried tea leaves, allowing the leaves to become infused with the flowers' scent, and then removing the expended flower petals. The type species of the genus is *J. officinale*, which is also the most commonly grown. *J. auriculatum* (Indian jasmine), *J. grandiflorum* (Catalonian jasmine), and *J. sambac* (Arabian jasmine) are also widely cultivated.

Jet

Jet is a lignite, a precursor to coal that was formed when wood was subjected to intense heat and pressure. It is very black, hard, and takes a high polish. It has been used in Europe since Neolithic times as a semiprecious stone in jewelry and other ornamentation. Like amber, jet generates a static charge when rubbed. The best-known source of jet is in Whitby, England. That deposit dates to the early Jurassic period, about 180 million years ago.

Jicama   *yam bean, Mexican turnip*
Pachyrhizus erosus

A ground vine in the pea (*Fabaceae*) family, native to Mexico but now widely cultivated elsewhere, mainly for its large edible tuberous root. Two other species in the genus are also cultivated, both are known as the yam-bean: *P. ahipa* and *P. tuberosus*.

Jimsonweed   *moonflower, thorn apple, false castor-oil*
Datura stramonium

Datura is a genus of several species of night-flowering plants in the nightshade (*Solanaceae*) family. *D. stramonium* is the best known of these. Its exact native range is unknown, but it is presumed to be native to Mexico. It is now widely naturalized to temperate and tropical regions, though its cultivation is highly restricted or banned in some areas. All species of the genus are poisonous, especially the seeds and flowers. The toxic alkaloids **atropine, hyoscyamine** (daturine), and **hyoscine** (scopolamine) are all derived from these plants. They are important medicinally, with atropine and hyoscine both on the World Health Organization's Model List of Essential Medicines. *D. metel* (metel) is also a well-known species cultivated as a source of these compounds. Metel has a long history of use as medicine in the Ayurvedic tradition, but its use is now banned due to its high toxicity.

Job's Tears   *adlay millet*
Coix lacryma-jobi

A relative of the maize plant in the grass (*Poaceae*) family, native to the temperate regions of the Near East and Asia. The beadlike seeds were a staple food of the hill tribes of India, have a history of use in traditional Chinese medicine, and in ancient Persia were used to make necklaces believed to possess magic powers.

Jojoba
Simmondsia chinensis

goat nut, wild hazel, coffeeberry

A small shrub native to the southwestern United States and Mexico, that is the sole species within the *Simmondsiaceae* family. It is widely cultivated in arid tropical and semi-tropical regions, almost exclusively for jojoba oil (not a true oil, but actually a liquid wax ester), which is extracted from its seeds. The plant is slow-growing and difficult to cultivate, so it is primarily used for small scale pharmaceutical and cosmetic applications.

Jujube
Ziziphus jujuba

A small deciduous tree or shrub in the buckthorn (*Rhamnaceae*) family, presumed native to southern Asia, but now extensively cultivated in many areas of the world, primarily for its small fruit, known by many names depending on where it is grown, but most commonly called the jujube. There are several cultivars of the species, and some of these are important nectar sources for honeybees. The closely-related Indian jujube (*Z. mauritiana*) is cultivated mainly in India, for similar purposes. This extremely hardy species is considered an invasive weed in some of the areas to which it has been introduced.

Juniper
Juniperus spp.

A genus of about 50-70 species of coniferous trees in the cypress (*Cupressaceae*) family, found widely distributed in the Northern Hemisphere. Several species are cultivated for a variety of purposes. Some species, notably *J. virginiana* (eastern redcedar) produces an aromatic timber traded as "cedar," though it is not a true cedar; the leaves and twigs are steam distilled to produce oil of juniper. The species *J. communis* is the most common source of juniper berries (actually female seed cones), which are used to flavor gin, and as a spice; the berries can also be steam distilled to produce an essential oil. Several species of juniper are sources of wood, essential oils, and resin. Among the Navajo, juniper ash was incorporated into food items as a flavoring, but it also provided an important source of calcium in their diet. A juniper forest in the Himalayas of southeastern Tibet, grows at 16,000 feet, making it one of the highest altitude forests in the world.

Kainite

A mineral that is a hydrated potassium-magnesium sulfate-chloride. It is usually formed as an evaporate, in cavities and fissures. It is found in relatively few places, but it is used as a source of potassium and magnesium in fertilizer.

Kale   see *Cabbage*

Kamut   see *Wheat*

Kaolin   *China clay*

Kaolin is the name for a clay rich in the mineral kaolinite, which is formed by the chemical weathering of aluminum silicate minerals. It is best known for the making of china and porcelain, but it is also used in the making of cosmetics, paint and kaolin poultice, and as a filler in the manufacture of paper, rubber and textiles.

Kapok   *silk-cotton tree*
Ceiba pentandra

A species of tropical tree in the mallow (*Malvaceae*) family whose exact native range is unknown but is presumed to be Central and South America. It is now widely naturalized to and cultivated in other tropical regions, particularly Southeast Asia. Kapoks are some of the largest trees in the world, growing up to about 240 feet high, with buttressed trunks that can be up to 19 feet thick (or more), above the buttresses. It is cultivated mainly for the fibers harvested from the outer casing of the seed; these fibers are called kapok and have a wide variety of uses. In addition, an edible oil is pressed from the seeds that has potential as an alternative to petroleum-based fuel. According to the folklore of Trinidad and Tobago, the demon of death (Bazil) lives in a huge kapok tree deep in the forest, where he was imprisoned through the clever trickery of a common carpenter.

Kapur tree
Dryobalanops spp.

Dryobalanops is a genus of flowering trees in the *Dipterocarpaceae* family, native to Sumatra, Malaysia and Borneo. It is harvested for its valuable hardwood. The species *D. aromatica* (Borneo camphor), was at one time an important source of **camphor**.

Karri
Eucalyptus diversicolor

A large evergreen tree in the myrtle (*Myrtaceae*) family, native to the wetter regions of Western Australia, and one of the many useful species in the *Eucalyptus* genus. It is one of the tallest trees in the world, sometimes reaching heights of up to 295 feet. It is harvested for its attractive hardwood, which is relatively rot-resistant, though can be vulnerable to termites. It is used for building roofs, furniture, and other items. In the past, it was cut into blocks used to pave roads. The tree is also an important source of nectar for honeybees.

Kauri
Agathis australis

A coniferous tree in the *Araucariaceae* family, native to the northern districts of New Zealand's North Island. Kauri forests are among the most ancient in the world. The trees are not cultivated, but they produce a resin called kauri gum, which falls from the tree and over time becomes semi-fossilized **copal**. Kauri gum copal is highly valued as an ingredient in varnish. The most famous and largest kauri tree is named Tane Mahuta (after the Maori god of the forest and birds), located in New Zealand's Waipoua Forest preserve. The tree is 168 feet high and is an estimated 1250 to 2500 years old).

Kava
Piper methysticum

A species of herbaceous plant in the pepper (*Piperaceae*) family, with a long history of cultivation in the cultural region of Oceania. *P. methysticum* is the domesticated version of the wild ancestor *P. wichmanii*. Kava is an important part of the spiritual beliefs of some of the cultures of the Pacific Islands. It is cultivated for its root, which is prepared into a drink that has psychoactive effects, most of which are described as being mildly narcotic. The precise effects depend on several factors, including the type of cultivar used. In many of the countries in which kava is culturally important, the production of kava is strictly controlled to protect its sanctity, and preserve the quality of the so-called noble cultivars.

Kelp
Laminariales

The name refers to large brown algae seaweeds that make up the order *Laminariales*. They are found in shallow temperate ocean waters around the world. Some species are edible, and in the past, they were an important source of nutritional potassium and iodine. It is claimed that edible kelp (called *kombu* in Asia), can help to soften beans and convert indigestible sugars, reducing flatulence. Previously, the word kelp was used to denote the ash produced when seaweed was burned, which was an important source of soda ash (sodium carbonate). Soda ash has a variety of uses including: glass manufacture, water softening, and as a raising agent in food, among others.

Kenari nut   *Java almond*
Canarium vulgare

A species of evergreen tree in the torchwood (*Burseraceae*) family, native to Southeast Asia and Indonesia, and cultivated elsewhere in the tropics. It is cultivated for its edible nut, the kenari nut. It is one of several members of the genus that is cultivated for this purpose, others include the galip nut or Java olive (*C. indicum*), and the pili nut (*C. ovatum*).

Khuskhus   *vetiver*
Chrysopogon zizanioides

A species of perennial plant in the grass (*Poaceae*) family, native to India but now naturalized to Australia and Central America, and cultivated elsewhere. It is mainly cultivated for its especially fragrant roots, which yield an the essential oil called **vetiver oil**, used in perfumery, and as an antiseptic and termite repellent. In India, the fibers of the roots are used to make mats. It is in the same genus as other grasses cultivated for their aromatic essential oils, including lemongrass (*C. citratus*), citronella (*C. nardus*), and palmarosa (*C. martinii*). It is also closely related to sorghum.

Kohlrabi   see *Cabbage*

Kola tree
Cola spp.

cola tree, goora-nut

A genus of tall evergreen trees in the mallow (*Malvaceae*) family, native to the tropical forests of Africa, and cultivated in that region. Two species in particular (*C. acuminata* and *C. nitida*) are cultivated for their nuts, called **kola nuts,** which (like cacao, also in the mallow family) contain the stimulants caffeine and theobromine. The nuts are either chewed or used to flavor beverages.

Korarima
Aframomum corrorima

Ethiopian cardamom, false cardamom

A species of herbaceous plant in the ginger (*Zingiberaceae*) family, native to East Africa and extensively cultivated in Ethiopia and Eritrea. It is cultivated for its seeds, which are dried and used as a spice. It is closely related to the spice known as Grains of Paradise (*Aframomum melegueta*).

Kumquat
Citrus japonica

A species of evergreen shrub or small tree in the citrus (*Rutaceae*) family, native to south Asia and the Asian Pacific region, but now widely cultivated elsewhere in the world. Once classified as several species in the genus *Fortunella*, the varieties are now consolidated into the single species. They are a cold-hardy citrus, cultivated for its edible fruit, which resembles an orange but is much smaller. Essential oil is cold pressed from the rind. Several cultivars exist, as well as hybrids with other citrus species.

Kutjera
Solanum centrale

Australian desert raisin

A species of perennial shrub-like plant in the nightshade (*Solanaceae*) family, native to Central Australia, where it was an important forage food for centuries. It is currently cultivated by some Australian Aboriginal people for its small edible fruit, called the desert raisin. Due to its pungency, it is popular for use in food flavoring and as a condiment. It is also high in vitamin C.

Lac insect
Kerria lacca

The most important commercial species within the lac family of insects. This insect is native to India and Asia, and produces the resin called **lac**, which is the only resin of animal origin. Lac insect farming is economically important in some regions of India and Southeast Asia, with several thousand tons of raw lac produced annually. Lac can be refined into **shellac** (a type of varnish) and other products. Lac bugs also exude a useful wax. The body fluid is used to make a strong red dye that is used in food and cosmetics. Several hundred species of plants are known to serve as host plants for lac insects, a few dominate as commercially important.

Lacquer tree   *varnish tree, Japanese sumac*
Toxicodendron vernicifluum

A species of tree in the cashew (*Anacardiaceae*) family, native to China and India. It is cultivated for its resin, which is used as a varnish or **lacquer** in creating lacquerware. Like many other species in the *Anacardiaceae* family, the resin and other parts of the tree contain the toxic compound urushiol, which can cause contact dermatitis. In applying the lacquer, breathing the fumes can cause an allergic reaction in the lungs. The urushiol is evaporated during the drying process, making the finished product much less likely to cause a reaction. The natural color of the varnish is dark brown, but the lacquer is often pigmented with magnesium or ferric oxide, to create a black or red color.

Lapis lazuli

A deep blue mineral consisting of sodium aluminum silicate and sodium sulfide, which occurs in metamorphic limestone. It has been used as a semiprecious stone since antiquity, prized for its intense color and fine polish. When powdered, it is used to make the highly-prized and extremely expensive blue pigment called ultramarine. During the Renaissance and Baroque periods, ultramarine was used by the best-known artists of the period, when they could afford it, but was often only used for the most important figure in the painting. Most notably, it was used to paint the blue robes of the Virgin Mary.

Larch
Larix spp.

A genus of coniferous trees in the pine (*Pinaceae*) family, native to the cooler temperate regions of the Northern Hemisphere. They are especially dominant in the boreal forests of Siberia and Canada. They are one of the few conifers that are deciduous, losing their needles in the fall. Larch wood is very durable and waterproof, and resistant to rot when in contact with the ground. It is used extensively in building houses, railway sleepers, fencing, and boats. If they are grown where the summers are fairly warm, the larch produces very clear turpentine. In Eurasian shamanism, the world tree is often depicted as a larch.

Lavender
Lavandula spp.

A genus of evergreen shrubs in the mint (*Lamiaceae*) family, native to a widespread distribution across the Old World and now widely cultivated and naturalized elsewhere in the world. The type species and most commonly cultivated is *L. angustifolia* (English lavender), with *L. latifolia* (broadleaf lavender) in second place. There are many cultivars and hybrids of the two species. Lavender is cultivated for the essential oil distilled from its flower spikes. The oil is used extensively in a variety of products for its scent, for its medicinal properties as an antiseptic and anti-inflammatory, and as a mosquito and insect repellent. Lavender is also an important nectar source for honey bees.

Laver   *zicai, slake*
Porphyra umbilicalis

A species of edible seaweed, classified as a red algae, in the *Bangiaceae* family, found in widespread distribution in coastal regions around the world. It has a very long history of cultivation for food, particularly in Britain and East Asia. Laverbread is a well-known traditional Welsh delicacy. Laver is high in many essential vitamin and mineral nutrients, and is a particularly good source of nutritional iodine.

Lead

A soft metallic element whose chief ore is galena. Its density, low melting point, ductility and relative resistance to oxidation have given it a number of uses. Lead is the basis of most solders and is alloyed with other metals to form type and shot metals, as well as pewter. It is used to make leaded glass, leaded gasoline, in the glaze of some ceramics, and in lead-acid batteries. Lead absorbs radioactive particles, and therefore is used extensively in shielding against radioactivity, such as in nuclear reactors. It is toxic to humans when ingested, so many of its previous uses have been discontinued in some parts of the world, for example as the white pigment in paint, but in other regions these uses remain.

Leek
Allium ampeloprasum

Leeks are a group of cultivars of the wild species *Allium ampeloprasum*, a member of the diverse onion/garlic/leek genus, within the amaryllis (*Amaryllidaceae*) family. The plant is native to southern Europe and western Asia, but is widely cultivated and naturalized elsewhere in the world. The various cultivars are known by several names (elephant garlic, kurrat, Persian leek, Tareh), that differ slightly in their uses, but they are mostly used as food similar to onions. The cultivation of the leek dates back to at least the second millennium B.C.E. This unassuming vegetable is one of the national emblems of Wales and has been worn as a symbol of national pride for centuries; the tradition continues today, as the emblem of the leek is worn as a cap badge by the Welsh Guards, a regiment of the British Army.

Lemon
Citrus limon

A small evergreen tree in the citrus (*Rutaceae*) family, whose exact native range is unknown, but was likely South Asia. It is now widely cultivated elsewhere in the world. It is cultivated almost exclusively for its edible fruit, although the leaves are also used to a much lesser extent. The fruit contains a high percentage of citric acid, and was once the main source of that compound. Essential oil extracted from the rind is used as a scent in perfumery, as a flavoring, and as an insecticide. The high acidity of the fruit gives it other uses, such as an ingredient in household cleaners.

Lemon verbena   *lemon beebrush*
Aloysia citrodora

A species of shrub in the verbena (*Verbenaceae*) family, native to
western South America but now widely cultivated in the tropical
regions. It was brought to Europe by the Spanish and Portuguese
explorers of the 17th century, and is cultivated for its essential oil,
used as a flavoring, in perfumery, and in traditional medicine.

Lemongrass   *Citronella grass, fever grass*
Cymbopogon spp.

A genus of plants within the grass (*Poaceae*) family whose native
region is unknown, but it is now widely naturalized to and cultivated in the tropical regions of Asia, Africa, South America, and
Australia. Some species are cultivated as culinary and medicinal
herbs (particularly *C. citratus* and *C. flexuosus*). The species *C.
nardus* and *C. winterianus* are also known as citronella grass, and
are cultivated for the essential oil **citronella**, which is used as an
insect repellent and antiseptic. In addition, the extract
lemongrass oil is used as a scent, a pesticide and a preservative,
most notably of the ancient palm-leaf manuscripts of India.

Lentil   *gram*
Lens culinaris subsp. culinaris

A species of annual plant in the pea (*Fabaceae*) family, native to
the Near East and Central Asia but now widely naturalized to
and cultivated in many temperate regions around the world.
They are cultivated mainly for their edible seed, the lentil. Lentils
are the oldest domesticated legume, and one of the first domesticated crops, with cultivation dating back to 11,000 BCE in Greece.
There are six species within the *Lens* genus, but five are wild; *L.
culinaris* is the only cultivated species, and has several cultivars.
Lentil is also grown as a fodder crop, and as nitrogen-fixing
plants is planted for soil improvement.

Lepidolite
One of the mica group of minerals, and the most abundant lithi-
um-bearing minerals. It occurs in high-temperature metamorphic
rocks. It is the chief source of medicinal **lithium salts**, and a secondary source of lithium. It is also one of the primary sources of
the rare alkali metals cesium and rubidium.

Leren
Guinea arrowroot
Calathea allouia

A species of perennial herbaceous plant in the arrowroot (*Marantaceae*) family, native to South America but now widely naturalized to and cultivated in the tropical regions of the Americas. It has been grown for its edible tuber since at least 7000 BC.

Lettuce
Lactuca sativa

A domesticated species of annual plant in the daisy (*Asteraceae*) family, native to and first cultivated in Egypt, with earliest evidence of cultivation dating to about 2680 B.C. It is now widely cultivated around the world and across many agricultural zones. There are many cultivars, which come in three main groups: leaf lettuce (*L. sativa var. crispa*), romaine (*L. sativa var. longifolia*), and head or cabbage lettuce (*L. sativa var. capitata*) types. Almost all are cultivated for their edible leaves and stems. A few varieties are cultivated for their seeds, for the production of seed oil.

Licorice
Glycyrrhiza glabra

An herbaceous perennial in the pea (*Fabaceae*) family, native to southern Europe, North Africa, and parts of Asia. It is widely cultivated for its root, from which is extracted the sweet, black-brown flavoring called licorice. It has traditionally been used medicinally, and is still a popular flavoring, particularly in confectionery. Some of the compounds found in licorice can cause adverse effects in large doses.

Lign aloes
Aloeswood, gharuwood, agarwood
Aquilaria spp.

A genus of several species of trees in the *Thymelaeaceae* family, native to the rainforests of Southeast Asia. They are harvested as the source of **agarwood**, a dark, fragrant, resinous wood used in incense, perfume, and small carvings. It is formed in the heartwood of several species of *Aquilaria* (especially *A. malaccensis*) when they become infected with a *Phialophora parasitica* mold; the resin is the tree's defensive response to the infection. First-grade agarwood is one of the most expensive materials in the world. Trade in the wood is restricted, to protect the tree population.

Lignum-vitae
Guaiacum spp.

guayacan, gaiac

A genus of slow-growing trees in the caltrop (*Zygophyllaceae*) family, native to the subtropical and tropical regions of the Americas and the Caribbean. All species of the genus are protected as endangered species, but in previous times the trees (especially *G. officinale*) were the source of **lignum vitae**, an extremely hard and dense wood of great value. The resin of the tree, gum guaiacum, has a history of use as a traditional medicine. The compound guaifenesin (an expectorant) found in the resin, is a common ingredient in modern cold medicines. Another phenolic compound in the resin is used to detect blood in human stool samples.

Lima bean
Phaseolus lunatus

Butter bean, Sieva bean

A species of herbaceous plant in the pea (*Fabaceae*) family, native to Central and South America but now widely naturalized to and cultivated throughout the world for its edible bean. The lima bean is named after Lima, Peru. It was of immense importance in Moche culture, which flourished in northern Peru from 1-800 CE. Like other species in the genus *Phaseolus* (including the common bean), lima beans contain a toxin that must be deactivated by cooking before it is eaten.

Lime

The name "lime" refers to a diverse group of fruit-producing trees, most of which are either species or hybrids within the genus *Citrus*. However, the name can also apply to species that are not true citrus, such as the Spanish lime (*Meliococcus bijugatus*).

Limeberry
Triphasia trifolia

triphasia

A species of evergreen shrub or small tree in the citrus (*Rutaceae*) family, likely native to Southeast Asia, though its origin is obscure. It has been widely introduced and naturalized to other tropical regions, particularly islands in the Pacific and Indian Oceans, and the Caribbean. It is cultivated for its edible small, citrus-like fruit, the limeberry.

Limestone

A sedimentary rock composed mainly of the skeletal remains of small sea animals such as corals and mollusks. As such, limestone is composed largely of the minerals calcite and aragonite, both of which are forms of calcium carbonate. Limestone has a long history of use as a building material. It is also used to make industrial lime, which has many uses: it is the primary ingredient in Portland cement; is used as a chemical feedstock; as a soil conditioner; and as a filler and pigment (such as in toothpaste). Crushed limestone used as a soil conditioner is called agricultural lime (which is difference from processed lime). Lithographic limestone is a variety with a very fine grain and homogeneous texture, which is used for lithography.

Linden
Tilia spp.

lime, basswood

A genus of about 30 species of deciduous shrub or tree in the mallow (*Malvaceae*) family, native to and widespread throughout many of the temperate zones of the Northern Hemisphere. Despite the common name of lime tree, the genus is unrelated to true citrus limes. The best known species of linden are *T. cordata* (European linden), and *T. americana var. americana* (American basswood). Both are cultivated for very similar purposes. Their flowers (lime blossoms) have a long tradition of use in herbal medicines in Europe, and are important sources of nectar for honeybees. The flower buds and young leaves are edible raw. The wood is soft, light, and easily workable, with a very fine grain; qualities which have made it the wood of choice for fine carvings for hundreds of years. It is still the wood of choice for making marionettes. The name "basswood" comes from the use of its bast fibers to produce a number of products. The Ainu of northern Japan use the fiber to produce their traditional clothing. Lindens can be coppiced and are among the fastest growing hardwoods. The trees are very long-lived: the Najevnik linden tree, a 700-year-old *T. cordata* specimen, is the thickest tree in Slovenia.

Lingonberry

see *Bilberry*

Lithium

A metallic element similar to sodium and potassium. It is the lightest of all the metals, and its silvery-white appearance tarnishes quickly. It is used for light alloys; it increases the strength of aluminum and is also used as a hardener for some stainless steels and for silver solders. **Lithium salts** are important medicines.

Llama
Lama glama

A species of domesticated animal in the *Camelidae* family, native to South America. They are in the same genus as the wild guanaco (*Lama guanicoe*), and are closely related to the domesticated alpaca and wild vicuna. Llamas are particularly used in the Andean region of South America for meat, as a pack animal, and for the wool, which is lanolin-free and therefore hypoallergenic. Llamas have been domesticated since pre-Columbian times, and were central to the economy of many cultures in South America.

Lobster

The name refers to a number of species of large crustaceans, widely distributed in oceans around the world. The most commercially important species are in the *Nephropidae* and *Homaridae* families. Lobsters are widely farmed and wild caught as food.

Lodestone   see *Magnetite*

Loganberry   see *Bramble*

Logwood   *campeachy wood, bloodwood*
Haematoxylum campechianum

A species of flowering tree in the pea (*Fabaceae*) family, native to southern Mexico and northern Central America. It was intensively harvested by British colonizers of the area now known as the country of Belize, from the 17th through 19th centuries. The wood was a source of valuable dye that gave purple, blue, and a rare fast black. It is still a source of haematoxylin, one of the most commonly used stains in histology (the microscopic study of plant and animal tissue). The tree's flowers are also a nectar source for honeybees.

Longan
Dimocarpus longan

A species of tropical evergreen tree in the soapberry (*Sapindaceae*) family, native to China, East Asia, India, and Southeast Asia. It is cultivated, mainly in those regions, for its edible fruit, the longan. Cultivation has recently been introduced in the United States and Australia. Like other members of the soapberry family, such as the genip and guarana, the fruit is a translucent fleshy pulp surrounding a black lacquer-like seed, which gives it the appearance of an eyeball. This appearance has given the fruit its name, which derives from the Chinese word meaning "dragon eye."

Loofa   *dishrag gourd*
Luffa aegyptiaca

A species of tropical vine in the cucumber (*Cucurbitaceae*) family, presumed native to Africa but now widely cultivated in tropical regions. It is cultivated for its fruit, the loofah gourd. The fruit is edible when harvested young, but if left to mature, it becomes very fibrous. Mature fruit left to dry leaving only the fibrous skeleton, are called **loofah** sponge. Two other related species, *Luffa acutangula* and *L. operculata*, are also grown for the edible gourd.

Loquat   *Japanese medlar, Chinese plum*
Eriobotrya japonica

A species of evergreen tree or small shrub in the rose (*Rosaceae*) family, native to the cooler hill regions of China, but now naturalized to Japan and many other regions of the world. It is cultivated primarily in China and Japan for its edible fruit, the loquat. There are hundreds of cultivars of the species. In Japan and China it has a history of use in traditional medicine. Elsewhere in the world, it is widely grown as an ornamental.

Lychee
Litchi chinensis

A species of evergreen tree that is the sole member of the genus *Litchi*, in the soapberry (*Sapindaceae*) family, native to the southeast region of China. It is cultivated in tropical regions, primarily in Southeast Asia and India, for its edible fruit, the lychee. Lychee seeds contain a compound that has toxic, sometimes fatal effects when consumed in large amounts.

Macadamia nut
Macadamia spp.

popplenut, Queensland nut

A genus of four species of tree in the protea (*Proteaceae*) family, native to Australia. Two of the species are commercially important (*M. integrifolia* and *M. tetraphylla*), and are grown for the edible, oil-rich nut. The macadamia nut industry was developed in Hawaii in the 1920's, and has since spread to other tropical and subtropical regions. The nut shell is so hard that it takes three hundred pounds of pressure per square inch to crack it.

Mackerel

Although there are many species of fish referred to as mackerel, the type species for true mackerel (tribe *Scombrini*, within the *Scombridae* family) is the Atlantic mackerel (*Scomber scombrus*). Mackerel is an important food fish worldwide. Its oily meat is rich in omega-3 fatty acids.

Madder
Rubia spp.

A genus of perennial herbs and scrub shrubs in the madder (*Rubiaceae*) family, native to the Old World, but now widely naturalized to and cultivated elsewhere in the world. Two species in particular (*R. tinctorum* and *R. cordifolia*) are cultivated for the extraction of **alizarin**, a red pigment that dates back to antiquity.

Magnesite
magnesium carbonate

A mineral that is the principal ore of magnesium. When burned in the presence of charcoal, it produces magnesium oxide, which is used to make refractory bricks to line blast furnaces, kilns, and incinerators. It has a secondary use as beads for jewelry.

Magnesium

A silvery metal element that is found in metamorphic silicate rocks. It is highly flammable, with a characteristic bright white light, and will burn in water. It is used in the manufacture of fireworks, marine flares, and other light-producing uses. It is used medicinally as magnesium salts. It is used to make a strong light alloy with zinc and aluminum, for the manufacture of aircraft. It is an essential mineral for the human body.

Magnetite
ferrous ferric oxide

A mineral that is one of the chief ores of iron. It is the most magnetic mineral on Earth. It is naturally attracted to a magnet, and can be magnetized so that it is a magnet itself. It is one of the few minerals that can be found in nature naturally magnetized. This naturally-occurring magnetized magnetite is called lodestone. The property of magnetism was discovered through lodestone, and the first compasses were made with lodestone. The name comes from Middle English and means "leading stone," lode being an archaic word meaning "journey" or "way."

Maguey   see *Agave*

Mahogany   *Genuine mahogany*
Swietenia spp.

The name genuine mahogany refers to three species of tropical hardwood tree in the *Swietenia* genus, within the chinaberry (*Meliaceae*) family, all native to Central and South America and the West Indies. These trees are cultivated and wild harvested for their wood, which is highly prized for its reddish-brown color, straight grain, and durability. Currently, the only commercial species is Honduran mahogany (*S. macrophylla*). Wild mahogany is on the endangered species list due to overharvesting. Timber from other trees may be called mahogany, but only wood from *Swietenia* can be traded as "genuine mahogany."

Maize   *corn, Indian corn, sweet corn*
Zea mays

An annual plant in the grass (*Poaceae*) family, native to southern Mexico, but now one of the most important food staples in the world, surpassing even wheat and rice in volume of production. Maize has been cultivated for at least 10,000 years in Central America, and was introduced to Europe in the 15th century. There are many cultivars and many uses, including: as a food crop for humans; as a fodder crop for livestock (especially pigs); for the production of sugar (**corn syrup**); for the production of fuel (**ethanol**); and a starch that can be made into non-edible products such as plastics, adhesives, and fabrics.

Malachite
copper carbonate

A mineral known today mainly as an ornamental gemstone. It
has a rich, banded opaque green color, and is easy to cut and
polish. In former times, it was used as a green pigment in paints,
but it is only moderately lightfast and is vulnerable to acid. The
name comes from its resemblance to the mallow plant. In ancient
times, malachite was mined as a copper ore; for example, at the
Great Orme mine in Wales, active from about 1800 to 600 B.C.E.

Mallard duck
Anas platyrhynchos

A species of freshwater duck in the *Anatidae* family, one of many
that is used as a food source. Almost all domesticated ducks de-
rive from the mallard. They are used mainly for their meat, as
their eggs have a strong flavor.

Mamey sapote   *red mamey*
Pouteria sapota

A species of evergreen tree in the gutta-percha (*Sapotaceae*) family,
native to southern Mexico and Central America, but now cultivated in other parts of the world, including the United States, South
America, and the Caribbean. It is cultivated for its edible fruit,
the mamey sapote. An edible oil known as sapote oil or sapayul
oil is pressed from the seeds, and is used as a cooking oil and in
cosmetics. Several other closely-related trees in the *Pouteria* genus, also native to Central and South America, are cultivated
mainly locally for their edible fruit. These include: the caimito (*P.
caimito*); the canistel, or eggfruit (*P. campechiana*); and the lucuma
(*P. lucuma, P. macrophylla*).

Mammee   *mamee apple, tropical apricot*
Mammea americana

An evergreen tree in the *Calophyllaceae* family, native to tropical
South America, but since the 16th century has been introduced to
West Africa, Southeast Asia, Hawaii, and Florida. It is cultivated
for its bitter yet edible fruit, which is known by several names,
most commonly mammee or mammee apple. Both the gum resin
from the bark and the powdered seeds have been used medicinally, and as an insecticide. The bark also contains tannin.

Mandrake
Mandragora officinarum

A species of herbaceous plant in the nightshade (*Solanaceae*) family, native to the Mediterranean region, but now widely naturalized to and cultivated in many other temperate regions. In modern times it is grown mainly as an ornamental, but mandrake is known as the oldest magic plant in botanical history. In Greek legends it is called the Plant of Circe, as it is believed that the goddess' magic potion to turn men into pigs was made from it. In Europe, mandrake was used as a narcotic and a love potion; it was believed that the root emitted loud shrieks when pulled from the ground, and anyone hearing the sound would be driven mad. Like other members of the nightshade family, mandrake is a source of the powerful neurotoxin **hyoscine** (scopalamine), which has important medicinal uses and is listed on the World Health Organization's Model List of Essential Medicines.

Manganese

A metallic element not found free in nature, but is often found in combination with iron. Among its many uses are: as an important metal in alloys, particularly stainless steels, and in the manufacture of paints and varnishes. Manganese oxide is an important element of alkaline batteries. Manganese is also an essential mineral in the function of living organisms, but in large amounts is a toxin.

Mangelwurzel   see *Beet*

Mango
Mangifera spp.

A genus of tropical evergreen trees in the cashew (*Anacardiaceae*) family, native to South Asia. It is cultivated for its fruit, the mango. There are several fruit-producing species, but the species *M. indica* (common mango or Indian mango) has gained worldwide cultivation and distribution, and is one of the most widely cultivated tropical fruits, with many cultivars. Like other members of the cashew family, the stems, leaves, and sap of the mango tree can cause contact dermatitis in individuals who are sensitive to its allergens. The mango is the national fruit of India, and in Hinduism, the Lord Ganesha is often depicted holding a perfectly ripe mango as a symbol of the attainment of perfection.

Mangosteen
Garcinia mangostana

A species of evergreen tree in the *Clusiaceae* family, native to Southeast Asia, but now cultivated in other tropical areas. It is cultivated for its edible fruit, the purple mangosteen. It is the most widely cultivated species within the *Garcinia* genus, though many other species also produce fruit and are cultivated for local consumption. The mangosteen is closely related to the **gamboge** tree (*G. hanburyi* and *G. morella*, both native to India), whose resin is used to make the yellow pigment of the same name.

Manna ash   *South European flowering ash*
Fraxinus ornus

A species of tree in the olive (*Oleaceae*) family, native to southern Europe and southwestern Asia. In modern times, it is cultivated mostly as an ornamental plant with showy flowers. However, in the past in Europe, at least as far back as the Middle Ages, a sugary sap called **manna** was extracted by making cuts in the bark of the tree. The sugar mannose and sugar alcohol mannitol are both derived from the sap of this tree. The narrow-leaf ash (*F. angustifolia*) is used for a similar purpose.

Manuka   *broom teatree*
Leptospermum scoparium

A species of small scrub-like tree in the myrtle (*Myrtaceae*) family, native to Australia and New Zealand. An essential oil is distilled from its leaves which traditionally has been used for medicinal purposes; its bark is also claimed to have medicinal value. It is also highly valued for the flavorful honey, called Manuka honey, produced by bees who feed on the flower nectar. The closely-related lemon-scent teatree (*L. petersonii*) is the source of an essential oil used as a flavoring and a scent.

The Magic of Honey

Though honey is mostly composed of simple sugars (fructose and glucose), the exact composition — including flavor and other attributes — is heavily influenced by the flowers from which the nectar is gathered. Honey made from rhododendron nectar is toxic to humans, while manuka honey is claimed to have a therapeutic effect for neuropathy and other disorders.

Maple tree
Acer spp.

Acer is a genus of over a hundred species of deciduous trees in the soapberry (*Sapindaceae*) family. Most are native to Asia, with some native to Europe, North Africa, and North America. Only one species, *A. laurinum*, is found natively in the Southern Hemisphere. The type species *A. rubrum* (red maple), is the most common species in Europe. Maple is commercially cultivated for a variety of uses. The sugar or black maple (*A. saccharum*) has a sugary sap, and is tapped to make syrup. Some of the larger species are timbers sources, like the big-leaf or Oregon maple (*A. macrophyllum*), the box-elder (*A. negundo*), and the silver maple (*A. saccharinum*). The wood is used for furniture and cabinetry, among other things. Maple wood is particularly known for its acoustical quality, and is often used to make musical instruments.

Marble

A metamorphic rock made mainly of recrystallized carbonate minerals, usually calcite or dolomite. Pure marble is white; the colors often found in marble come from various impurities in the rock. It is often used for sculpture and other interior work, as opposed to an outdoor building material, as it weathers easily; though in a dry climate it is relatively durable. Some areas have become well known for their unique varieties of marble, such as the Italian Carrara marble used by the Renaissance sculptor Michelangelo, and the Pentelic marble of Greece, used to construct the Athenian Acropolis.

Marigold
Tagetes spp.

The name commonly refers to a genus of perennial herbaceous plants in the daisy (*Asteraceae*) family, native to Mexico, Central and South America but now widely naturalized to and cultivated elsewhere. It can also refer to *Calendula officinalis* (pot-marigold), which is native to Eastern Europe and Asia. It is a common ornamental plant, but several species, especially *T. erecta* (African marigold), *T. lucida* (Mexican tarragon), and *T. minuta* (Mexican marigold) are cultivated as a culinary herb. Recent studies suggest that menthol extracts from the plant have antimicrobial and antifungal properties. In Aztec culture, the plant was connected to the rain god, Tlaloc, and was an ingredient in a sacred incense.

127

Marijuana
Cannabis sativa subsp. indica

Indian hemp, bhang, ganja

C. sativa is a species of annual herbaceous plant in the cannabis (*Cannabaceae*) family, which also includes hops and hackberries. There are two main subspecies of *C. sativa*: *indica* and *sativa*. The name marijuana generally refers to the subspecies *indica* and its many cultivars, which are the varieties bred for the psychoactive and medicinal compounds, such as TCH and **cannabidiol** (or CBD), extracted from the leaves and flowers. The name hemp generally refers to the subspecies *sativa*, which is grown mainly for its fiber and edible seeds.

Marjoram
Origanum majorana

sweet marjoram

A perennial herb in the mint (*Lamiaceae*) family, native to Cyprus and southern Turkey. It is widely cultivated throughout the world, and is used fresh or dried as a culinary herb. An essential oil is steam distilled from the leaves. It is closely related to oregano (*Origanum vulgare*); the herb "hardy sweet marjoram" or "Italian oregano" (O. x majoricum) is a hybrid between the two.

Marl

A loose or unconsolidated rock or mud consisting of a mixture of mostly clay, with lime (calcium carbonate), and sometimes other carbonates. It is formed at the bottom of lakes and seas, either prehistorically, or in the present day. It is used as a soil conditioner, especially for acidic soils. Some types are used in the manufacture of Portland cement, and as an insulator.

Marram grass
Ammophila spp.

beachgrass, bent grass

A genus of two or three closely related species of perennial plant in the grass (*Poaceae*) family. The species are native to the North Atlantic region, North Africa, the Arabian Peninsula, West Asia and Europe, and are found almost exclusively on the sand dunes of the sea coast. The genus name comes from the Greek meaning "sand friend." The grass is of great importance in stabilizing sand dunes, especially where they lie close to agricultural land.

Marri tree   *Port Gregory gum*
Corymbia calophylla

A member of the myrtle (*Myrtaceae*) family, closely related to the
genus *Eucalyptus*, and formerly included in that genus. Native to
Western Australia, it is a type of tree known as a bloodwood because of the red gum (**kino**) it exudes in response to mechanical
damage. This gum contains tannins, and has a history of use in
traditional medicine. The marri, and other trees in the genus, are
harvested for their wood; the closely related lemon-scent gum (*C.
citriodora*), is cultivated for its essential oil.

Marron   *yabbies*
Cherax tenuimanus, Cherax cainii

Two closely related species of freshwater crayfish native to Western Australia, considered to be a food delicacy. Wild capture of
these crayfish is strictly regulated, due to the critically endangered status of *C. tenuimanus*. Farming of the crayfish is a devel-
oping industry in Western Australia.

Marrow   see *Squash*

Marsh mallow   *white mallow*
Althaea officinalis

A species of perennial herb in the mallow (*Malvaceae*) family, native to the marshy areas near the seacoasts of Europe, Western
Asia, and North Africa. The leaves, flowers, and root of the plant
have been used medicinally as relief for irritation of the mucous
membranes. A sticky extract of the root known as *halawa* was
originally used in the Middle East to make a medicinal confection
called *halva*. The recipe was modified in France to include egg
white meringue and rose water, and was the forerunner of the
confection we know today as marshmallows.

Marsh marigold   *kingcup, cowslip, meadowbright*
Caltha palustris

A species of perennial herb in the buttercup (*Ranunculaceae*) family, native to marshes and other marsh-like habitats in the temperate regions of the Northern Hemisphere. Its young flower buds
are harvested as a caper-like culinary herb. Like all members of
the buttercup family, it contains a toxin that can cause illness
when consumed in anything other than very small amounts.

Marula
Sclerocarya birrea

A species of tree in the cashew (*Anacardiaceae*) family, native to certain woodland regions in Southern Africa, West Africa, and Madagascar. Its edible fruit has been an important food source in those regions for centuries. A cooking oil is rendered from the seeds that is unusually resistant to oxidation, giving it a particularly long shelf life.

Mastic tree   *lentisk, Chios mastictree*
Pistacia lentiscus

A small evergreen tree or shrub in the cashew (*Anacardiaceae*) family, native to the arid, rocky regions of the Mediterranean, although it has now been naturalized to Mexico. It is cultivated mainly on the Greek island of Chios for its resin, known as **mastic**. Mastic has been used medicinally for thousands of years, as an antifungal and antibacterial. It is also used as a spice, as a chewing gum, as an ingredient in cosmetics and varnish, and in the holy oil *myron*, used by the Greek Orthodox Church.

Medlar tree
Mespilus germanica

A species of deciduous shrub or small tree in the rose (*Rosaceae*) family, native to Iran, southwest Asia, and Southeastern Europe, but naturalized and cultivated elsewhere. It has been cultivated since Roman times for its fruit, the medlar. It is unusual in that it is a winter fruit, and in that the fruit is harvested and eaten when bletted (that is, nearly rotten).

Meerschaum   *sepiolite*

A complex magnesium silicate-based clay mineral, found mostly in Greece and Turkey. It is sometimes found floating in the sea, which gives it the name meerschaum, which means "seafoam" in German. Since the 18th century, it has been a preferred material for making the clay tobacco pipes known meerschaum pipes. It is also used in East Africa to make the traditional incense burner called the *dabqaad*.

Melon
Cucumis melo subsp. melo

A domesticated species of annual vine within the cucumber
(*Cucurbitaceae*) family, native to Central Asia and India, but now
widely grown throughout the world for its edible fruit, the melon. It has many cultivars, which include most of the culinary
melons. The general categories of cultivars include the varieties:
C. melo var. inodorus, the smooth-skinned varieties such as honey-
dew, crenshaw and casaba; *C. melo var. cantalupo* (or var. *reticula-
tus*), the netted cultivars such as North American cantaloupe and
muskmelon ; *C. melo var. flexuosus*, which includes the Armenian
cucumber, or snake melon.

Menhaden   *mossbunker, bunker*
Brevoortia spp., Ethmidium spp.

Menhaden refers to two genera (containing seven species) of
small forage fish within the herring (*Clupeidae*) family. Of these,
the most commercially important are the Pacific menhaden (*E.
maculatum*), the Atlantic menhaden (*B. tyrannus*), and the Gulf
menhaden (*B. patronus*). These fish are mostly used as fertilizer
and animal feed, though they are also used as human food.

Mercury   *quicksilver*

A metallic element that is liquid at most ambient temperatures.
Most of the world's mercury comes from the mineral cinnabar. In
its pure form, mercury is mainly used in the manufacture of electrical items such as rectifiers and circuit breakers. It is also used
in the extraction of gold, and in barometers and thermometers.
Its compounds are used in the manufacture of fungicides, drugs,
and paints. It is toxic to the human body even in small amounts.

Mesquite   *algarroba-bean, ironwood*
Prosopis juliflora

A species of tree in the genus commonly known as mesquite, in
the pea (*Fabaceae*) family. It is native to the arid regions of Mexico, Central America, and northern and western South America,
but is now widely naturalized to and cultivated in other arid
tropical regions. In some areas, it has become an invasive weed.
Like other members of the genus, mesquite is very drought tolerant. It serves many purposes: as a nectar source for honeybees; as
fuel (charcoal and firewood) and wood; and as a source of tannin.

Metel

see *Jimsonweed*

Methane

marsh gas, natural gas
carbon tetrahydride, hydrogen carbide

A gas formed either as the byproduct of decomposition of plant material, or through geologic processes. It forms the main constituent of natural gas, which is an important fuel source.

Mexican mint

Cuban oregano, country borage
Plectranthus amboinicus

An herbaceous perennial plant in the mint (*Lamiaceae*) family, native to tropical and southern Africa, but now widely naturalized to and cultivated in tropical regions around the world. It is cultivated as a culinary herb, and for its essential oil, which is used as a scent, and as a mosquito and insect repellent.

Mica

A group of closely related sheet silicate minerals. Due to the nature of their crystalline structure, it is possible to divide the crystals into very thin, transparent, and flexible sheets. These sheets are very resistant to heat and electricity. The clear variety, known as muscovite, is the most widely used in the electrical industry, especially as an insulator. Ground mica provides a glitter effect to many products, including paints and cosmetics. It is also used in construction as a joint compound and filler for gypsum board.

Microcline

A type of feldspar commercially valuable in the manufacture of porcelain. It is ground very fine, then mixed with kaolin and quartz; upon firing, the microcline fuses the materials together.

Milkvetch

Astragalus spp.

Astralagus is a large genus of about 3000 species of plants within the pea (*Fabaceae*) family. The genus is best known as a source of gum **tragacanth**, which comes primarily from two species native to West Asia and the Middle East: *A. gummifer* (gum tragacanth), and *A. brachycalyx* (Persian manna). Tragacanth is a highly useful gum resin with uses and properties slightly different from other traditionally important gum resins like gum arabic. Several other species of *Astragalus* are also sources of various gums and resins.

Milkweed

silky swallowwort

Asclepias syriaca

A species of herbaceous perennial plant in the dogbane (*Apocynaceae*) family, native to southern Canada and much of the United States east of the Rocky Mountains. The mature plant's latex contains large enough amounts of glycosides to be toxic to livestock and humans, but the young shoots, leaves, flower buds and immature fruit are all edible. The seed floss (when compressed) has been used traditionally as the background material for mounted insects. Native Americans have used the seed floss and bast fiber for cordage and textiles. The seed oil contains cinnamic acid, which can act as a sunscreen in cosmetics.

Millet

The term "millet" is used for a large number of species of small-grained cereal grasses in the *Poaceae* family, which are generally cultivated in drier climates ranging from warm temperate to tropical. Millets are indigenous to many parts of the world, and are some of the oldest cultivated grains, with evidence for cultivation dating back 7000 years. When ground into flour, it is used extensively as human food in Africa and Asia, but in other countries the whole seed is more commonly used as animal fodder. The most commonly cultivated species are: *Eleusine coracana* (Finger millet); *Panicum miliaceum subsp. miliaceum* (common millet, Proso millet); *Panicum sumatrense* (little millet); *Pennisetum glaucum* (Pearl millet); and *Setaria italica* (Foxtail millet, Italian millet).

Mindanao gum

rainbow gum, deglupta

Eucalyptus deglupta

A species of tree in the myrtle (*Myrtaceae*) family, native to Indonesia, New Guinea, and the Philippines. It is the only *Eucalyptus* species whose natural range extends into the Northern Hemisphere. The common name "rainbow gum" comes from its bark, which is colored in stripes of bright green, maroon, orange, and dusky blue. It is one of the fastest growing trees in the world, growing up to ten feet per year. It is widely grown in tropical regions as pulpwood for paper.

Mint
Mentha spp.

Mentha is s genus of roughly fifteen perennial herbaceous species within the mint (*Lamiaceae*) family, with a widespread distribution across Europe, Africa, Asia, Australia, and North America. Species identification is tricky, as hybridization occurs naturally, and there are many cultivars. The genus is cultivated for its strong aroma, which is used as a food flavoring, medicinally, and in cosmetics and perfumery. It is used fresh, and as an essential oil steam distilled from its leaves. Some of the more widely cultivated species include: *M. x piperita* (peppermint); *M. spicata* (spearmint); *M. pulegium* (pennyroyal); *M. aquatica var. citrata* (bergamot mint, yerba buena, lemon mint). All members of the genus may cause allergic reactions in some people, and can cause adverse effects in large doses.

Miracle fruit   *sweet-berry agbayun, asaa, ledidi*
Synsepalum dulcificum

A species of evergreen shrub in the gutta-percha (*Sapotaceae*) family, native to tropical West Africa. There, it has a long history of traditional use as a food flavoring. Its berries contain the compound **miraculin**, which is a taste-modifier that has the effect of making sour foods taste sweet. Since the 1970's it has been banned from import or sale in the United States, as it is classified as an unapproved sweetener.

Molybdenite
molybdenum disulfide

A mineral that is the primary ore of molybdenum. The mineral itself had use in early semiconductor diodes.

Molybdenum

A metallic element that is used primarily in ferrous alloys to produce high-strength and corrosion-resistant steels.

Monazite

A phosphate mineral known mainly as an ore for the rare-earth metals thorium, lanthanum, and cerium. Formerly, it was used in the manufacture of incandescent gas mantles.

Monkeypod
Albizia saman
cow-tamarind

A species of tree in the pea (*Fabaceae*) family, native to the tropical regions of the New World from Mexico to Peru and Brazil, but widely introduced to and cultivated in other tropical regions throughout the world. Its wood is used for fine woodworking, such as furniture. It is also a host for lac insects. Many other species within the *Albizia* genus are also important sources of wood in their native regions.

Mopanie
Gonimbrasia belina

The name "mopanie" refers to the caterpillars of a species of emperor moth native to southern Africa. In its native regions, it is an important source of both wild-harvested and cultivated protein. In some areas, it is an important cash crop, with hundreds of tons of caterpillars being traded annually. The name derives from the fact that the caterpillar feeds mainly, though not exclusively, on the mopane tree (*Colophosperum mopane*).

Mountain pepper
Tasmannia lanceolata
peppertree

A species of evergreen shrub in the *Winteraceae* family, native to the cool temperate rainforests of southeastern Australia and Tasmania. Its leaves and berries are coming into wider use as a spice with a flavor similar to pepper.

Mulberry
Morus spp.

A genus of about fifteen species of deciduous flowering trees and shrubs in the mulberry (*Moraceae*) family. Most species are native to Asia and the Asian subcontinent, but some are indigenous to North and South America, and Africa. The best-known species is white mulberry (*M. alba*), which is widely cultivated as its leaves are the preferred food stock for the silkworm (*Bombyx mori*). The species *M. nigra* (black mulberry, native to Asia) and *M. rubra* (red mulberry, native to North America) produce edible fruit; the berries are poisonous when unripe, but edible when ripe. The leaves are used to make tea in some cultures, and the bark has in the past (especially in Southeast Asia) been used to make paper.

Mule

A sterile hybrid between a male donkey and a female horse, mules have been valued for centuries as hardy pack and draft animals, able to carry heavy loads for long distances over rough terrain, on less and coarser food than horses can tolerate.

Mung bean   *green gram*
Vigna radiata var. radiata

A species of annual vine in the pea (*Fabaceae*) family, thought to have originated in Asia, but now widely cultivated throughout the world, particularly in the tropics. It is closely related to the adzuki bean, cowpea, and Bambara groundnut. It is cultivated for its highly nutritious edible bean (the mung bean), which is eaten whole or sprouted. The starch extracted from the bean is also used to make transparent cellophane noodles. Mung beans are a particularly important food source in Asia and the Middle East.

Muscadine grape
Vitis rotundifolia

A species of perennial plant in the grapevine (*Vitaceae*) family, native to North American and cultivated there since the 16th century. It is one of several grape species native to North America that is cultivated for its edible fruit, the grape. The fruit is eaten raw, and made into preserves, juice, and wine. Other species include the Concord grape (*V. labrusca*), and the Arkansas grape (*V. aestivalis*). North American grapes are closely related to the wine grape (*V. vinifera subsp. vinifera*), and like many other species, are used as graft stock and to breed desirable characteristics such as disease resistance into wine grape cultivars.

Muscovy duck   *Barbary duck, pato criollo*
Cairina moschata

One of two species of duck in the *Anatidae* family that is domesticated (the other is the mallard). It is native to Mexico, Central, and South America, but is now found in many other parts of the world, both feral and domesticated. They are a tropical bird, but are highly adaptable to cooler regions. They are raised primarily for their meat, and have been domesticated in the Americas for several centuries at least. In the culinary context, the meat is known as Barbary duck.

Mushroom

"Mushroom" is a term that encompasses a wide variety of macro-fungi, and refers specifically to the spore-producing fruit body. Some species are cultivated or wild harvested for food, or for medicinal use. A great many are poisonous. There are over twenty species of mushroom that are commercially cultivated for human consumption, for example, white or portabello (*Agaricus bisporus*, the most widely-grown mushroom species in the world) and shitake mushrooms. There are at least twenty species that are difficult or as yet impossible to cultivate, and are wild-harvested for commercial consumption; these include the chanterelle (genus *Cantharellus*, among others) and morel (genus *Morchella*) mushrooms. There are many more that are cultivated or wild harvested simply for local use. In addition, some varieties are consumed for their psychoactive properties, such as several mushrooms of the genus *Psilocybe*. Due to the difficulty of discerning edible from toxic varieties, care and expertise are required when wild-harvesting mushrooms, in order to prevent poisoning.

Musk deer
Moschus moschiferus

A species of deer in the *Moschidae* family, native to the mountain forests of northeast Asia. A gland found in the male deer is the original source of the scent material known as musk. The animal is now endangered due to poaching for this valuable material, and trade in true musk is strictly regulated.

Musk mallow   *musk okra*
Abelmoschus moschatus

A species of perennial herbaceous plant in the mallow (*Malvaceae*) family, native to Asia and Australia but now cultivated in other tropical regions. The seed oil of the plant was at one time used as a substitute for animal-sourced musk, due to the similarity of fragrance. In modern times, the seeds and to a lesser extent the flowers are used as a food flavoring. The unripe pods, leaves, and new shoots can be eaten. The mucilage from the roots is used as paper sizing.

Mustard
Brassica spp., Sinapis spp.

The name refers to several species in the cabbage (*Brassicaceae*) family, native to the tropical regions of the Northern Hemisphere. Black mustard (*Brassica nigra*) and brown mustard (*Brassica juncea*) are the most commonly cultivated for their pungent seeds, which are used as a spice and to make the condiment known as prepared mustard. Mustard oil is produced either by pressing the seeds (seed oil), or by steam distillation (essential oil). The meal left after pressing is used as an insecticide. White mustard (*Sinapis alba*) is grown as a cover crop, a forage crop, and for its seedlings, which are eaten as a fresh vegetable.

Myrrh tree   *African myrrh, herabol myrrh*
Commiphora myrrha

The genus *Commiphora*, within the torchwood (*Bursuraceae*) family, contains many species known for their aromatic resins. *C. myrrha*, native to the Arabian Peninsula and northwest Africa, is the best-known source of the resin known as **myrrh**. Myrrh has been used since antiquity for incense, perfumery, and medicine. It has a particular place in the sacred rituals of Judaism and Christianity: it was an ingredient in ketoret, an incense used in the temples of Jerusalem; in the New Testament, it is one of the three gifts presented by the magi to the Christ child at his birth. For more information, see the separate entry for *Commiphora*.

Myrtle
Myrtus communis

An evergreen tree in the myrtle (*Myrtaceae*) family, native to the Mediterranean region, but widely naturalized and cultivated elsewhere. Its fragrant white flowers produce an essential oil used in perfumery. The purple berries are edible; on the Mediterranean islands they are used to make the popular liqueur called Mirto. In ancient times, the tree was considered sacred to the cultures of the eastern Mediterranean. The ancient Hebrews covered the tent of the Tabernacle with myrtle boughs in bloom. To the Egyptians, it was the tree of Hathor, goddess of love, mirth, and joy. In Greece and Rome, it was sacred to Aphrodite and Venus, the goddesses of love. This association continues in the tradition of brides wearing wreaths of myrtle-blossoms.

Nasturtium
Tropaeolum spp.

A genus of plants in the family *Tropaeolaceae*, all native to western South America but now widely cultivated elsewhere. The common name comes from the similarity in smell to watercress (genus *Nasturtium*). The most common species is *T. majus*, which is mainly cultivated as an ornamental. All parts of the plant are edible, and are often eaten fresh as greens; the seed pod is pickled as an alternative to capers. Several species are cultivated as food, such as *T. tuberosum* (mashua), which is grown in the Andean region for its tuberous root. Other species have a history of use in traditional medicine; *T. minus* (dwarf nasturtium) is a source of essential oil used as a flavoring, in perfumery, and in pest control.

Nectarine   see *Peach*

Neodymium
A metallic element that occurs in the minerals monazite and cerite. It is a silver-white metal that tarnishes easily. Its salts are used to give a mauve color to glass and porcelain. It is also used to make alloys that are neodymium magnets, which are powerful permanent magnets.

Neon
An inert, colorless and odorless elemental gas found only in the atmosphere. It is used in electric lights, as it will glow a bright reddish-orange in the presence of an electric field. It is also used in other varieties of vacuum tubes and lasers.

Nettles
Urtica spp.

The name "nettle" is used to describe many plants that have fine stinging hairs; however, plants of the *Urtica* genus, in the *Urticaceae* family are the most commonly known as nettle. These plants have fine hairs coated with a caustic fluid that causes a dermatological reaction in humans and animals. *Urtica* is used as a minor food source and in traditional medicine in several cultures in Europe. Nettles are also the subject of folklore, such as the fairy tale *The Wild Swans* in which a princess must weave coats of nettles in order to free her enchanted brothers.

New Zealand flax
harakeke, New Zealand hemp
Phormium tenax

A species of herbaceous perennial plant in the *Asphodelaceae* family, native to New Zealand and cultivated mainly there and in Australia. Its leaves, which can grow up to 9 feet long, produce a long, strong fiber that has long been used by the Maori people to produce cloth. The plant is now widely cultivated in temperate zones as an ornamental and a source of the fiber, which is used mainly for cordage (ropes, twine, and fishing nets)

Nickel

A metallic element commonly found in association with iron and copper. It is hard, ductile, and corrosion-resistant. It is used primarily in creating heat-resistant steel alloys, and as plating to provide corrosion protection. It is ferromagnetic at room temperature, and is used to create magnets. It is used in batteries, and in pigments. The name comes from that of a mischievous sprite that appears in the folklore of German miners.

Niobium

A gray metallic element formerly known as columbium, often found in association with tantalum. The chief ore is columbite. It is used for hardening steels, and for the manufacture of stainless steel and high-speed steels, as it is highly resistant to corrosion. It is also used in superconducting materials. It has the unusual property of becoming iridescent upon anodization, which has made it popular in jewelry making.

Nitrate

Potassium nitrate (saltpeter), and sodium nitrate (Chile saltpeter) are important nutrients for humans, although overexposure can cause adverse effects. Nitrates are used as fertilizer, and as oxidizing agents in explosives, such as gunpowder. They are important preservatives for cured meat. Nitrates are used in the manufacture of **celluloid**, one of the first thermoplastics.

Noni
Morinda citrifolia

Indian mulberry, cheese fruit

A species of tree in the madder (*Rubiaceae*) family, presumed native to Southeast Asia and Australasia, but now widely cultivated and naturalized throughout the tropics. It is cultivated mainly for the medicinal properties of its pungent fruit, which is also edible and served as a famine food for some South Pacific cultures. A brownish-purple dye used in batik is made from its bark, and in Hawaii, a yellow dye is made from its roots.

Nori
Pyropia spp.

A species of edible seaweed, classified as a red algae, in the *Bangiaceae* family. It is cultivated primarily in East Asia, where it is an important traditional food source. The main cultivated species are *P. tenera* and *P. yezoensis*.

Nutmeg
Myristica fragrans

true nutmeg

A species of evergreen tree in the nutmeg (*Myristicaceae*) family, native to the Moluccas (formerly known as the Spice Islands) of Indonesia, but now widely cultivated throughout the tropical regions. It is the best-known member of the *Myristica* genus, as it is the primary source of the spices nutmeg and mace. Nutmeg is made from the seed, whereas mace is made from the red seed coat (the aril). Both are dried and ground into powder to make the spice. The fruit (the pericarp of the seed) is edible. An essential oil steam-distilled from the seed is used in perfumery. Nutmeg butter, produced by cold-pressing the seed, is used as a substitute for cocoa butter.

Nux vomica
Strychnos nux-vomica

strychnine tree

A species of deciduous tree in the *Loganiaceae* family, native to India and Southeast Asia. Like many members of this family, the plant is extremely poisonous. The seeds of its fruit are the source of the toxic alkaloids **strychnine** and brucine. Strychnine is a common ingredient in rat poison. It has been used as an herbal medicine in India and Asia, but its use is extremely hazardous.

Oak
Quercus spp.

A large genus of deciduous trees, containing several hundred species, within the oak and beech *(Fagaceae)* family. The genus is widespread throughout the temperate regions, but is also found in North Africa, the Andes, the Himalayas, and in Indonesia. Several species are noted for their hard, durable, and rot-resistant wood. In North America, the white oak *(Q. alba)* is of particular importance as a hardwood; in Britain and other parts of Europe, the English oak *(Q. robur)* has the same importance. The fruit (acorn) of some species is used for fodder; for example, four species of oak found in the Iberian peninsula provide the main food source for the Black Iberian pig, the source of a famous ham. Some Native Americans have used acorns as a staple food, though they require processing before they are edible by humans. The bark of some species is a significant source of tannins used for tanning. The bark of the cork oak *(Q. suber)* supplies cork.

Oakmoss
Evernia prunastri

A species of lichen found throughout the temperate regions of the Northern Hemisphere. It grows primarily on the trunks and branches of oak trees, but is also found on conifers such as pine and fir. It is commercially important as a source of oleoresin that is used extensively in the perfume industry, both as a scent, and as a fixative.

Oat
Avena sativa

A species of annual plant in the grass *(Poaceae)* family, native to the Fertile Crescent, but now widely cultivated in the Northern Hemisphere, particularly in areas that are further north, with wetter, cooler summers than those required for other cereals, such as wheat. Oat is cultivated for its edible seed. The majority of oats are used as animal fodder, but they are also commonly consumed by humans. Other edible species in the genus include *A. abyssinica* (Abyssinian oat), and *A. nuda* (naked oat), cultivated in China and processed into a flour known as *youmian*. Oats are also used in cosmetics for their emollient properties.

Obsidian

A mineral that is a naturally-occurring form of volcanic glass. It is formed when lava with a high silica content cools quickly. By using the process called knapping, it can be shaped into cutting tools that have extremely sharp edges, sharper than any metal edge. Obsidian is the basis of some of the oldest tools known to mankind, with the earliest known tools dating back to 700,000 B.C. In modern times, obsidian is used as a stone in jewelry and for other ornamental purposes.

Ochre

A family of natural earth pigments whose basis is the mineral limonite (iron oxide-hydroxide) mixed with varying amounts of clay and sand. The variety of color is due to the presence of other minerals. Yellow ochre contains mainly limonite; red ochre contains hematite; purple ochre is chemically identical to red ochre, but has a larger particle size, which creates a different hue; brown ochre is mainly goethite (partially hydrated iron oxide); sienna contains limonite and a small amount of manganese oxide, producing a darker yellow; umber contains a higher percentage of manganese oxide, producing a dark brown. Ochre is an ancient pigment, with evidence of use in cave paintings dating to 75,000 years ago. Many cultures throughout history have used ochre for a variety of purposes, both sacred and secular.

Okra *gumbo, lady's fingers*
Abelmoschus esculentus

A domesticated species of perennial plant in the mallow (*Malvaceae*) family, of disputed native origin, but now widely cultivated in tropical, subtropical, and warm temperate zones of the world. It is mostly grown for its edible seed pods, though it has other uses. The seed oil is edible; the seeds themselves are roasted and ground for use as a coffee substitute; the bast fibers of the stem are used industrially, for example to reinforce polymer composites; research is being conducted on the use of the mucilage produced by the plant as a flocculant, which could be used to remove the turbidity from waste water.

Old fustic   *Dyer's mulberry*
Maclura tinctoria

A species of medium to large tree in the mulberry (*Moraceae*) family, native to Central and South America. A dye known as fustic is made from the bark; it is very colorfast and produces shades from yellow to green. It was used to dye the uniforms of the U.S. military in World War I. The leaves can also be used to feed silkworms. It is closely related to the osage orange (*M. pomifera*).

Olive tree
Olea europaea

The type species of the genus *Olea*, within the olive (*Oleaceae*) family. This evergreen tree is native to the eastern Mediterranean region, but is now widely naturalized to and cultivated throughout the Mediterranean region, and elsewhere in the world. It is cultivated mainly for its edible fruit, the olive. Ninety percent of cultivated olives are used to produce the popular edible oil. Olive wood is highly prized for its hardness, beauty, and durability, but cultivated trees are rarely harvested for this purpose. Olive trees can be extremely long-lived, with the oldest confirmed tree on the island of Brijuni in Croatia, which has an estimated age of 1600 years. The olive tree and olive oil have significant connotations in the religious traditions originating in the regions around the Mediterranean.

Onion   *bulb onion, shallot*
Allium cepa

A domesticated species of biennial herbaceous plant in the amaryllis (*Amaryllidaceae*) family. It has been cultivated for at least 7000 years, and it is presumed to have originated somewhere in western Asia. It is now the most widely cultivated species of the genus *Allium,* and is grown in the cooler temperate regions all over the world. It is cultivated for its edible bulbous stem and leaves. The many cultivars of the species are divided into two groups: the common onion group (*A. cepa var. cepa*), which produce a single bulb and are the most commercially important group; and the aggregatum group (*A. cepa var. aggregatum*), which produce multiple bulbs and includes the potato onions and shallots. Onions contain the compound thiosulfate, which is toxic to dogs, cats, and other animals.

Onyx

see *Chalcedony*

Opal
hydrated silica

A form of amorphous silica that is colored by impurities. There are two classes of opal: precious, which displays the iridescent play of light, and common, which does not. The changing colors observed within the stone are due to the varying water content of the thin layers in which the fragments of silica were deposited. Opals are used as a gemstone, usually polished into a cabochon.

Opium poppy
breadseed poppy

Papaver somniferum subsp. somniferum

A species of annual plant in the poppy (*Papaveraceae*) family. Its origins are obscure due to a long history of cultivation, but it presumed to be native to the eastern Mediterranean or western Asia. It is now widely naturalized to and cultivated in many temperate regions. The plant is cultivated for three separate purposes, each of which has produced its own set of cultivars: for the edible seeds (poppy seeds), and the edible oil from the seeds; for the recreational drug opium (and its derivative, heroin), which is derived from the latex of the seed pod; for opiate alkaloids contained in the latex, including codeine, morphine, thebaine, noscapine, and papaverine, which are used by the pharmaceutical industry to make narcotics. All poppies produce edible seeds, but many varieties within the cultivar groups that are ornamental or grown specifically for the seeds, do not produce the latex.

Orange tree
sweet orange

Citrus sinensis

A species of deciduous tree in the citrus (*Rutaceae*) family that is a hybrid between the pomelo (*C. maxima*) and mandarin (*C. reticulata*). Like most members of the genus *Citrus*, it is interfertile with almost all other species within the genus, which has led to a great many hybrids and cultivars. The sweet orange hybrid has been in cultivation since at least the fourth century B.C. (in China), and now it is the most widely cultivated fruit tree in the world. It is cultivated in the tropical and subtropical regions. Additional uses include an essential oil distilled from the rind of the fruit, and as an important source of nectar for honeybees.

Oregano
Origanum vulgare

A perennial herb in the mint (*Lamiaceae*) family, native to temperate Western and Southwestern Eurasia and the Mediterranean region. It is widely cultivated throughout the world, and is used as a culinary herb, either fresh or dried. The leaves are steam distilled to produce an essential oil. There are two main subspecies: Greek oregano (*subsp. hirtum*), and European oregano (*subsp. vulgare*), each with several cultivars. The European variety is an important source of nectar for honeybees.

Oregon myrtle   *California bay laurel, pepperwood*
Umbellularia californica

The sole species in the genus *Umbellularia*, in the laurel (*Lauraceae*) family, it is a large evergreen hardwood native to the northern coast of California and southern Oregon. Its wood is highly valued as a tonewood for making musical instruments. The leaves have historically been used medicinally by Native Americans of the region. The leaves also have insect-repelling properties. The bitter fruit and seed (the bay nut) have been used as food, and still are, to a limited extent. It is the only wood ever used to produce currency in the United States. The so-called "Myrtlewood money," was a series of wooden coins issued in 1933 as a local currency by the city of North Bend, Oregon, in response to the sudden bank closure that effectively shut down the town's cash economy. The coins are still valid today within the boundaries of the town, but are much more valuable as collector's items.

Orris   *Dalmatian iris, sweet iris*
Iris pallida

A species of annual plant in the iris (*Iridaceae*) family, native to Southeastern Europe. It is widely cultivated elsewhere in the world, and is one of the two iris species (the other is *Iris x germanica*, a domesticated hybrid known as the Florentine iris) that is the source of **orris root**, which is made from the dried rhizome of the plant. Orris was once used medicinally, but in modern times its primary use is as a base note in perfumes, and as a fixative in perfumery and potpourri.

Osage orange
hedge apple, bow-wood
Maclura pomifera

A species of deciduous tree or shrub in the mulberry (*Moraceae*) family, native to the east and central United States. Despite the common name, it is not closely related to the true orange, and its fruit, though large and technically edible, is not very palatable and is not often eaten by humans or animals. The tree became well-known for its use as a windbreak and cattle barrier in the large-scale projects of the 1930's that attempted to stop agricultural soil loss in the Great Plains region. Its wood is valued for its hardness, durability, and resistance to rot. It is commonly used as fence posts and tool handles. Some Native Americans, such as the Comanche and the Osage, used the wood to make highly-valued bows. Like its close relative, the old fustic tree (*M. tinctoria*), a yellow dye can be extracted from the wood.

Osier
Salix spp.

The term is a general name given to any willow tree or shrub (genus *Salix*) that has been cut back (coppiced) so that the shoots, known as **withies**, grow long and slender enough for use in the making of baskets and bags. In particular, the species common osier or basket willow (*S. viminalis*), and purple osier (*S. purpurea*) are used for this purpose.

Osmiridium

This naturally occurring alloy of osmium and iridium is hard wearing and is used for fountain pen nibs, instrument pivots, electrical contacts, and other uses that require extreme durability and hardness. It occurs in gold dust as pale steel gray grains.

Osmium

A brittle, bluish-white metallic element; it is the rarest element in the Earth's crust, and has the highest density of all the stable elements. It is used as a catalyst and as a filament for electric light bulbs. It also occurs as the natural alloy osmiridium.

Ox

Ox (plural oxen) is a term used for a bovine that has been specifically trained as a draft or riding animal. In the European tradition, oxen are usually castrated male cattle (*Bos taurus*), although female cattle are also used.

Oyster

There are many shellfish that are called "oyster," usually due to the fact that they look or taste like true oysters. However, true oysters belong to the *Ostreidae* family. Edible oysters are mainly of the genera *Ostrea, Crassostrea, Ostreola, Magallana,* and *Saccostrea.* Oysters are widely farmed as edible shellfish. Pearl oysters are of the genus *Pinctada,* in the *Pteriidae* (feather oyster) family. It is a genus of saltwater oysters notable for their strong inner shell composed of **nacre** (mother-of-pearl), which gives them the ability to produce pearls. Pearls occur naturally, or they can be cultured by placing an irritant in the oyster, which causes it to make a pearl. Two species in particular are used to culture pearls: *P. maximus,* and *P. margaritifera.*

Ozokerite   *earthwax*

A naturally-occurring **paraffin wax** found in beds of bituminous coal. When refined, it produces **ceresine** wax, which is commercially important as an adulterant of beeswax. During distillation, it also produces light oils similar to vaseline. The material remaining after distillation is a hard black waxy substance that is combined with rubber to make **okonite**, an electrical insulator.

Palladium

A rare metallic element that is harder and stronger than platinum. Most of the palladium produced is used in the catalytic converters of car exhaust systems. It is also used in photography, jewelry, and electronics.

Panama hat palm   *toquilla, jipipapa*
Carludovica palmata

A species of perennial plant in the *Cyclanthaceae* family, native to and cultivated in Central America. Despite the name, it is not a true palm. It is cultivated for the long, flexible and durable fibers obtained from its leaves, which are woven into (most famously) Panama hats, as well as other items.

148

Pandan
screw pine

Pandanus spp.

Pandanus is a large genus of plants in the *Pandanaceae* family,
native to the Old World tropics. Many species are of tremendous
importance to local economies, especially throughout Oceania. In
this region, all parts of the plant are used. The leaves can be harvested and used to weave various items like mats and baskets;
the species *P. tectorius* and *P. utilis* are the best known for this use.
The leaves are also used as food, and flavoring is extracted from
the leaves of some species, especially *P. amaryllifolius,* and *P. fas-
cicularis.* Many species provide edible fruits or nuts, such as the
karuka nut (*P. julianettii*), and *P. dubius.*

Papaya
pawpaw

Carica papaya

A small species of evergreen tree in the *Caricaceae* family, native
to Mexico and northern South America. It is widely cultivated
and has become naturalized to many tropical and subtropical
regions. It is cultivated for its edible fruit, the papaya. Both the
unripe fruit and the plant's latex contain the chemical compound
papain, which has a long history of use as a meat tenderizer. Papain is also the primary ingredient in the medication Accuzyme,
which is used for the debridement (cleaning) of wounds. The
seeds of the fruit are edible, and are sometimes dried and ground,
and used as a spice similar to black pepper.

Paper mulberry
tapa cloth tree

Broussonetia papyrifera

A species of deciduous shrub or tree in the mulberry and fig
(*Moraceae*) family, cultivated widely in East Asia and the Pacific
Islands for food, wood, fiber, and medicine. Its inner bark is used
to make tapa cloth, traditionally the primary source of clothing in
the South Pacific Islands. The inner bark was also commonly
used to make paper in Japan and China.

Paprika
see **Chili pepper**

Papyrus

Cyperus papyrus

Egyptian paper plant

A species of aquatic herbaceous plant in the sedge (*Cyperaceae*) family, native to Africa. In modern times, it is grown mostly as an ornamental. However, it has a long history of cultivation in the Nile Delta, earning the name "Gift of the Nile." Its long thin stems were used to make baskets, clothing, reed boats and, of course, paper. Its woody roots were used to make bowls and other utensils. It was also used to make medicine and incense.

Parsley

Petroselinum crispum

A species of herbaceous biennial plant in the parsley (*Apiaceae*) family, native to the Mediterranean region, but widely cultivated and naturalized elsewhere in the temperate regions. There are many cultivars, which fall into two broad categories: leaf parsley (*var. crispum*), which is cultivated for its edible leaves and stems, and its essential oil; and root parsley (*var. tuberosum*), which is cultivated for its tuberous root, which is eaten as a vegetable.

Parsnip

Pastinaca sativa

A species of herbaceous biennial (though usually grown as an annual) plant in the parsley (*Apiaceae*) family, native to Eurasia, but widely naturalized to and cultivated in other temperate regions. It is grown for its edible root, which is very similar to a carrot, but is sweeter. In Europe, it was used as a sweetener until cane sugar became broadly available in the 18th century.

Passion fruit

Passiflora edulis

maracuja, granadilla, liliko'i

A species of vine in the passion flower (*Passifloraceae*) family, native to southern South America, but widely cultivated in tropical and semitropical regions of the world. It is grown for its edible fruit. It is the most common and widely grown of all the fruit-bearing members of the *Passiflora* genus, but other cultivated species include: *P. maliformis* (sweet calabash or conch apple); *P. quadrangularis* (giant granadilla or grenadine); and *P. laurifolia* (water lemon, Jamaican honeysuckle, orange liliko'i). Several other species in the genus are cultivated locally for their fruit.

Patchouli
Pogostemon spp.

Several species of herbaceous plant in the mint (*Lamiaceae*) family, native to Southeast Asia, but now widely cultivated in other tropical regions. The primary cultivated species are *P. cablin, P. benghalensis, P. hortensis, P. heyneasus, and P. plectranthoides*. It is cultivated mainly for the essential oil distilled from its leaves, known as patchouli oil. The oil is used extensively in perfume and incense. It is also used as an insect repellent.

Pawpaw
Asimina triloba

A species of small deciduous tree in the custard apple (*Annonaceae*) family, native to the Eastern United States and Canada. They produce the largest edible fruits indigenous to the U.S. (not including gourds, which are botanically fruits, but considered vegetables for culinary purposes). It is cultivated for its nutritious fruit, which contains an unusually high percentage of protein. Native Americans in the past used fibers of the inner bark to make ropes, fishing nets, and mats. The bark and leaves contain chemicals that act as insect repellents.

Pea
Pisum sativum

A domesticated species of annual vine in the pea (*Fabaceae*) family, native to the Mediterranean basin and Near East, but now widely cultivated in temperate zones all over the world. Archaeological evidence suggests that peas have been cultivated since at least 4000 BC. It is cultivated for its edible seeds, and in some of the many cultivars (such as the sugar snap pea), the edible seed pod. When the peas are dried, they are called split peas. Some varieties are grown as fodder or forage plants. The name "pea" is also given to other unrelated plants, like the cowpea or chickpea.

Peach palm   *chonta*
Bactris gasipaes

A species of tree in the palm (*Arecaceae*) family, native to the tropical regions of South and Central America. It has been domesticated in those regions for centuries, being cultivated for its edible fruit and for hearts of palm. It is also used for animal fodder, and its leaves can be woven into mats, hats, and other items.

Peach tree
Prunus persica

A species of deciduous flowering tree in the rose (*Rosaceae*) family, in the same genus as the cherry, almond, apricot, and plum. It is native to northwestern China, but was cultivated in Persia before it was brought to Europe. It is now widely cultivated and naturalized, grown for its edible fruit, the peach. There are hundreds of cultivars of peaches and nectarines, which are a smooth-skinned variety of peach. There is tremendous cultural significance to peaches in Asia, particularly China. For example, seals and figures made of peach wood were affixed to gates and doors to guard against evil spirits. Momotaro, the "Peach Boy," is a hero of Japanese folklore whose mother gave birth to him after eating a magical peach that caused her to grow younger.

Peanut   *groundnut, goober*
Arachis hypogaea

A domesticated species of annual plant in the pea (*Fabaceae*) family, native to the West Indies and South America, but now widely cultivated in the tropical and subtropical regions of the world. The current species is a likely domesticated hybrid of two wild species, with the likely progenitor being *A. duranensis*. The earliest evidence of this domesticated species was found in Peru and dates back almost 8000 years. The plant is grown for its edible seed, the peanut, which is high in oil and protein. It is unusual in that once the plant flowers, the flower head buries itself in the ground, and the seed matures underground. The peanut itself is valued as food, and for the oil expressed from the seed, and the pulp that is left after the oil has been removed, which is pressed into rich feed cake for animals. The protein from the seed is also used to make the synthetic fiber known as Ardil. Peanut shells are used in the manufacture of plastic, wallboard, abrasives, fuel, cellulose (used to make rayon and paper), and mucilage (glue). There are many cultivars of the species, such as the Valencia, Spanish, and Virginia peanuts. There are several other species in the genus are also grown for their nuts, but *A. hypogaea* is by far the most commonly cultivated.

Pear
Pyrus spp.

The name "pear" generally refers to number of species within the genus *Pyrus*, in the rose (*Rosaceae*) family. The genus is native to the milder coastal and temperate regions of the Old World, but is now widely cultivated globally for its edible fruit, the pear. Pears have been used as food since antiquity. The most commonly cultivated species is *Pyrus communis*, the European pear, which has many cultivars, though the Bartlett cultivar represents the majority of pears produced commercially. The fruit is prepared in many ways, including as a base of the fermented beverage known as perry. The European pear is also cultivated for its hardwood timber. Another commonly cultivated species is the nashi pear or Asian pear (*Pyrus pyrifolia*), and its hybrids.

Peat   *turf*

Peat is formed by the accumulation of decayed vegetation in swamps. It is a precursor to the formation of coal. It is found particularly in areas called peatlands, which are a type of bog. It takes thousands of years for the peat to accumulate to what is in current times its average depth, which is about 5-7 feet. In some regions, particularly in Britain and other parts of Europe, peat is harvested: that is, cut into blocks, dried, and used as fuel. Peat is not considered a renewable energy source, since the rate of extraction greatly outstrips the rate of accumulation.

Pecan tree
Carya illinoinensis

A species of large deciduous tree in the hickory (*Carya*) genus, within the walnut (*Juglandaceae*) family. It is presumed native to Mexico and the Southern United States, but is now widely naturalized to and cultivated in other temperate regions. It is cultivated for its edible "nuts" (actually a type of fruit called a drupe), called pecans. Pecan wood is used for flooring and furniture. The pecan tree was domesticated only as recently as the late nineteenth century in the United States, although the wild pecan has a long tradition of use by Native Americans.

Peridot
chrysolite

A silicate mineral that is a magnesium-rich olivine, classified as a precious gemstone. It is one of the few gems that only occurs in one color (olive green), but the green can vary from yellow-green to brown-green, depending on the amount of iron. Peridot has been mined since about the first century B.C. in the region of the Red Sea. Peridot is found in in igneous rock in various parts of the world. Large peridot crystals also occur embedded in an iron-nickel matrix in a rare type of meteorite known as pallasites.

Perilla
Perilla frutescens

A species of annual plant in the mint (*Lamiaceae*) family, native to East Asia and popularly cultivated there as an herb, and a leaf vegetable. Since it was introduced to the United States, it has escaped cultivation and become a noxious weed; it is toxic to cattle.

Persimmon
Diospyros spp.

A genus of deciduous trees in the ebony (*Ebenaceae*) family, native to the temperate regions of the Northern Hemisphere. Several species are cultivated for their edible fruit (actually a large berry), called the persimmon. The most widely cultivated species is the Japanese persimmon (*D. kaki*), but others include *D. lotus* (date-plum), *D. digyna* (black sapote, or black persimmon), and *D. texana* (Texas persimmon). The American persimmon (*D. virginiana*) is cultivated for its fruit and wood, used as a substitute for ebony, to which it is closely related.

Petroleum

A complex hydrocarbon that was formed over the course of millions of years, when decaying organic matter at the bottom of ancient seas became trapped in layers of what would become sedimentary rock. Over time, and with temperature and pressure, these became sometimes very large deposits of the thick, black liquid we know as petroleum. Petroleum is the source of the so-called "fossil fuels": gasoline, diesel, and kerosene; as well as lubricating oil, paraffin wax, and asphalt. It is also the basis of many synthetic materials such as plastic. Because petroleum is a non-renewable resource, many plants are under investigation as alternative renewable sources of fuel oil.

Phosphates

Phosphates are a type of sedimentary rock containing predominately phosphorus compounds, such as the mineral apatite. They are usually associated with limestones and shales. Phosphates have many uses, such as fertilizer, as matches, and in the manufacture of a variety of chemicals.

Pig
domestic pig, swine, hog
Sus scrofa domesticus

A species of domesticated pig within the pig, hog, and boar family (*Suidae*). Archaeological evidence suggests that pigs were domesticated from wild boars around roughly 13,000 BC in Mesopotamia. Today, they are widely farmed as a livestock for their meat (pork and ham); the hide, bones, and bristles are also used in the manufacture of commercial products.

Pilinut
see *Kenarinut tree*

Pimento
see *Chili pepper*

Pine tree
Pinus spp.

Pinus is a genus of over a hundred species of coniferous evergreen trees and shrubs in the pine (*Pinaceae*) family. They are widespread throughout the temperate to subarctic regions of the Northern Hemisphere; some species extend to the subtropical and tropical regions, and cross over into the Southern Hemisphere. Some species are extremely long lived, particularly the Great Basin bristlecone pine, of which there are two specimens, both in California, known to be over 4000 years old. All pine trees are resinous, and that resin has found many uses throughout the ages, especially as an important source of **turpentine** and **rosin**. The wood is a fast-growing softwood with many indoor commercial uses including furniture, cabinetry, flooring, and especially wood pulp; it is one of the most important commercial woods. Some species produce large edible seeds called pine nuts, and the outer layer of wood (the cambium just beneath the outer bark) is also edible. The leaves (needles) have been used to make tea that has nutritive and medicinal properties. In the long-leaf species, the needles have traditionally been used as a weaving material for ornamental baskets and other items.

Pineapple
Ananas comosus

A species of herbaceous perennial plant in the bromeliad (*Bromeliaceae*) family, native to South America, presumably the region between Brazil and Paraguay. The Spanish and Portuguese colonizers brought the pineapple to the Old World and Hawaii, where it is now an important international fruit crop. The Red Spanish cultivar was once grown in the Philippines for its leaf fibers, which were woven into a textile used for clothing and other items. Pineapple is also a source of the compound bromelain, which is used as a meat tenderizer, and is under investigation for potential medicinal uses.

Pistachio tree
Pistacia vera

A species of small tree in the cashew (*Anacardiaceae*) family, native to Central Asia but now widely cultivated for its edible nut, the pistachio. Like other members of the cashew family, the tree contains urushiol, an irritant that can cause an allergic reaction in some people. The pistachio is closely related to the mastic tree (*P. lentiscus*), which, like several species of the genus, is cultivated for its aromatic resin. It is also in the same genus as the terebinth (*P. terebinthus*), one of the earliest known sources of **turpentine**.

Pitahaya   *dragon fruit, night-blooming Cereus*
Hylocereus undatus

Hylocereus is a genus of perennial night-blooming plants in the cactus (*Cactacae*) family, native to the hot, arid regions of the Americas. It is now widely naturalized to and cultivated in the tropics, mainly in the Pacific region. One of the most famous specimens is the *Panini O Ka Punahou,* planted on the campus of the Punahou School in Honolulu in 1925. Several species produce edible fruit, but *H. undatus* is the most common species, grown as an ornamental vine, as well as for its large edible fruit known as dragon fruit, pitahaya, or pitaya (though this name usually refers to fruit from the plant *Stenocereus gummosus*). Trade in dragon fruit is regulated in order to protect the species from overexploitation.

Pitaya
Stenocereus spp.

Stenocereus is a genus of columnar, night-blooming cacti in the cactus (*Cactaceae*) family, native to the hot, arid regions of the southwestern United States and Mexico, with one species also native to the Caribbean. The species are generally known as "pitaya," with variations on the name depending on the characteristics of the plant. The organ-pipe cactus (*S. thurberi*) is one of the most recognized and characteristic plants of the American Southwest. Several species of the genus produce edible fruit, but all species are currently protected to avoid overexploitation.

Pitchblende   *uraninite*
uranium oxide

This radioactive mineral is the chief ore and source of the elements uranium and radium. The development of the atomic bomb spurred a "uranium rush" in the United States in the early 1950's, with the most important deposit discovered by prospector Charles Steen near the town of Moab, Utah. The discovery made Steen a fortune, which he lost when the government stopped paying premium prices for uranium just a few years later.

Plaice
Plaice is a common name for a group of flatfish species, right-eyed flounders within the *Pleuronectidae* family. Two species are commercially important food fish: European plaice (*Pleuronectes platessa*), and American plaice (*Hippoglossoides platessoides*). The stocks of both species are declining due to overfishing.

Plantain   see *Banana*

Platinum
A relatively rare metallic element that is one of the precious metals. It is one of the least reactive metals, and is highly corrosion resistant, even at high temperatures. It is used in catalytic converters, jewelry, electrical contacts and electrodes. In alloys, it imparts corrosion resistance and hardness. Several compounds containing platinum, such as cisplatin (which appears on the World Health Organization's Model List of Essential Medicines), oxaliplatin, and carboplatin, are important chemotherapy drugs.

Plum tree
Prunus prunus spp.

Prunus is a subgenus of *Prunus*, within the rose (*Rosaceae*) family. It contains many species, some of which are widely cultivated for their edible fruit. When fresh, the fruits are called plums, when dried, they are called prunes. Archaeological evidence of plums found associated with Neolithic era human settlements suggest that plums were among the oldest fruits cultivated. Today, the species are generally divided into three sections, each with many cultivars: *Prunus* (Old World plums), which contains the species *P. domesticus*, the most commonly cultivated plum; *Prunocerasus* (the New World plums); and *Armeniaca* (the apricots), which includes *P. armeniaca*, the most commonly cultivated apricot.

Plutonium

Plutonium is the heaviest element to occur in nature. It is found in trace quantities with uranium. It is radioactive and highly reactive. It is used as a fuel source in nuclear reactors, nuclear weapons, and has a small specialized use as a power source in spacecraft. The amount of plutonium is increasing due to its manufacture as a byproduct of uranium fission.

Polish cochineal
Porphyrophora polonica

A scale insect native to the Central Europe and Eurasia. In the past, it was of great economic importance in Europe as the source of the red pigment known as **carmine**. It has since been largely replaced by the Mexican cochineal (*Dactylopius coccus*).

Pollock
Pollachius spp.

A genus of two species of fish within the cod (*Gadidae*) family. Both are native to the North Atlantic and highly valued as food fish. The two species are: the Atlantic pollock (*P. pollachius*), also known as the European pollock, lieu jaune, or lythe; and the coley (*P. virens*), also known as the Boston blue, silver bill, or saithe.

Pomegranate
Punica granatum

A species of deciduous shrub or small tree in the *Lythraceae* family, native to the region stretching from Iran to northern India, but now widely cultivated in the temperate regions of the Northern and Southern Hemispheres. It is cultivated for its edible fruit, the pomegranate. The pomegranate's unusual fruit is composed of a hard rind surrounding many small seeds, each of which is encapsulated by a juicy red aril. The pomegranate has become a symbol of fruitfulness in many European and Asian cultures.

Poplar
Populus spp.

A genus of roughly 30 species of deciduous trees in the willow (*Salicaceae*) family. They are widespread throughout the temperate regions of the Northern Hemisphere. This diverse genus is generally divided into six sections of species: *Populus*, the white poplars and aspens; *Aigeiros*, the black poplars and some cottonwoods; *Tacamahaca*, the balsam poplars; *Leucoides*, the necklace or bigleaf poplars; *Turanga*, the subtropical poplars; and *Abaso*, the Mexican poplars. The trees are widely grown as ornamentals, and cultivated for their relatively soft, flexible, and close-grained wood. The wood is mainly used for pulp and non-durable items such as boxes and pallets, but its flexibility has made it popular for such applications as snowboard cores and musical instruments. Poplar trees can be coppiced and grow quickly, which has created interest in using them as a biomass energy source.

Potassium

A metallic element that occurs in nature only as salts, and not as a free element. Potassium is a critical nutrient for the function of living things. Potash is a mixture of potassium salts (e.g., potassium chloride or potassium nitrate) found in the ashes of burned organic matter, and in mineral deposits. Potassium salts have many important uses, such as soap making, glass manufacture, fertilizer, explosives, tempering steel, and others.

Potato
Solanum tuberosum

A species of perennial herbaceous plant in the nightshade (*Solanaceae*) family, native throughout the United States and much of South America. Potatoes were domesticated in the Americas roughly 7000 - 10,000 years ago, cultivated for their edible tuber. The plant was introduced to Europe by the Spanish in the 16th century. Today, they are widely cultivated and are the fourth-largest food crop in the world (behind maize, wheat, and rice), with at least 1000 cultivars of the species. Potatoes are also commonly used as animal fodder. Potato starch is used in the food industry as a thickener and binder, in the textile industry as an adhesive, and in the manufacture of paper and board.

Poultry

"Poultry" is a term that refers to domesticated birds usually farmed for their meat, eggs, and feathers. The most common poultry are the chicken (*Gallus gallus domesticus*), the duck (*Anas platyrhynchos domesticus*), and goose (*Anser anser domesticus* or *Anser cygnoides domesticus*). Less common examples are the quail, guinea hen, swan, emu, ostrich, and peafowl.

Prickly pear   *Indian fig, nopal*
Opuntia ficus-indica

A species of perennial plant in the cactus (*Cactaceae*) family, presumed to be native to Mexico, but now also naturalized to and cultivated in other hot, arid regions of the world. Although other species of the *Opuntia* genus are also called prickly pear, *O. ficus-indica* is the most commonly cultivated, mainly for its edible fruit, called the prickly pear in English, and *tuna* in Spanish. The young cactus pads (called *nopal* in Spanish) are also eaten in some cultures. Prickly pear is useful as animal fodder, and is an important host plant for cultivated cochineal insects (see separate entry for cochineal). The mucilage extracted from the plant is being investigated for use as a flocculant (a material that causes particles to adhere, forming masses that are easier to remove) for the treatment of waste water.

Pumice

A very light, porous stone that is created when molten rock is violently ejected from a volcano, and is subjected to both rapid depressurization and rapid cooling. The resulting rock is rough-textured and so full of air pockets that it can be light enough to float on water. It has many uses: as an abrasive, both in powdered form (such as in polishes, erasers, toothpaste and soaps), and in natural form; and as an ingredient in lightweight concrete and cinder blocks.

Pumpkin   see *Squash*

Purslane   *verdolaga, little hogweed*
Portulaca oleracea

A species of annual succulent plant in the *Portulacaceae* family, very widely distributed in the Old World and assumed to have originated there, though its exact origin and native range is unknown. It has a long history of extensive use in the Eastern Mediterranean, and is now widely used as a leaf vegetable and fodder plant throughout Europe, the Middle East, Asia, and Mexico.

Pyrethrum
Tanacetum spp.

The name "pyrethrum" refers to two species of herbaceous perennial or subshrub plants in the daisy (*Asteraceae*) family, *Tanacetum cinerariifolium* and *T. coccineum*. The plants have a long traditional use as an insecticide called **pyrethrum**, which is made from the dried and pulverized flower heads. Pyrethrum is one of the few insecticides approved for use in organic gardening.

Pyrite   *fool's gold*
iron sulfide

Pyrite is the most common of the sulfide minerals. It is an important source of sulfur dioxide and sulfuric acid. Because it creates a spark when struck against steel, it was once used as an ignition source in firearms. It is a semiconductor, and has been used as a mineral detector in crystal radio sets, which were the precursor to vacuum tube radios. It is currently used as a cathode material in lithium ion batteries. It is also used to make the so-called "marcasite" jewelry.

Pyrolusite
manganese dioxide

A mineral that is an important ore of manganese. It is also used in the preparation of permanganate (a disinfectant), and in the manufacture of metal alloys. It is used as a coloring material to impart violet, amber, or black colors to glass, pottery and bricks; and to manufacture green and violet paints.

Quartz
silicon dioxide

Quartz is the second most abundant mineral in the Earth's crust, behind feldspar. Many gemstones, such as amethyst, citrine, and elbaite are quartz crystals with trace impurities. Quartz is used in the manufacture of glass and porcelain, cement and other building materials. Pure quartz crystals are used for lenses and prisms. Quartz has piezoelectric properties, and is used as a crystal oscillator, especially in electric clocks and watches.

Quassia   *bitterwood tree*
Quassia amara

A species of deciduous shrub or small tree in the *Simaroubaceae* family, native to tropical South America and widely cultivated elsewhere. Its wood and bark are the source of **quassin**, one of the most bitter compounds found in nature. Quassin is used as an insecticide in organic farming, and to kill mosquito larvae in ponds. It is used medicinally as an anti-malarial drug and against lice and fleas. It is also used as a food flavoring.

Quebracho

The Spanish term *quebracho* ("axe-breaker") is used generically in South America to describe any extremely hard wood, or a tree that produces such wood. There are three commercially important species of tree grown in the Gran Chaco region of South America that are traded as Quebracho: red quebracho (*Schinopsis lorentzii* and *Schinopsis balansae*, of the *Anacardiaceae* family); and white quebracho (*Aspidosperma quebracho-blanco*, of the *Apocynaceae family*). These trees are cultivated for their timber, and for the tannin extracted from the wood.

Quince
Cydonia oblonga

A species of deciduous tree that is the sole member of the *Cydonia* genus, within the rose (*Rosaceae*) family. It is native to West Asia, the Caucasus, and Middle Asia, but is now widely naturalized to and cultivated in other temperate regions. It has been cultivated for at least two thousand years for its edible fruit. Its fruit is very bitter if eaten raw, and is most often cooked or prepared into jams or jellies. In the Greek mythological tradition, the quince is the sacred symbol of the goddess Aphrodite.

Quinoa
Chenopodium quinoa

A species of annual plant in the amaranth (*Amaranthaceae*) family, native to the Andean region of South America, and now widely cultivated elsewhere. It has been cultivated for at least 3000- 4000 years for its edible seeds. The outer seed coating contains saponins, which are processed out prior to consumption, but which have been used traditionally as a detergent, and as an anti-septic. Several other species within the goosefoot (*Chenopodium*) genus are also cultivated for food, such as: *C. album* (lamb's quar-ters); *C. berlandieri subsp. nuttalliae* (huauzontle), of Mexico; and *C. pallidicaule* (kaniwa), also of the Andean region.

Rabbit   *European rabbit*
Oryctolagus cuniculus

The European rabbit is the only widely domesticated rabbit. There are many breeds within the species, selectively bred for various purposes. Some breeds are raised for food. The Angora rabbit is known primarily for its coat of long, silky fibers, known as **Angora wool**, which are used as a textile fiber.

Radish
Raphanus raphanistrum subsp. sativus

A species of annual or biennial plant in the cabbage (*Brassicaceae*) family, presumed to native to the Mediterranean region, but now widely distributed and cultivated in many parts of the world. Most of the many cultivars are grown for their edible tuber, and some varieties are grown for their edible seeds. Radish seed oil is a potential source of biofuel.

163

Radium

A metallic element found in nature in trace amounts in uranium ores. It is highly radioactive. Its only current use is in nuclear medicine. In former times it was used in radioluminescent devices, such as the glowing numbers on watch dials. However, because of its toxicity, it is no longer used for those purposes.

Raffia palm
Raphia spp.

The name refers to several species of tree in the genus *Raphia*, within the palm (*Arecaceae*) family, native to the tropical regions of Africa, but also grown in parts of Central and South America. It is the source of the **raffia** fiber, made from the veins of the leaves, which are some of the longest in the plant kingdom. This coarse fiber is used for basketry, twine, hats, shoes, mats, and other items.

Ramie   *China grass, white ramie*
Boehmeria nivea

A species of herbaceous perennial plant in the nettle (*Urticaceae*) family, native to East Asia, but naturalized to and cultivated elsewhere around the world. It is the best-known of several species in the genus that are cultivated for their bast fiber. Ramie is one of the oldest cultivated fiber crops, and is primarily used for textiles. Ramie fiber is the strongest natural fiber, though it is neither very durable nor flexible, so it is most often used in combination with other fibers, such as cotton. Ramie is being explored as a source of cellulose for use in the manufacture of bioplastics.

Ramin   *melawis*
Gonystylus spp.

Gonystylus is a genus of about thirty species of hardwood tree in the *Thymeleaceae* family, native to Southeast Asia, Indonesia, and Melanesia. The trees are highly valued for their yellow hardwood, which has been used to make furniture, window blinds, children's furniture, and decorative items. Due to overexploitation, the trees and the ecosystems surrounding them are now endangered, and trade in the wood is strictly controlled.

Rape
canola, colza

Brassica napus subsp. napus

A species of herbaceous plant in the cabbage (*Brassicaceae*) family, widely cultivated in temperate zones, primarily for its oil-rich seeds. It is the third-largest source of vegetable oil in the world, after soybean and palm oil. It is the second-largest producer of protein meal after the soybean. Its cultivars are divided into two groups: the original rapeseed, which produces the non-edible but highly useful **colza oil**; and canola, a variety bred to produce edible **canola oil**. Once the oil has been expressed from the seeds, the remaining pulp is used to make animal fodder.

Raspberry
see *Bramble*

Rattan
Calamus spp.

"Rattan" refers to a group of 600 species of plants in 13 genera within the *Calamoideae* subfamily of the palm (*Arecaceae*) family. They are climbing palms native to the Old World. The strong flexible stems (called **cane**) of many species are widely used for a variety of building and manufacturing purposes. The most commercially important species are in the genus *Calamus*, native mainly to East and Southeast Asia, with the canes of each species having slightly different properties and uses. Some species, like *C. rotang*, produce edible fruit; the fruit of some species produces a resin called **Dragon's Blood**, which has a history of use in traditional medicine, and is also used to make varnish.

Realgar
arsenic sulfide

A highly toxic mineral that was in previous times used for several purposes: to create white flashes in fireworks, in the preparation of leather, and as a pigment. It was used in Chinese medicine, and mixed with rice wine to make realgar wine, which is drunk during the annual Dragon Boat Festival. It has largely been replaced with safer alternatives in most of its uses, though it is still an important source of arsenic.

Redwood
see *Coast redwood, Giant sequoia*

165

Reed (common)
Phragmites australis

A species of fast-growing perennial plant in the grass (*Poaceae*) family. Its native range is not known, but it is widely distributed throughout the temperate wetlands of the Northern and Southern Hemispheres. It has found many uses in the different regions of the world, for example: it is used to make the mouthpieces of various musical instruments; some parts of the plant are edible, though the use as food is not widespread; it is used to make fishing poles, spears, fences, thatching, pen tips, and paper. It is used extensively in phytoremediation projects, most notably in wetlands wastewater treatment. Due to its aggressive growth habit, it is considered an invasive weed and is cultivated with caution.

Reed (giant)
Arundo donax

A species of tall perennial grass in the *Poaceae* family, native to temperate Asia, and now widely naturalized to and cultivated in many temperate and subtropical regions around the world. It has traditionally been cultivated as a source of **cane** and fiber, but more recently has been investigated as a potential source of biomass for energy generation.

Rhodium

One of noble metal elements, it is the rarest and most valuable of the precious metals. It is chemically inert and is usually found in its free form in nature. It is hard and corrosion-resistant at high temperatures, and so is often used as an alloy with platinum or palladium for use in coating or plating. Most rhodium is used in the catalytic converters of car exhaust systems. It is also used for plating silver to prevent tarnishing, and in the preparation of the silvered surface of mirrors.

Rhodochrosite
manganese carbonate

A mineral whose primary value is as an ore of manganese. It is pink to rose-red in color, and its banded form is sometimes used as an ornamental stone.

Rhubarb
Rheum rhabarbarum

An herbaceous perennial plant in the buckwheat (*Polygonaceae*) family, native to and cultivated in China for thousands of years, but now widely cultivated in other temperate regions for the edible leafstalks. The stalks have a tart flavor due to the presence of acidic compounds, including the toxic oxalic acid. The leaves of the plant are inedible due to much higher concentrations of oxalic acid than is found in the leafstalks. For millennia, rhubarb had an important place in Chinese medicine. It was brought to Europe as a medicine, but in the 17th century became a food source when sugar became readily available, and the two could be paired to offset rhubarb's tartness. The root is also used as a source of dark brown dye.

Rice (African)
Oryza glaberrima

An annual plant in the grass (*Poaceae*) family, native to West Africa and brought to the United States during the slave era. It is one of two domesticated rice species. It has largely been supplanted by Asian rice, though it is still grown to some extent in West Africa as a subsistence crop, and the United States as a heritage crop. Though it is lower-yielding than Asian rice, it is also hardier and more pest-resistant.

Rice (Asian)
Oryza sativa

An annual plant in the grass (*Poaceae*) family, native to Asia. It is the most widely grown of the rice species, and consists of two major subspecies (*indica* and *japonica*) and over 40,000 varieties. It is grown for its edible seed. Asian rice arose from the domestication of the wild rice (*O. rufipogon*) in China, which occurred somewhere between 8,000 and 13,500 years ago. Today, other wild and cultivated members of the genus native to various parts of the world are used to breed characteristics such as disease resistance and higher yields into Asian rice. Today, rice is the third largest food crop in the world (behind maize and wheat), and the largest human food crop. Rice is also used to make a wide variety of wines, mostly in East and Southeast Asia.

Rice (Wild)
Zizania spp.

A genus of four species of annual plants in the grass (*Poaceae*) family, known collectively as wild rice. Three of the species are native to North America and have a history of being wild-harvested as food, a practice that continues in modern times. Of these, one species, *Z. palustris*, has been domesticated and is currently cultivated as a food and forage crop. The fourth species, *Z. latifolia*, is native to China, where it is a minor food crop.

Rice-paper plant
Tetrapanax papyrifer

A species of evergreen shrub in the *Araliaceae* family, native to Taiwan but also widely cultivated in East Asia and a few other tropical areas. It is grown as an ornamental, but also for the pith of the stem, which is used to manufacture a lightweight paper known as **rice paper**, though the plant is not closely related to true rice. Rice paper is used to make ornamental flowers, as a watercolor medium, and other mainly decorative purposes.

Rooibos
Aspalathus linearis

A species of shrub in the pea (*Fabaceae*) family, native to the west coast of the Western Cape province of South Africa, and still mainly cultivated there. The tea made from the processed leaves is consumed in various places throughout the world.

The Art and Science of Healing

There are thousands of plants, animals, and minerals that have a history of use in many systems and traditions of folk medicine in cultures throughout the world. An attempt to include all of them would have resulted in a book about ten times longer than this one. Still, a significant portion of the natural resources included here have a medicinal use: in fact, medicinal use is second only to food in importance. Some of these medicinal substances have undergone extensive systematic testing to further the understanding of how they work and to test their effectiveness. Some of them have not, and our understanding comes mainly through anecdotal evidence or traditional lore.

Rose
Rosa spp.

There are about 300 species and thousands of cultivars in the *Rosa* genus, within the *Rosaceae* family. Most of the species are native to Asia, but some are native to other temperate regions, including Europe, North America, and Africa. Roses are widely grown throughout the world, mainly as ornamentals for their showy and sometimes fragrant flowers. Some select species and cultivars produce scented oils. Rose oil (or attar of roses), an essential oil steam-distilled from the flowers, is used in perfumery and cosmetics. Rose water, made by steeping rose petals in water, is used as a food flavoring, in cosmetics, traditional medicine, and in some religious practices. Rose absolute is a more concentrated extract of essential oil produced through the use of solvents. Rose hips are the accessory fruit, and in some species (especially *R. canina*) are edible and contain a high vitamin C content. Rose petals are edible, and are also used to make tea.

Rose geranium
Pelargonium graveolens

A domesticated flowering shrub in the geranium (*Geraniaceae*) family, cultivated in South Africa, Zimbabwe, and Mozambique. Along with other members of the genus, it is grown for its fragrant foliage, from which is extracted the essential oil known as **geranium oil**. Geranium oil is widely used in the perfume industry, as a food flavoring, and as a pipe tobacco flavoring.

Rosemary
Rosmarinus officinalis

A species of evergreen shrub in the mint (*Lamiaceae*) family, native to the Mediterranean region. Its many cultivars are popular in several regions of the world for its aromatic leaves, which are used as a food flavoring. The essential oil from rosemary is used as a fragrance in perfumes; it has also been shown to improve the shelf life and heat stability of omega-3-rich oils. Rosemary was one of the many ingredients in Four Thieves vinegar, a mixture of vinegar and a variety of herbs, spices, and garlic, popular in the Middle Ages as a ward against the black plague.

Rosewood
Dalbergia spp.

True rosewood comes from a dozen or so species of trees of the genus *Dalbergia*, in the pea (*Fabaceae*) family. The best-known and most valuable species is *D. nigra*, or Brazilian rosewood. The wood is highly prized for its hardness, grain, deep reddish color, and rose-like scent. This species of rosewood is currently protected and trade is highly regulated due to overexploitation. Other valued timber species with slightly different characteristics and uses include Brazilian kingwood (*D. cearensis*), Brazilian tulipwood (*D. decipularis*), Indian blackwood (*D. latifolia*, native to the Indian subcontinent), and sissoo (*D. sissoo*, native to Western Asia and the Arabian peninsula).

Rubber tree
Para rubber tree, hevea
Hevea brasiliensis

A species of tree in the spurge (*Euphorbiaceae*) family, native to the Amazon region, but now intensively cultivated mainly in Malaysia and Thailand. It is cultivated for its latex, which is an important source of natural rubber, also known as **caoutchouc**.

Rubidium
A metallic element with several high-technology applications, including in atomic clocks and lasers.

Ruby
see *Corundum*

Runner bean
scarlet runner bean, ayocote
Phaseolus coccineus

A species of herbaceous perennial plant in the pea (*Fabaceae*) family, native to Central America but now widely cultivated in temperate zones around the world. It is popularly cultivated as an ornamental, but the subspecies *coccineus* is also cultivated for its edible beans; the green peas, pea pods, and tuberous root are also edible. Like its close relative the common bean (*P. vulgaris*), the beans contain a toxin and must be cooked before being eaten.

Rutabaga
Brassica napus subsp. rapifera

swede, Swedish turnip

A species of annual plant in the cabbage (*Brassicaceae*) family, native to the cool temperate regions of Europe. It is closely related and very similar to the turnip. It is widely cultivated for its edible tuberous taproot, as well as its edible leaves. It is also used as fodder for livestock.

Rutile
titanium dioxide

One of the chief ores of titanium. The high refractive index of its crystalline form, particularly large birefringence and high dispersion give it the potential for use in some optics, particularly polarization of the longer light wavelengths.

Rye
Secale cereale

A species of cereal grain in the grass (*Poaceae*) family, closely related to both wheat and barley. It is native to Turkey and was originally domesticated there during the Neolithic Era, somewhere around 7500 - 5600 BC. Today, it is widely grown (primarily in Eastern, Central, and Northern Europe) as a food grain, as fodder, and as a cover crop. The grains are most often ground into flour, but they are also used to make the alcoholic beverages rye whiskey and rye beer, among other things.

Safflower
Carthamus tinctorius

bastard saffron

A species of annual plant in the sunflower (*Asteraceae*) family. The use of its flowers as a source of the orange-red pigment called **carthamin** dates back to about 2000 BC in Egypt, and continues today. In modern times, safflower is widely cultivated mainly for its seed oil (safflower oil) which is used as food and in cosmetics. Its dried flowers are occasionally used as a substitute for the spice saffron, which gives it the name bastard saffron.

Saffron crocus
Crocus sativus

autumn crocus

A species of annual plant in the iris (*Iridaceae*) family. Its wild ancestor is unknown, and its place of origin is uncertain, though suspected to be Western or Central Asia. It is an entirely domesticated plant and requires direct human intervention to reproduce, as the plant is sterile. It has been cultivated for about 3500 years, for use as the spice **saffron**, which is produced from the filaments that grow inside the flower. It is also used as a yellow dye. Saffron is the most expensive spice in the world, by weight.

Sage
Salvia officinalis

common sage, garden sage, culinary sage

A species of evergreen subshrub in the mint (*Lamiaceae*) family, native to the Mediterranean. It is now widely cultivated and naturalized elsewhere, with a long history of use as a culinary herb and medicinal plant. There are many cultivars of the species. Clary sage (*S. sclarea*) is also commonly grown, also with a long history of medicinal use; it is grown for its essential oil. The name "sage" is also used to refer to a variety of plants, some closely related, some not, but sharing characteristics of *Salvia*.

Sagebrush
Artemisia spp.

wormwood, mugwort

Artemisia is a diverse and important genus within the daisy (*Asteraceae*) family. The species that are native to North America are generally known as "sagebrush," while those native to Europe and Asia are generally known as "wormwood" (see separate entry). Several species of sagebrush have a history of use as traditional medicine; currently they are cultivated mainly as ornamentals. Tarragon (see separate entry) is a species of Artemisia that is found in both Europe and North America.

Sago palm
Metroxylon sagu

A species of tree in the palm (*Arecaceae*) family, native to Southeast Asia and the southwestern Pacific. It is cultivated for the starch product called **sago**, which is extracted from the trunk of the tree. Sago as a staple food in that region, as well as an important export; each tree produces about 800 pounds of sago.

172

Salmon

The term "salmon" is used for a variety of fish species within the *Salmonidae* family. Of these, the Atlantic salmon (*Salmo salar*), and the Pacific salmon (*Oncorhynchus* spp.) are the most important commercially. Most of the Atlantic salmon consumed worldwide is farmed (about 99%); while most of the Pacific salmon consumed is wild caught (about 80%). Salmon is an oily fish, rich in omega-3 fatty acids and vitamin D.

Salsify   *oyster plant*
Tragopogon porrifolius

A species of herbaceous biennial plant in the daisy (*Asteraceae*) family, native to the Mediterranean region, but widely cultivated in other areas of the world. It is grown mainly for its edible root, whose flavor is similar to oyster; other parts of the plant, including the shoots, flowers, and sprouted seeds are also edible.

Salt   *common salt*
sodium chloride

Although "salt" is a generic term referring to a specific kind of chemical compound (an acid radical with a base radical), what we commonly know as salt, is sodium chloride. It is one of the most important compounds known to man. In nature, it is formed from the evaporation of sea water, and can be found in deposits all over the world. It is essential to human nutrition, and besides that has very many uses, including: as is a food preservative; in the manufacture of soap, glass, baking powder; as a flux in metallurgy; and as one of the most important raw materials in the chemical industry.

Saltree
Shorea robusta

Shorea is an important genus of large trees in the *Dipterocarpaceae* family, native to the Indian subcontinent, Southeast Asia, Indo-China, and Malesia. *S. robusta*, native to India, is among the most versatile. Like many of the species within the genus, it is an important source of hardwood. Like some other species in the genus, it produces **dammar gum**, a resin used for incense and as a caulk. In addition, a cooking oil is obtained from the seeds. The tree is also a host for silkworms.

Samphire   *sea fennel*
Crithmum maritimum

A species of perennial plant in the parsley (*Apiaceae*) family, native to the coastal areas of the North Atlantic and Mediterranean
regions. It is less commonly cultivated in modern times, and col-
lection of wild plant is illegal in Great Britain. The plant is edible;
its stems, leaves, and seed pods are pickled; its fleshy leaves have
a salty taste and can be used fresh in salads.

Sand

The term refers to small particles of mineral that have been created by erosion, but especially to mica, feldspar, quartz, basalt, and
calcium carbonate (from the shells of sea creatures). Sand has
many uses, depending on its chemical composition. These include: glass manufacture, pottery, as an abrasive, concrete, cement, and mortar.

Sandalwood
Santalum spp.

A genus of several species of slow-growing, semi-parasitic trees
in the sandalwood (*Santalaceae*) family, native to India, Southeast
Asia, Melanesia, and the South Pacific. Many species are charac-
terized by fine-grained, highly scented hardwood that, unlike
other aromatic wood, retains its scent for years. The best-known
species is *S. album* (Indian sandalwood or white sandalwood),
which has been prized for centuries and is now a threatened species. It is the second most expensive wood in the world. Australian sandalwood (*S. spicatum*) is also commercially cultivated for
its essential oil.

Sandarac cypress   *arartree*
Tetraclinis articulata

A species of evergreen tree in the cypress (*Cupressaceae*) family,
native to the Mediterranean region, especially the Atlas mountains. It is known mainly as the source of the resin **sandarac**,
which has been used for centuries to make incense, and a varnish
used mainly for preserving paintings. The tree is one of the few
conifers that can be coppiced. The wood was known historically
as thyine wood, and was used for decorative woodwork; the
wood from burls was particularly valuable.

Sandstone

A type of sedimentary rock composed mainly of quartz grains cemented together by temperature and pressure. It is primarily used as a building material, and to manufacture the bricks used to line kilns. The rock is relatively vulnerable to weathering.

Sapodilla tree   *chicle, zapote, naseberry*
Manilkara zapota

An evergreen tree in the gutta-percha (*Sapotaceae*) family, native to southern Mexico, Central America, and the Caribbean, but now widely cultivated in other tropical regions of the world. It is cultivated for its latex (**chicle**), and its edible fruit, the sapodilla. It is closely related to other trees native to the same region and used for similar purposes, such as the balata (or bulletwood) tree (*M. bidentata*).

Sappanwood   see *Brazilwood*

Sapphire   see *Corundum*

Sardine   *pilchard*

"Sardine" is a term that refers to a variety of species of small, oily food fish of the *Clupeidae* family (which also includes herring, shad, and menhaden). The exact meaning of the term, and what species and or size of fish it refers to, depends on the region.

Sarsaparilla
Smilax ornata, Smilax aristolochiifolia

The name refers to two species of perennial trailing vine in the greenbrier (*Smilacaceae*) family, native to Mexico and Central America; both species have similar uses. An extract of the root was the basis of patent medicines from the late nineteenth and early twentieth century reputed to cure skin and blood problems, as well as syphilis. Currently, it is used mainly as a flavoring, and is still the basis of a soft drink called sarsaparilla, and (in conjunction with sassafras root) of root beer.

Sassafras
Sassafras albidum

A species of deciduous tree in the laurel (*Lauraceae*) family, native to eastern North America. All parts of the plant (roots, stems, leaves, flowers, and fruit) have a long history of use in traditional medicine, and as food. Its wood has been used in shipbuilding and furniture making. Steam distillation of the root bark produces an essential oil comprised mainly of the compounds safrole, **camphor**, and eugenol. This aromatic extract (along with sarsaparilla) is one of the primary ingredients in root beer. Sassafras oil is also used as an insect and pest repellent. Trade in sassafras oil is restricted in the United States, as the compound safrole is the precursor to the recreational drugs MDA and MDMA.

Savory
Satureja spp.

The name "savory" refers to two species in the genus *Satureja*, in the mint (*Lamiaceae*) family. Both are native to Southern Europe and western Asia, and both used as a culinary herb. Summer savory (*S. hortensis*), is an annual; winter savory (*S. montana*), is a perennial.

Scheelite
calcium tungstate

A mineral that is one of the chief ores of tungsten. It fluoresces a bright blue under ultraviolet light, a property that has made it useful as a substitute for radium paint, as the coating for glass on fluoroscopes.

Sea buckthorn   *sallowthorn*
Hippophae rhamnoides

A species of deciduous shrub in the oleaster (*Eleagnaceae*) family, native to the cold temperate regions of Europe and Asia. It is cultivated for a variety of purposes, including: its edible berries, which are high in Vitamin C; the fruit and seed oil, which is used as a dietary supplement and in the cosmetics industry; the leaves are used to make tea, and as animal fodder. As a nitrogen-fixing plant with extensive roots, capable of growing in poor soil, it is used in soil remediation and as a shelter plant.

Sea kale
Crambe maritima

A species of halophytic (salt-loving) perennial plant in the cabbage (*Brassicaceae*) family, native to and cultivated in the coastal regions of Europe as a vegetable. It is also naturalized to the northwestern United States. It is closely related to crambe (*Crambe hispanica subsp. abyssinica*), which is an important oilseed crop.

Selenium

A nonmetallic element that is widely distributed on Earth, but is fairly rare. In trace amounts, selenium salts are a necessary nutrient for all living organisms; in large amounts, they are toxic. Selenium is a semiconductor, and was formerly used in electronic components, but is now largely replaced by silicon. Its primary use today is in glassmaking and in pigments.

Serpentine
hydrous magnesium iron phyllosilicate

The name refers to a subgroup of rock-forming minerals that are usually green or brown and come in a variety of forms. Serpentine is an important source of magnesium. The chrysotile variety (a fibrous form) is an important source of asbestos. Some varieties are easily workable and can be highly polished, and are used to make ornamental items.

Servicetree
Sorbus domestica

A species of deciduous tree in the rose (*Rosaceae*) family, native to much of Europe, northwest Africa, and southwest Asia. It is cultivated for its edible fruit, called **sorbs**, which are made into jams, jellies, and an alcoholic drink resembling cider.

Sesame   *benniseed, gingelly*
Sesamum indicum

A species of annual plant in the sesame (*Pedaliaceae*) family, native to India but now widely cultivated for its edible seed. The seed is an important food source, and the source of sesame oil. Sesame oil is edible, and is also used as a natural pesticide. Sesame is the oldest known cultivated oil plant, with domestication occurring over 3000 years ago.

Shad
Alosinae subfamily

The name "shad" refers to a subfamily of fish within the herring (*Clupeidae*) family. The commercially important species include the genus *Alosa* (river herrings), genus *Brevoortia* (menhadens), and the species *Tenualosa ilisha* (hilsa).

Shale

A type of rock composed of clay that has been hardened with temperature and pressure. There are many types of shale, each with its own use. Some shales are used for firebricks; limestone shales are used to manufacture Portland cement; iron shales are used as a paint pigment; bituminous shales yield petroleum.

Shallot   see *Onion*

Shark
Selachimorpha superorder

The name "shark" refers to a very large group of cartilaginous fishes. Many species of shark are hunted for food around the world. Because many of these species are apex predators, their flesh can have high mercury levels, and is not recommended to be eaten by pregnant women or children. In addition, shark fishing is not well regulated and many species hunted for food have suffered stock depletion and some are threatened or endangered.

Shea tree   *karite-nut, bambouk-buttertree*
Vitellaria paradoxa

A species of evergreen tree in the *Sapotaceae* family, native to the savannahs of tropical Africa; is mainly cultivated or wild harvested there. Of particular value is the large nut inside the fruit, which is the source of **shea butter**, an edible oil the consistency of butter. Shea butter is widely used as a cosmetics ingredient. In parts of Africa, it is a food source. A tree takes 15-18 years to produce its first fruit, and can produce fruit for up to 200 years. The species is considered vulnerable to overexploitation.

Silver

A metallic element that has the highest electrical conductivity, thermal conductivity, and reflectivity of any metal. Since antiquity, it has been considered a precious metal in many different cultures. It has many uses, including but not limited to: bullion coins, jewelry, the manufacture of specialized mirrors, in electrical contacts and conductors. Compounds of silver are used in photography and in medicine as antimicrobials.

Silver fir
Abies alba

A species of coniferous tree in the pine (*Pinaceae*) family, native to the mountain forests of central and southern Europe, but now widely cultivated elsewhere. It is valued for its timber, which is strong and lightweight, with a fine grain and even texture. The wood is used in building construction, furniture, plywood, pulp, and paper. It was the first tree used as a Christmas tree. Its resin yields **turpentine** and a fragrant essential oil.

Silverberry   *wolf-willow*
Elaeagnus commutata

A species of shrub in the oleaster (*Eleagnaceae*) family, native to western and boreal North America. It is cultivated mainly as an ornamental, but the fruit (both pulp and seed) is edible. The fruit is high in vitamins A, C, and E, and in certain fatty acids that are rarely found in fruit. As a nitrogen-fixing plant, it is sometimes planted in orchards as a companion plant to improve the soil.

Sisal
Agave sisalana

A species of succulent in the *Asparagaceae* family, native to the hot, arid regions of Mexico and the Southwestern United States. It is commercially valuable as the source of sisal, a hard fiber commonly used in the production of rope, twine, paper, cloth, footwear, hats, bags, and carpets. Sisal is the leading material for agricultural twine, and is known for its strength, durability, stretch, affinity for dye, and resistance to salt water. *A. sisalana* is a sterile hybrid and must be propagated by human action.

Slate

Slate is shale that has been subjected to high temperature and pressure. The rock can be split into thin sheets along its cleavage planes. It is used for a roofing material, a paving material, and in powdered form as an ingredient in cement, bricks, and pottery.

Slippery elm   *red elm*
Ulmus rubra

A species of deciduous tree in the elm (*Ulmaceae*) family, native to eastern North America. It is known primarily for its medicinal properties. The mucilaginous inner bark of the tree has tradition-ally been used to sooth irritation of mucous membranes.

Soapbark   *quillaja*
Quillaja saponaria

A species of evergreen tree in the *Quillajaceae* family, native to warm temperate central Chile. The powdered inner bark is known as **quillaia**, and has many uses as a substitute for soap, a food additive, a natural agricultural spray, and in pharmaceuti-cals to increase the effectiveness of vaccines.

Soapwort   *bouncing-bet*
Saponaria officinalis

A species of herbaceous perennial plant in the carnation (*Caryophyllaceae*) family, native to Europe and Asia, but now widely naturalized to and cultivated in other temperate regions. Like the other members of the genus, it contains the toxic chemi-cal saponin. This gives the plant the ability to produce a foam which binds to fats, and therefore acts as a mild soap. Plants con-taining saponin are commonly used as fish poison. Despite its potential for toxicity, the root has culinary use as an emulsifier in the traditional sweet halvah, and in tahini. It is also used as a foaming agent in beer.

Sodium

A metallic element that never occurs free in nature, but its salts are very common and have many uses. Sodium chloride is the compound commonly known as salt (see separate entry); sodium nitrite (saltpeter) is used as fertilizer and in gunpowder; sodium peroxide is used in bleaching and dyeing; sodium sulphate is a food preservative; borax (sodium borate) is a cleaning agent.

Sole
Solea solea

Dover sole, black sole

The type species for the genus *Solea*, a type of bottom-dwelling flatfish within the *Soleidae* family. They are native to the Northern Atlantic and Mediterranean Sea, and are highly valued as a food fish.

Sorghum
Sorghum bicolor

great millet, durra, broomcorn, milo

A domesticated species of cereal crop within the grass (*Poaceae*) family. It is the single cultivated species within the genus *Sorghum*. Wild sorghum is native to Africa, where it was originally cultivated and domesticated about 5000 years ago; domesticated sorghum is now the fifth most important cereal crop in the world. The grain has a number of uses. The sweet sorghum cultivars within the subspecies *bicolor* are variously grown for fodder, food, syrup production, and ethanol production. The Sudangrass cultivar in the subspecies *drummondii* is widely grown as animal forage. More recently, the stalks of the plant are being used to make a pressed board building material.

Sorrel
Rumex spp.

dock

Rumex (sorrel or dock), is a genus of herbaceous perennial plants in the buckwheat (*Polygonaceae*) family, native to Europe and Asia and widely introduced to North America. Several species are grown as a garden herb and salad vegetable, including: common sorrel (*R. acetosa*), spinach dock (*R. patientia*), and French sorrel (*R. scutatus*). *R. hymenosepalus* (Arizona dock, or tanner's dock), native to North America, is a source of tannin and a brown dye.

Soybean
Glycine max

soya bean

A species of perennial plant in the pea (*Fabaceae*) family, native to East Asia and cultivated there for at least 3000 years. In the late 19th century it was introduced to western countries and is now widely cultivated for its edible seed. Soybeans are high in protein and are widely used as food and fodder. Most soybeans are grown for their seed oil, which has many uses as food, industrially, and as a possible substitute for petroleum-based fuel.

Spelt
see *Wheat*

Sphalerite
zinc blende

zinc sulfide

A mineral whose main use is as the chief ore of zinc. About 95% of all zinc comes from sphalerite. It is also a source of other rare metals such as gallium, cadmium, and indium, which are often included in the mineral as trace elements.

Spinach
Spinacia oleracea

A species of annual plant in the amaranth (*Amaranthaceae*) family, native to central and western Asia. It is widely cultivated in temperate zones around the world as a leaf vegetable. It is a very rich source of several essential vitamins and minerals.

Spindle tree
Euonymus, wahoo

Euonymus spp.

A genus of small deciduous and evergreen shrubs, trees, and lianas in the staff vine family (*Celastraceae*), native to Europe, Australasia, North Africa, and Madagascar. In Europe, the very hard wood of some species could be filed to a sharp point, and were traditionally used to make the spindle for spinning yarn, which gives the plant its name. It was also used to make charcoal, and in joinery. In modern times, they are mostly used as ornamentals. The plant, including the small brightly-colored fruit, contains a poisonous latex.

Spinel
magnesium aluminum oxide

A gemstone that often occurs in association with sapphires and rubies, and is often confused with ruby. Spinel occurs in many colors, including shades of red, blue, green, yellow, brown, and black. Some of the most famous gems in the world are spinel, including the "Black Prince's Ruby" on the British Crown, which has been in the possession of British rulers since the 14th century, and the 500-carat Samarian Spinel of the Iranian crown jewels, which is the largest spinel in the world.

Sponge
Spongia spp.

A genus of marine animals (most notably, the species *S. officinalis*) whose soft, porous, fibrous skeletons have a long history of use as cleaning implements and other tools. By the mid-20th century, overfishing had reduced the population to near extinction. In modern times, most "sponges" are made of synthetic materials.

Sprat
Sprattus spp.

Sprat are a genus of small, oily saltwater forage fish in the herring (*Clupeidae*) family. The type species and most important commercial species is the European sprat (*Sprattus sprattus*). They are a valued food fish, high in omega-3 fatty acids.

Spruce
Picea spp.

A genus of about 35-40 species of coniferous evergreen trees in the pine (*Pinaceae*) family, native to the temperate and boreal regions of the world. The trees are valuable commercially for their many uses. The wood is classified as a softwood, and is neither rot nor insect resistant after logging. Nevertheless, it is important for indoor uses, such as drywall framing, furniture, and as a tonewood in the production of musical instruments. As a lightweight, flexible wood, it was used in the construction of early aircraft, such as the Wright brothers' first aircraft, the *Wright Flyer*. It is also one of the most important sources of pulp for paper. The first shoots and needles of the spruce are edible, and are a significant source of vitamin C; they are also used to make spruce beer (a beverage that can be made either alcoholic or non-alcoholic). Spruce resin (pitch) was traditionally used as waterproofing and adhesive. The Sitka spruce (P. sitchensis), native to the northern Pacific coast of North America, is by far the tallest of the spruces (at a maximum height of about 300 feet), and is the fifth largest conifer in the world.

Squash
marrow, pumpkin
Cucurbita spp.

A genus of mostly domesticated herbaceous vines in the gourd (*Cucurbitaceae*) family. It is native to the Americas, and has been in cultivation for thousands of years as one of the "Big Three" domesticated food staples of the New World (maize, beans, and squash). The best known cultivated species are *C. maxima* (winter squash), *C. moschata* (butternut squash), and *C. pepo. C pepo* is by far the most common, and its many cultivars can differ so widely from each other that they were previously misidentified as separate species. The general categories of the cultivars are: acorn squash; cocozelle; crookneck; pumpkin; scallop; straightneck; vegetable marrow; zucchini (courgette); and ornamental gourds.

Squid

The name "squid" refers to a number of species of ocean-swelling cephalopods, several of which are important food sources in a variety of cultures around the world. Calamari is the culinary name given to several squid and octopus dishes, particularly fried dishes. Squid ink is edible, and has been an important source of writing and drawing ink since antiquity.

Star anise
badiane
Illicium verum

A species of evergreen shrub or small tree in the *Schisadraceae* family, native to southern China and Indochina. It is cultivated for its fruit, which is dried and used as a spice. Its essential oil is used as a fragrance in soap, cosmetics, and perfumery. Most star anise is cultivated as the source of **shikimic acid**, which is extracted from the fruit and is used to produce the influenza medication known as Tamiflu (oseltamivir).

Star apple
cainito, caimito blanco
Chrysophyllum cainito

A species of evergreen tree in the gutta-percha (*Sapotaceae*) family, native to the Caribbean, but now widely naturalized to and cultivated in the tropical regions, especially of Central America and Southeast Asia. It is cultivated for its small edible fruit, whose skin and rind contain an inedible latex. Other species in the genus also produce edible fruit, notably: *C. albidium* (white star-apple); and *C. oliviforme* (damson plum, or satinleaf).

Stevia   *sweetleaf, candyleaf*
Stevia rebaudiana

A species of herbaceous perennial plant in the daisy (*Asteraceae*) family, native to parts of Brazil and Paraguay. It has been used for centuries by the native people of those regions as a sweetener. Currently, it is widely used to produce the non-nutritive sweetener known as stevia, which is an extract of the leaves. This extract tastes like sugar, but is not metabolized by the body, and so provides no nutrients.

Stibnite   *antimonite*
antimony trisulfide

A mineral that is the chief ore of the metalloid element antimony. When powdered and mixed with fat, it is the cosmetic paste known as **kohl**, which has been used for centuries in North Africa, the Middle East, and South Asia as eyeliner and to darken the brows. It is also used in pyrotechnic displays, and is a component of safety matches.

Strawberry
Fragaria x ananassa

An annual plant in the rose (*Rosaceae*) family, it is the most widely grown species within the genus *Fragaria*. Wild or woodland strawberries (*F. vesca*) are native to temperate Europe and were the first cultivated species of strawberry. The garden strawberry (*F. x ananassa*) is a domesticated hybrid that was developed in France in the mid-18th century, and is now widely cultivated in temperate regions throughout the world, with hundreds of cultivars. Strawberries are a source of both vitamin C and nutritional manganese.

Strontianite
strontium carbonate

A mineral that is the principle source of the element strontium. It is fluorescent under ultraviolet light, and is sometimes thermoluminescent. It is used for the refining of sugar, and in the manufacture of fireworks, to give a deep red color.

Strontium

A relatively rare metallic element. Previously, its primary use was in the cathode ray tubes of television sets, as it prevented the emission of x-rays. Strontium aluminate is used in glow-in-the-dark toys, due to being biologically inert. Strontium chloride is used in toothpaste. Radioactive strontium, which is a byproduct of nuclear fission, has application in medicine, and in radioisotope thermoelectric generators.

Sugarcane
Saccharum spp.

Several species of perennial grasses in the *Poaceae* family. Sugarcane is native to South Asia and Melanesia but is widely cultivated in the tropics as the source of 80% of the world's sugar. Other products include **molasses** (a brown syrup drained from raw sugar), **ethanol** (a biofuel), and **bagasse** (the fibrous residue left after sugar extraction, usually used as fuel for furnaces). The most commonly-cultivated species is *S. officinarum*, but several other species are either cultivated directly as sugar or fodder crops, or provide genetic material to improve sugarcane characteristics such as drought-resistance and productivity.

Sulfur

A non-metallic element which usually occurs naturally in volcanic areas. It has many commercial uses, including: sulfuric acid; an insecticide; an ingredient in medicine; and in paper manufacturing. Its compounds, mainly sulfides and sulfates, have many uses.

Sumac
Rhus spp.

A genus of about 35 species of shrubs or small trees within the cashew (*Anacardiaceae*) family, native to the Middle East, Asia, Australia, and North America. The fruit of the type species, *R. coriaria* (tanner's sumac), is dried and used as a spice in the Middle East. The leaves of some species (especially *R. coriaria*, *R. pentaphylla*, and a gall on *R. chinensis*) contain **tannin**; they were also historically used to make a yellow dye. In North America, the fruit of smooth sumac (*R. glabra*) and staghorn sumac (*R. typhina*) are used to make a beverage known as sumac-ade. Sumac is closely related to poison sumac (*Toxicodendron vernix*), but does not contain the allergenic compound urushiol.

Sunflower
Helianthus annuus

A species of annual plant in the daisy and sunflower (*Asteraceae*) family, first domesticated in the Americas and brought to Europe in the sixteenth century. They are now widely naturalized to and cultivated in many parts of the world, with many cultivars. They are grown mainly for their edible seeds, which are eaten whole, crushed to form a nut butter, or pressed to extract an edible oil. The oil is also a potential biofuel. The cake remaining after oil extraction is used to feed livestock, as are the leaves. The seeds are also used a bird feed. The flowers produce a yellow dye, and are an important source of nectar for honey bees.

Sunn hemp   *brown hemp, Indian hemp, Madras hemp*
Crotalaria juncea

A species of annual plant in the pea (*Fabaceae*) family, native to India, but now widely grown in tropical regions. It is cultivated primarily for the fiber obtained from its stem, which is used for canvas, cordage and other similar applications. It is also used as fertilizer and fodder, and is being explored as a possible source of biofuel. It is potentially invasive, and in some regions it is con-sidered a noxious weed.

Sunroot   *Jerusalem artichoke, topinambour*
Helianthus tuberosus

A species of herbaceous perennial plant in the daisy (*Asteraceae*) family, native to eastern North America, but now naturalized to many other parts of the world, including Australia, New Zealand, South America, and Europe. It is widely cultivated for its tuber, which is eaten as a root vegetable and used as fodder. It is being investigated as a potential fuel source. In some regions it is con-sidered a weed and a potential seed contaminant of sunflowers.

Sweet birch   *black birch*
Betula lenta

Birch (*Betula*) is a genus of many species of deciduous hardwood trees native to the Northern Hemisphere's temperate and boreal climates. Sweet birch is a species from which **wintergreen oil** (methyl salicylate) is made. The oil is a food flavoring and has medicinal purposes, most notably as a topical analgesic.

Sweet boronia
Boronia megastigma

A species of shrub in the citrus (*Rutaceae*) family, native to and cultivated in Australia. It is cultivated primarily for the essential oil distilled from its flowers, which is used in perfumery and as a food flavoring.

Sweet flag   *calamus, flagroot*
Acorus calamus

A species of tall, rush-like plant in the *Acoraceae* family, native to the Southeast Asia and India but naturalized elsewhere, particularly in the Eastern Mediterranean region. An aromatic oil from the roots of the plant was a primary ingredient in the sacred anointing oil of the ancient Hebrews, and was used at the Tabernacle in Jerusalem. The root and oil are still used today as flavoring; in crystalline form, it is known as German ginger. In former times, the leaves were used to cover the floor of houses of worship; in Europe they were also used as roof thatching material.

Sweet potato   *koumara, yam*
Ipomoea batatas var. batatas

A species of herbaceous perennial vine in the morning glory (*Convolvulaceae*) family, native to the tropical Americas, but now widely naturalized to and cultivated in many tropical regions. It is grown mainly for its edible tuberous root, which is high in starch and other nutrients. Despite its common names, it is not closely related either to the potato (*Solanum tuberosum*) or the true yam (*Dioscorea* spp.) Many other species within the genus *Ipomoea* are locally cultivated as a food source, but *I. batatas* is the only species currently of widespread commercial importance.

Sweetfern
Comptonia peregrina

A species of deciduous shrub in the *Myricaceae* family, native to eastern North America. In modern times, it is cultivated mainly as an ornamental plant, but in earlier times the aromatic leaves were used to make a tea, and it had a history of use in traditional medicine. The plant also produces small edible nuts.

Sweetgale
Myrica gale

bog-myrtle, meadow-fern

A species of perennial plant in the *Myricaceae* family, native to northern and western Europe and parts of North America. Its natural habitat is peat-bogs and intertidal zones. Its leaves contain an essential oil that is used as an insect repellent, for medicinal purposes, and in perfumery.

Sweetgum tree
Liquidambar styraciflua

American storax, alligatorwood

A species of deciduous tree in the *Altingiaceae* family, native to North America and Mesoamerica, and cultivated mainly in those regions. It is an important source of hardwood, particularly in the American southeast. It is also cultivated to produce a balsamic resin called **storax** (or styrax), which is used as flavoring, fragrance, and in pharmaceuticals.

Sweetsop
Annona squamosa

custard apple

A species of small deciduous tree or shrub in the custard apple (*Annonaceae*) family, most likely native to the tropical Americas and the West Indies. It is now widely naturalized to and cultivated in tropical regions around the world. It is the most commonly cultivated species of the genus *Annona* and is grown for its fruit, called the sweetsop or custard apple. a name it shares with the fruit of a number of other species of the genus (especially *A. reticulata*). It is closely related to the soursop (*A. muricata*), and the cherimoya (*A. cherimola*).

Sycamore
Platanus occidentalis

American planetree, buttonwood

A species of large deciduous tree in the planetree (*Platanaceae*) family, native to the eastern and central United States, southern Ontario, and northeastern Mexico. It is the largest hardwood tree in the eastern United States. Its timber, though coarse-grained, is used to build furniture (especially butchers' blocks) siding, and musical instruments. It shares the name "sycamore" with many other unrelated species of trees. A hybrid of eastern (*P. orientalis*) and western *Platanus*, known as the London plane (*P. x acerifolia*), is grown extensively as an urban shade tree.

Tabasco pepper   see *Chili pepper*

Talc
hydrated magnesium silicate

A soft clay mineral widely distributed throughout the world. In powdered form, it is the principle ingredient (along with corn starch) in baby powder. It has many industrial uses as a solid lubricant, a flux, in the manufacture of plastics, paper, and pottery. It is heat resistant, and is used to make refractory materials such as stoves and firebricks. It is used as a food additive, and in the pharmaceutical industry. In compact metamorphic form, it is known as soapstone, and is carved into ornaments and utensils.

Tamarind   *kilytree*
Tamarindus indica

A species of tree in the pea (*Fabaceae*) family, native to tropical Africa and the Arabian peninsula, but now widely naturalized to and cultivated in other tropical and subtropical regions throughout the world. The timber is used for woodworking. The leaves are edible, and produce a yellow-red dye. The pulp of the podlike fruit is edible, as is the seed oil. The kernel powder remaining after oil extraction is used as a sizing material for textile manufacture, as well as the manufacture of gum and adhesives.

Tanbark oak   *tanoak*
Notholithocarpus densiflorus

A species of evergreen tree in the oak and beech (*Fagaceae*) family, closely related to the North American temperate oak genus (*Quercus*). It is native to the northwest Pacific Coast and the inland ranges of California and Oregon. It has not been widely cultivated, but at one time its edible nuts were a staple food source for the Native Americans of the region. Its high tannin content makes the nuts easier to store. In addition, its bark was, for a time, an important local source of tannin for tanning leather. In modern times, it is mostly used as an ornamental. The leaves, when crushed into a mulch, serve to repel slugs and grubs.

Tantalum

A hard grayish-white metallic element, notable for its resistance to corrosion. It is used to make containers for corrosive substances, and for surgical and dental instruments.

Taro
cocoyam, dasheen

Colocasia esculenta

A species of perennial plant in the arum (*Araceae*) family, presumed native to Southeast Asia. For an estimated ten thousand years, taro was the most important food source for the Polynesians, who cultivated it primarily for its edible corms (the tuberous underground stem). The plant is still revered by the Hawaiian people, who have developed over 300 cultivars. The Hawaiian term *'ohana*, meaning "family" has roots in the name for the taro corm, *'oha*. It is still widely cultivated today in Oceania, Southeast Asia, and Africa.

Tarragon
estragon, silky wormwood

Artemisia dracunculus

A species of herbaceous perennial plant in the wormwood or sagebrush genus (*Artemisia*), within the daisy (*Asteraceae*) family, native to much of Eurasia and North America. It is widely cultivated for its aromatic leaves, which are used as a culinary and medicinal herb. The essential oil extracted from the leaves is also used as a flavoring, and as a traditional medicine. There are many subspecies and cultivars; the most commonly-grown variety for culinary purposes is *A. dracunculus var. sativa*.

Tea plant
Camellia sinensis

A species of evergreen shrub or small tree in the tea (*Theaceae*) family, native to East Asia, India, and Southeast Asia, but now widely cultivated in tropical and subtropical regions around the world. It is grown for its leaves, which are used to make *the* tea, the second most widely consumed beverage in the world, after water. Black, green, and white tea all come from *C. sinensis*. Tea has a long history of cultivation in China, originating in southwestern China during the Tang dynasty (from the 7th to 10th centuries A.D.). It was brought to Europe by Portuguese priests in the 16th century. There are three main varieties of the tea plant used to make commercial tea: common tea (*C. sinensis*); Chinese tea (*C. sinensis var. sinensis*); and Assam tea (*C. sinensis var. assamica*). Within these varieties, there are hundreds of cultivars.

193

Teak
Tectona grandis

A species of large deciduous tree in the mint (*Lamiaceae*) family, native to south and Southeast Asia, and other areas of the Pacific. It is one of the world's most valuable timber trees; it has an unusual combination of properties, as it is easily worked, but the wood is very hard and resistant to weathering, moisture, rot, and fungi. Its high oil content helps prevent iron (such as nails) from rusting. For these reasons, teak has been important in shipbuilding for over 2000 years.

Tellurium

An extremely rare metalloid element whose main use is in alloys with copper and steel (to improve machinability), and aluminum (to improve ductility). It is a poor conductor of both heat and electricity. The main source of the metal is as a byproduct of the refining of copper and lead, with 1000 tons of copper ore yielding about two pounds of tellurium.

Terebinth   *Turpentine tree*
Pistacia terebinthus

A species of deciduous tree or small shrub in the cashew (*Anacardiaceae*) family, native to the Mediterranean region. The tree is the earliest known source of turpentine, and is still used for that purpose. The fruit is important in various Mediterranean countries; it is eaten directly, or used to make brandy, or dried to make a coffee-like beverage. The bark is rich in tannins and is used for tanning leather, as is a gall that is found on the bark. The tree has been used for a variety of medicinal purposes for centuries. Bittim soap is made from the seed oil.

Thorium

A weakly radioactive metallic element that was once used in the production of gas mantles and arc welding electrodes, but has now been largely replaced due to safety concerns. It has been proposed as a substitute for uranium as the fuel in nuclear reactors, and several thorium-based reactors have been built. The first of these was the Indian Point Energy Center in Buchanan, New York, built in 1962 and still operating today.

194

Thyme
Thymus vulgaris

The most commonly grown species of the genus *Thymus* of the mint (*Lamiaceae*) family, native to the Mediterranean region. In both ancient Greece and Europe during the Middle Ages, thyme was associated with courage. It is now widely cultivated as a culinary herb. It also yields an essential oil rich in the compound **thymol**, which is used as an antiseptic, primarily in mouthwashes. Other important culinary species include *T. citriodorus* (lemon thyme), *T. herba-barona* (caraway thyme), *T. mastichina* (mastic thyme), and *T. zygis* (sauce thyme).

Tiare   *Tahitian gardenia*
Gardenia taitensis

A species of evergreen tropical shrub in the madder (*Rubiaceae*) family, native to Melanesia and the western Pacific islands. It is one of the few cultivated plants that is native to those islands, and was brought to the other Pacific islands by the colonizing Polynesians. Its primary use is for producing **Monoi oil**, which is made by soaking the unopened flower in coconut oil for fifteen days. The scented oil is used as a perfume. In Polynesia, the plant is used medicinally to treat a variety of illnesses, including inflammation and ghost sickness.

Tilapia
The *Tilapiine* tribe within the *Cichlidae* family includes various genera and species of fish, collectively known as tilapia. Some species, particularly within the genera *Oreochromis*, *Sarotherodon*, and *Tilapia*, are of commercial importance as farmed fish.

Tin
A metallic element that has been used by humans since prehistoric times. The first alloy to become widely used was bronze, an alloy of tin and copper developed about 3000 B.C. Pewter, an alloy of tin, copper, antimony, and lead, was used to make eating utensils from the Bronze Age until the 20th century. In modern times, the main use of tin is in tin-lead solders, and as a corrosion-resistant plating on steel, such as the interior of food cans.

Titanium

A hard white metallic element that is ductile and resistant to corrosion. Its strength-to-density ratio is the highest of any metallic element. It is only found in nature as an oxide. Titanium is combined with many metals to produce strong, lightweight alloys, such as are used in aircraft engines. Titanium dioxide is used as a white pigment. Titanium carbide is used for high-speed cutting tools. Titanium chloride is used as a bleaching agent. It is also used in the ceramic industry to produce a yellow glaze.

Tobacco
Nicotiana tabacum

A domesticated species of annual plant in the nightshade (*Solanaceae*) family, whose wild ancestor is native to the Americas. It is widely cultivated in the tropical and subtropical regions of the world for its leaves, which contain the compound nicotine, a powerful stimulant. The leaves are dried and processed to produce tobacco, which is either smoked or chewed. Tobacco smoke and tobacco juice are known carcinogens. Nicotine is also used as an insecticide. The tobacco plant has a long history of ethnomedicinal use in the Americas, and was considered a sacred plant by some cultural groups, including the ancient Mayans.

Tomatillo   husk tomato, miltomate
Physalis philadelphica

A species of annual plant in the nightshade (*Solanaceae*) family, native to Central America and Mexico, where it has been cultivated since pre-Columbian times. It is cultivated commercially mainly in Mexico and Guatemala, but it is also grown on a small scale and in home gardens in many regions around the world. It is cultivated for its edible berry (usually green or purple), called the tomatillo or miltomate.

Tomato
Solanum lycopersicum

A species of perennial herbaceous vine in the nightshade (*Solanaceae*) family, native to western South America, but now widely cultivated worldwide. It is grown for its large edible berry, which is classified in many cuisines as a vegetable, due to its relatively low sugar content. Currently, there are over 7000 cultivars of the species.

Topaz
aluminum silicate, with fluorine

A mineral usually found in granite and often associated with mica, cassiterite, and tourmaline. It is the hardest of the silicate minerals. Pure topaz is a transparent golden brown to yellow, but impurities present can cause variation in color from blue to pink to orange and purple. It is used as a semiprecious gemstone. In England, it was once believed that topaz could cure insanity.

Tourmaline

A crystalline borosilicate mineral that comes in a wide variety of colors, depending on presence of trace amounts of iron, aluminum, magnesium, sodium, lithium, and potassium. It is classified as a semiprecious gemstone. Most gem-quality tourmalines are of the elbaite variety. Some varieties of tourmaline are potentially magnetic, due to the presence of iron and magnesium

Travertine
calcium carbonate

A type of limestone that is deposited in mineral springs, especially hot springs. This mode of deposition often creates a pattern of concentric circles when the material is cut and polished. The stone is used as a decorative building material.

Truffle

Truffle is a name give to several varieties of edible fungus that are native to Europe and grow under the soil. Truffles are prized as a delicacy in some European cuisines. Trained dogs and pigs are used to find truffles by their scent, as there is no visible above-ground indication of their presence.

Tuliptree   *canary whitewood, tulip poplar*
Liriodendron tulipifera

A species of deciduous tree in the magnolia (*Magnoliaceae*) family, native to eastern North America and cultivated in that region for its hardwood, which is used for interior finish and is a wood of choice for pipe organs. The flowers produce large quantities of nectar for honey bees.

Tuna
Thunnus spp.

A genus of eight species of fish in the mackerel (*Scombridae*) family, known as the true tunas. Of these, six species are commercially important as food fish; two of these are endangered, one critically so. The remaining four are vulnerable or near threatened, due to overfishing.

Tung oil tree   *Chinese wood-oil tree*
Vernicia fordii

A species of deciduous tree in the spurge (*Euphorbiaceae*) family, native to China, but now widely cultivated elsewhere in the temperate regions. It is cultivated for the oil (**tung oil**) made by pressing the seeds of the fruit. Tung oil is popularly used as a wood varnish, and is known as a drying oil, meaning that it hardens to a solid film on exposure to air. The oil can also be processed to remove the gums and used as a fuel oil. All parts of the plant are toxic, and the leaves can cause contact dermatitis.

Tungsten

A metallic element also known as wolfram, obtained mainly from the ores scheelite and wolframite. It has the highest melting point of all the elements, at 6192°F (3422°C), and is extremely hard and dense. It is useful mainly as an alloy; its main use is in the production of a very hard steel used for high-speed cutting tools; it is also used as the filament in light bulbs and X-ray machines.

Turkey
Meleagris gallopavo

A domesticated species of ground-dwelling bird in the *Phasianidae* family, and the largest bird in the order *Galliformes* (which includes pheasant, quail and chickens). Turkeys are native to the New World, from southern Mexico to the eastern United States and Canada. The domesticated turkey is descended from a subspecies of the wild turkey, and was domesticated by the Mayans of Central America by at least 800 BC. Today there are eight recognized breeds of turkey, with many varieties of each breed. Turkeys are farmed almost exclusively as food.

Turmeric
Indian saffron

Curcuma longa

A species of perennial herb in the ginger (*Zingiberaceae*) family, native to India and Southeast Asia, but now cultivated in many tropical and subtropical regions. It is cultivated mainly for its tuberous rhizome, which is used as a spice. It is also used as a yellow food coloring and a fabric dye, though it is not light-fast. An indicator paper (used to test for alkalinity and acidity) called curcuma paper is made by steeping paper in tincture of turmeric. Turmeric has a history of use in the Ayurvedic system of traditional medicine in India; however, studies have not yielded any support for the claimed medical or nutritional efficacy.

Turnip
Brassica rapa

A species of annual plant in the cabbage (*Brassicaceae*) family, native to the cool temperate regions of Europe. It is widely cultivated for its edible tuberous taproot, as well as its edible leaves. Turnips are also used as fodder for livestock. It is believed that the turnip was first domesticated in the 15th century BC as an oilseed crop, rather than for the edible root. The turnip is closely related to the rapeseed plant (*Brassica napus subsp. napus*), an important oilseed plant and the source of canola and colza oil.

Turquoise
hydrous aluminum sulfate

An opaque blue-green mineral composed of hydrous aluminum sulfate colored with copper or iron sulfate. It can be carved and highly polished, and for centuries in many different cultures it has been considered a precious or semi-precious gemstone.

Tussar moth
Antheraea spp.

The name refers to several species within the genus *Antheraea* in the *Saturniidae* family, that produce the silk fiber known as Tussar or Kosa silk; particularly, the species *A. assamensis, A. mylitta, A. paphia, A. pernyi, A. roylei,* and *A. ramamai*. Most Tussar silk is wild-harvested from the forests of China, India, Sri Lanka, and Japan, where the larvae feed on the leaves of a variety of trees, especially those in the genus *Terminalia*.

Upas tree
Antiaris toxicaria

ancar, bemu, sackingtree

A species of small tree that is the sole member of the genus *Antiaris*, in the mulberry (*Moraceae*) family. It has a wide distribution in tropical regions, but especially in Australia, Indonesia, tropical Asia, and the Philippines. The plant is best known as the source of the deadly poison called upas, which is derived from its latex. However, the tree has many other uses: as a source of fast-growing lightweight timber similar to balsa, tannins for dying, bast fiber for making cloth, and edible fruit.

Uranium

A metallic element, highly radioactive, that is obtained primarily from the ore pitchblende. It is used to power nuclear reactors, and in the manufacture of nuclear weapons.

Valerian
Valeriana officinalis

garden-heliotrope

A perennial herbaceous plant in the honeysuckle (*Caprifoliaceae*) family, native to Europe and Asia, and naturalized elsewhere in the world. An extract made from the root oil has a long history of use in traditional medicine, particularly as a mild sedative, but this effect has not been well-studied. The plant also contains the chemical compound actinidine, which is a cat attractant.

Valonia oak
Quercus ithaburensis

Tabor oak

A species of tree in the beech and oak (*Fagaceae*) family, native to Southern and Eastern Europe and the Mediterranean region. It is one of three oak trees common to Israel. The acorn caps were traditionally used for dyeing and tanning; ripe acorns are edible.

Vanadium

A metallic element, widely distributed but relatively rare in the Earth's crust. It is used mainly in steel production, as a hardening and purifying agent. Some vanadium alloys have superconducting properties. Vanadium compounds have many industrial uses, including, among others: as a catalyst in industrial chemistry; in the redox battery, used commercially for grid energy storage; as a glass coating to block infrared radiation.

Vanilla orchid
Vanilla spp.

Vanilla is a genus of vines in the orchid (*Orchidaceae*) family, native to Mexico, Central America, the Caribbean, and northeastern South America. Three species in particular, *V. planifolia* (Bourbon vanilla), *V. tahitensis* (Tahitian vanilla), and *V. pompona* (West Indian vanilla) all of which are derived from a single wild species, are cultivated for the essential oil contained in the fruit pod or "bean." The oil is used as a spice, in perfumery, and to make the food flavoring known as **vanilla extract**. **Vanilla** is the second most expensive spice, after saffron. Vanilla had long been used as a flavoring by Mesoamerican cultures when it was introduced to Europe by the Spanish explorers of the sixteenth century. Today, most vanilla is grown in Madagascar, Mexico, and Indonesia. The latex causes contact dermatitis in most people. All species are protected in order to avoid over-exploitation.

Verawood
Bulnesia spp.

A genus of slow-growing trees in the caltrop (*Zygophyllaceae*) family, native to South America. It is a close relative of true lignum vitae (genus *Guaiacum*), and its wood shares similar characteristics of hardness and durability. Two main species produce wood that is traded as "lignum vitae": *B. sarmentoi* (gaiacwood, Paraguay lignum vitae), native to the Grand Chaco region of South America; and *B. arborea* (verawood, Maracaibo lignum vitae), native to Columbia and Venezuela.

Verbena   *vervain*
Verbena officinalis

Verbena is a genus of roughly 250 species of herbaceous plants in the verbena (*Verbenaceae*) family, native mainly to the Americas and Asia. In modern times, most species are cultivated as ornamentals. However, *V. officinalis* is cultivated for its essential oil, known as "Spanish verbena oil." The plant has a long history of use as an herbal remedy, and as having supernatural powers. Early Christian folklore claims that verbena was used to staunch Jesus' wounds after his crucifixion, which gave the plant divine powers to repel evil spirits and Satan himself.

Vermiculite

The name given to a variety hydrous phyllosilicate minerals (biotite micas) which when heated, swell to more than ten times their original volume. One of its main uses is as wall insulation, sound proofing, and fire-proofing. It is also used as a soil conditioner, and for many other agricultural and industrial purposes.

Walnut
Juglans spp.

A genus of deciduous trees within the walnut (*Juglandaceae*) family, native to the temperate zones in the New and Old Worlds. Though several species are cultivated for their nuts and wood, the two most commonly cultivated species are: *J. regia* (English walnut), native to Persia, grown for timber and its highly nutritious edible nuts; and *J. nigra* (black walnut), native to eastern North America, grown mainly for its finely-grained, durable hardwood. There are many cultivars of each of these species, as well as hybrids with other species. Less commonly seen is J. *cinerea* (butternut), native to eastern North America, which produces the edible white walnut or butternut. The green husk surrounding the nut (usually of *J. nigra*) is used to make both an ink and a brown dye. Crushed walnut shells are used as a non-toxic abrasive cleaning agent.

Wasabi   *Japanese horseradish*
Eutrema japonicum

An herbaceous plant in the cabbage (*Brassicacea*) family, native to far eastern Asia, and still mainly cultivated only in that region, as cultivation is very difficult. It is grown as a spice, which is prepared as a paste similar to horseradish (*Armoracia rusticana*), which is in the same botanical family. Like horseradish, the flavor of wasabi is due to the presence of the compound sinigrin, which converts to aromatic mustard oil when the root is grated.

Water buffalo
Bubalus bubalis

A domesticated species of buffalo in the *Bovidae* family, native to South Asia, Southeast Asia, and China, but now found in many countries throughout the world. They are important as beasts of burden, and for their meat, dairy, hide, horn and bone products.

Water caltrop
bullnut, water chestnut

Trapa natans

A species of annual aquatic plant in the loosestrife (*Lythraceae*) family, native to Asia, North Africa, and Europe. It is widely naturalized to and cultivated elsewhere for its large and starchy edible nut. It shares the common name "water chestnut" with the unrelated plant *Eleocharis dulcis* (see separate entry for water chestnut).

Water chestnut
Eleocharis dulcis

A species of perennial aquatic plant in the sedge (*Cyperaceae*) family, native to a large region of the tropics in the Northern and Southern Hemispheres. It is widely cultivated for its edible corm (underground stem), which is eaten either raw or cooked, and may be pickled or tinned; it may also be dried and ground into flour. It is one of the few vegetables that remains crisp even after cooking. The above-ground leaves can be used as cattle fodder.

Watercress
Nasturtium officinale

A species of rapidly-growing aquatic or semi-aquatic perennial plant in the cabbage (*Brassicaceae*) family, native to Europe and Asia but widely naturalized to and cultivated in other temperate zones. It is grown for its edible peppery-flavored leaves. It is in the same family as other plants known for their pungent flavor, such as radish, mustard, garden cress, and wasabi.

Watermelon
Citrullus lanatus var. lanatus

A domesticated species of annual vine in the cucumber family (*Cucurbitaceae*), whose wild ancestor is native to southern Africa, but is now widely cultivated all over the world. Evidence of cultivation in Egypt dates back to the second millennium B.C. Watermelon is grown for its large fruit, which is eaten raw; there are many cultivars, including seedless varieties, very large varieties, and those with thinner rinds.

Wax gourd
Benincasa hispida

winter melon, tallow gourd

A species of annual vine in the cucumber (*Cucurbitaceae*) family, and the single species in the *Benincasa* genus. It is native to South and Southeast Asia, and is widely cultivated throughout Asia, as well as parts of the Pacific region and North America. It is cultivated for its edible fruit, which is notable for its long shelf life after harvesting. It is also used as graft stock for watermelon.

Wax myrtle
Morella cerifera

candleberry, tallow shrub

A species of small tree or large shrub in the *Myricaceae* family, native to North and Central America and the Caribbean. The bark, roots, and berries have been used medicinally. The berries are the source of a wax used to make bayberry candles. Several closely-related species native to other regions have similar uses, such as: *M. cordifolia* (waxberry), native to South Africa; and *Myrica pensylvanica* (northern bayberry), native to the eastern United States and Canada.

Whale
infraorder Cetaceae

The term "whale" refers to an informal grouping of large marine mammals within the infraorder *Cetaceae*. Whales have been hunted by humans for millennia, particularly in the northern reaches of the Northern Hemisphere. But in the 18th century, Europeans began hunting whales, particularly sperm whales and humpback whales, on a large-scale basis for their blubber (a source of whale oil), bone, **spermaceti** (a type of wax found in the head cavity of the sperm whale, used to make candles and pharmaceuticals), and **ambergris** (a waxy substance found in the digestive tract of sperm whales highly valued as a fixative in perfumery). Several species of whales were hunted nearly to the point of extinction, and today the hunting of most whales is illegal in most countries. Whale products have been replaced in most of their uses by other natural or synthetic products.

Wheat
Triticum spp.

Triticum is a genus of about twenty species of annual cereal plants in the grass (*Poaceae*) family. Wheat is one of the oldest domesticated crops, with evidence for cultivation dating back to about 9600 BCE, in the Levant. Today, wheat is the most important crop in the world, with world trade exceeding that of all other food crops combined. The most commonly cultivated species is common wheat, *T. aestivum*. The second most common is *T. durum* (durum wheat), representing about 5-8% of total wheat production. Other cultivated species include spelt (*T. spelta*), emmer (*T. dicoccon*), khorasan or kamut (*T. turanicum*), einkorn (*T. monococcum*). The latter three are ancient grains that are still grown today, but not commonly.

White dammar
Vateria indica

A species of tree in the *Dipterocarpaceae* family, native to India. It is cultivated for the **dammar gum** obtained by tapping the bark, and for the edible oil known as Indian copal or **dhupa fat**, pressed from the seeds.

White mulberry
Morus alba

A species of deciduous tree in the mulberry (*Moraceae*) family, native to China, Korea, and Japan, but now widely cultivated and naturalized to many temperate regions. It is the preferred food stock for silkworms, the larvae of the silkmoth (*Bombyx mori*), which are a source of commercially important silk fiber.

White rubber vine   *Congo rubber, landolphia rubber*
Landolphia spp.

A genus of several species of liana in the dogbane (*Apocynaceae*) family, native to tropical central Africa. On the savannah, it grows as a shrub, but in among trees it grows as a vine that can reach a meter in diameter and 100 meters long. It was commercially important (especially *L. owariensis*) for its latex, a source of natural rubber (**caoutchouc**), similar to that produced by the rubber tree (*Hevea brasiliensis*). It was also traditionally used for its edible fruit (especially *L. heudelotii*) and the medicinal properties of its leaves and stems.

White sapote   *casimiroa, Mexican apple, cochitzapotl*
Casimiroa edulis

A species of evergreen tree in the citrus (*Rutaceae*) family, native
to Eastern Mexico and Central America as far south as Costa Rica.
It is cultivated there and in Australia for its edible fruit. The
seeds and leaves contain toxic compounds that were traditionally
used as poison by the Aztecs, but one of these (zapotin) is currently being investigated as an anti-colon cancer medication.

Whiting   *merling*
Merlangius merlangus

A species of fish in the *Gadidae* family, native to the eastern North
Atlantic, north Mediterranean, western Baltic, and Black Sea. It is
an important food fish, although it has generally been considered
inferior to cod, a close relative.

Willow   *sallows, osiers*
Salix spp.

Salix is a genus of about 400 species of deciduous trees and
shrubs in the *Salicaceae* family, with a widespread distribution
throughout the temperate zone of the Northern Hemisphere. The
bark of almost all species contain the compound salicin, which is
the precursor to **salicylic acid**, a compound with many important
medical applications. Some of the earliest manufactured items
were made from willow, and many of those uses continue today.
Withies (long slender branches) are used to make wicker, fences,
and other items. Willow wood is used as a building material, a
source of tannin, fiber, paper, and cordage. Willow is grown for
biomass or biofuel. The trees are also used in biofiltration and
phytoremediation projects.

Winter's bark
Drimys winteri

A species of evergreen tree in the *Winteraceae* family, native to the
temperate rainforests of Chile and Argentina. It was introduced
to other temperate regions, particularly Great Britain, for its bark,
which is high in vitamin C and which was carried on ships to
prevent scurvy. Today it is grown mostly as an ornamental, but
the wood is used for indoor furniture and musical instruments,
and the bark is used as a peppery spice in Argentina and Chile.

Wisteria
Wisteria spp.

A genus of perennial woody climbers in the pea (*Fabaceae*) family, native to East Asia but now widely cultivated elsewhere in the temperate zones. Many species (for example, *W. floribunda*) are cultivated for their scented flowers, which yield an essential oil used in perfumery, soap, candles and other cosmetics.

Witch hazel
Hamamelis virginiana

Hamamelis is a genus of about six species of deciduous trees or small shrubs, collectively known as witch hazels. Four of the species are native to North America, two are native to East Asia. The North American species *H. virginiana* has a long history of medicinal use by Native Americans, particularly decoctions made from the leaves and bark. This use continues today, as witch hazel is sold as an over-the-counter astringent, and as an ingredient in several topical medications intended to soothe irritated skin.

Witherite
barium carbonate

A mineral toxic to humans, that was considered without use (except as a rat poison), until Joseph Wedgwood used it in the 1770's to create a fine porcelain known as Jasperware. It is a source of barium, as an alloy to harden steel, and in the manufacture of glass and porcelain.

Woad   *dyer's woad*
Isatis tinctoria

A species of annual plant in the cabbage (*Brassicaceae*) family, native to the steppe and desert zones of Western and Central Asia, but naturalized to and widely cultivated in Europe. In China, it has a long history of use as a medicinal plant. In Europe, it was grown for the blue dye extracted from its leaves. It was brought to North America by European settlers and has since become naturalized; it is now considered a noxious weed and invasive species.

Wolframite
iron manganese

A mineral most often found in association with granite intrusives, it (along with the mineral scheelite) is important primarily as an ore of tungsten.

Woodruff   *sweetscented bedstraw*
Galium odoratum

A species of perennial plant in the madder (*Rubiaceae*) family, native to the temperate regions of Asia, but now widely naturalized to other areas of the world. It is cultivated for use as a food flavoring, particularly in Germany, where it is used to flavor various alcoholic beverages (especially May wine), as well as ice cream, candy, and jams and jellies. It has a history of use in traditional medicine, and is also known to be a moth deterrent.

Wormwood   *absinthe, mugwort*
Artemisia spp.

Artemisia is a diverse genus in the daisy (*Asteraceae*) family. The species native to Europe and Asia are generally known as "wormwood," while those native to North America are generally known as "sagebrush." *A. absinthium* is one of the best-known of the European wormwoods, as it is the most famous ingredient in the spirit absinthe. Wormwood contains the chemical compound thujone, which imparts a menthol flavor and acts as a mild stimulant (though is toxic in large doses). It has a long history of use in traditional medicine. Several other species of wormwood are used as food flavoring. A few are also important sources of traditional and modern medicine, notably: *A. annua* (annual wormwood), which is the source of the compound artemisinin, an antimalarial drug; *A. brevifolia*, which is the source of santonin, a drug for expelling parasitic worms; and *A. abyssinica*, which is being explored for use as an antimicrobial and antioxidant.

Yacon
Smallanthus sonchifolius

A species of annual plant in the daisy (*Asteraceae*) family, native to the Andean regions of South America. It is traditionally grown in those regions for its edible tuberous root, similar to the jicama.

Yak
Bos grunniens

A species of domesticated animal in the *Bovidae* family, native to the Himalayan region but also found in Mongolia and Russia. In those regions, the yak has been important for thousands of years as a source of meat, milk, fiber, and as beasts of burden. Their droppings are a valuable source of fuel for heat and cooking.

Yam
Dioscorea spp.

Although there are many plants and vegetables around the world that are known by the common name of "yam," the term is most commonly used to refer to species in the *Dioscorea* genus, within the *Dioscoreaceae* family. These are perennial herbaceous vines cultivated in the temperate and tropical zones for their starchy edible tubers. There are 870 known species in the genus; the vast majority of these are cultivated in Africa. The most important cultivated species are: *D. rotundata* (white Guinea yam); *D. cayanensis* (yellow Guinea yam); *D. alata* (greater yam); *D. bulbifera* (air potato); and *D. polystachya* (Chinese yam). The species *D. nipponica*, native to China, is the source of the compound diosgenin, used to synthesize a variety of medical steroids such as cortisone (an anti-inflammatory) and progesterone (used in oral contraceptives). Yams can become invasive or noxious weeds when introduced outside of cultivated areas. In Papua New Guinea, yams are so important that the cultivation, harvest, and storage of yams is circumscribed by complex religious rituals and taboos.

Yam bean   see *Jicama*

Yeast
Saccharomyces cerevisiae

A species of fungus in the *Saccharomycetaceae* family that has been instrumental in human food production for millennia. It occurs naturally on the skin of some fruits, such as grapes and plums. It is believed that it was first used in winemaking, and from there the organism was isolated for other uses. It is now widely used for fermentation in many products (such as winemaking, brewing, and kombucha tea), as well as a leavening agent in baking.

Yellowwood
Podocarpus latifolius

A species of evergreen tree in the *Podocarpaceae* family, native to the wetter southern and eastern regions of South Africa, where it is the national tree. It is a very slow-growing and long-lived tree that grows up to 100 feet tall, and produces wood of exceptional quality. Due to overexploitation, the tree is no longer used for timber, but is mainly grown as an ornamental.

Yerba mate
Ilex paraguariensis

An evergreen flowering shrub or tree in the *Ilex* (holly) genus, which is the sole living genus within the *Aquifoliaceae* family. It is native to Brazil and southern South America and is still largely cultivated there, almost exclusively for its leaves, which are dried and used to make the caffeinated tea known as mate or yerba mate. Similarly, the leaves of the guayusa (*Ilex guayusa*), also native to Brazil, is used to make a caffeinated beverage, though it is not as widely known.

Yew tree
Taxus spp.

Taxus is a genus of evergreen trees within the yew (*Taxaceae*) family, native mostly to the cooler temperate zones of the Northern Hemisphere. All yews are very similar, with the type species being the European yew, *T. baccata*. All parts of the yew, except for the berry-like aril surrounding the seed, are highly toxic to humans and livestock. It is known primarily for its wood, which is used in cabinet making. In former times, the flexible wood was used to make long bows. The Pacific yew (*T. brevifolia*) was the original source of the chemotherapeutic drug **paclitaxel** (Taxol), which is on the World Health Organization's Model List of Essential Medicines. The trees can be extremely long-lived, with the oldest known yew (and the oldest known tree in Europe) being the 2000-year-old Fortingall Yew in Perthshire, Scotland.

Yucca
Yucca spp.

A genus of perennial plants in the asparagus (*Asparagaceae*) family, native to the hot, arid regions of the southwestern United States, Mexico, and the Caribbean. In modern times, they are cultivated mostly as ornamental plants, but they have a history of use as a source of food and fiber. Some species are notable for the high level of saponins found in their stems and roots, and were traditionally used as soap and shampoo by some Native American groups. The Joshua tree (*Y. brevifolia*), endemic to the Mojave desert of the Southwestern United States, is one of the most recognizable and famous desert plants.

Yuzu
Citrus junos

A species of deciduous tree in the citrus (*Rutaceae*) family native to China and East Asia and cultivated mainly there for its edible fruit. It is one of several similar species of slow-growing and cold-hardy citrus native to Asia. Other well-known members of this group include the kaffir lime (*C. hystrix*), and the shangjuan or ichang lemon (*C. ichangensis x C. maxima*).

Zanzibar copal   *amber tree*
Hymenaea verrucosa

A species of tree in the pea (*Fabaceae*) family, native to tropical East Africa and Southern Africa, and cultivated mainly in those regions. It is cultivated for its particularly hard resin, known as **copal**, which is used for incense and varnish. Copal is also found in semi-fossilized form, buried in the ground beneath live trees.

Zedoary   *white turmeric*
Curcuma zedoaria

A perennial herbaceous plant in the ginger (*Zingiberaceae*) family, native to India and Indonesia, but now naturalized to other wet tropical and subtropical regions. It was once widely cultivated for its edible tuberous rhizome, which was used as a spice and for medicinal purposes. It is now largely replaced by ginger (*Zingiber officinale*) and turmeric (*Curcuma longa*), to which it is closely related. Another closely related plant, *C. aromatica* (yellow zedoary or wild turmeric), is used for similar purposes.

211

Zinc

This metallic element is not found in its free state in nature. Its most abundant ore is zinc blende (sphalerite). Its primary use is for galvanizing iron to protect it from oxidation. Zinc is also used for other metal alloys (particularly brass), in roofing material, batteries, and engraving plates. Zinc oxide is used as a paint pigments, in cosmetics, ointments (such as calamine lotion and sunscreen), and dental cements.

Zircon
zirconium silicate

A mineral whose transparent varieties are used as gemstones; those that are colorless are used as substitutes for diamonds. Its primary use is in making materials opaque, as in ceramics. It is also a precursor to zirconium dioxide, a synthetic mineral commonly known as cubic zirconia; it is one of the most refractory (heat-resistant) materials known, and is also used as a substitute for diamond gemstones.

Zirconium

A metallic element used in electrical appliances, refractories, and in nuclear energy piles due to its low absorption of neutrons. Zirconium carbide is used as an abrasive for cutting glass.

Zucchini   see *Squash*

PRODUCTS

Activated carbon
A form of carbon (either from charcoal or other sources) that has been processed to give it a highly porous surface area. It has many uses, particularly in filters and purification systems, and in medicine as an emergency treatment for the ingestion of poison.

Agar
A jelly-like substance obtained from certain types of algae and seaweeds, especially the *Gelidiaceae* family and the *Gracilaria* genus of red algae. It is produced by boiling the plant and letting the resulting liquid cool and set to a gel. Agar is used as a thickening or gelling agent in many food products, and also as a substrate medium for microbiological cultures.

Agarwood
A dark, fragrant, resinous wood used in incense, perfume, and small carvings. It is formed in the heartwood of several species of lign aloe trees (genus *Aquilaria*) when they become infected with a *Phialophora parasitica* mold. The production of the resin is the tree's defensive response to the infection. As of 2010, first-grade agarwood was one of the most expensive materials in the world.

Alginate
Also known as alginic acid or algin, it is a hydrophilic, edible, nontoxic substance refined from brown algae such as giant kelp. Its many uses include: as sodium alginate, a dye thickener; calcium alginate, used for wound-dressings and other medical products; and as a food additive in dehydrated products.

Alizarin

A red dye used since ancient times, prepared from the roots of several species of madder (genus *Rubia*), especially *R. tinctoria*.

Alkanet

A red pigment obtained from the roots of the alkanet plant (*Alkanna tinctoria*), which is cultivated in parts of North Africa, West Asia, and the Middle East. It has been used since antiquity as a food coloring, in varnish, and in cosmetics. In a strongly alkaline solution, the pigment turns blue.

Aloe vera

The common name of the translucent mucilaginous sap obtained from the leaves of the true aloe (*Aloe vera*). It is used cosmetically as a moisturizer, and as a food ingredient, primarily in beverages.

Aloin

A bitter, yellow-brown compound found in the latex of primarily two species of aloe: bitter aloe (*A. ferox*) and socotrine aloe (*A. perryi*). It has a history of use as a laxative, but its use is somewhat controversial due to its potential toxicity.

Alum

A double sulfate salt of aluminum and either potassium, aluminum, or sodium. The name usually refers to potassium alum, which is widely used industrially as a mordant to give permanency to dyes, in tanning, in making paper and baking powders, as a flocculant to purify piped water, and as an astringent.

Amber Oil, Amber Pitch

Amber oil is made by heating amber to above 200°C. In the past, it was combined with nitric acid to produce a musky scent used in perfumery. The same process also produces amber pitch, a black residue that can be combined with turpentine or linseed oil to produce amber varnish.

Ambergris

A solid, waxy substance produced in the intestines of sperm whales. It is sometimes found floating in tropical seas, or cast up on tropical coasts. Its main use was as a fixative in the manufacture of perfumes.

Amboyna wood

A highly valued hardwood used mainly for decorative purposes, obtained from the burls of the Amboyna-wood tree (*Pterocarpus indicus*) and its close relative Burmese rosewood (*Pterocarpus macrocarpus*).

Anatto

A bright orange substance obtained from the waxy coating of the seeds of the achiote tree (*Bixa orellana*). It is used mainly as a food coloring, but also a dye.

Angora wool

The long, silky fibers of the coat of the Angora rabbit, used to make yarn and textiles.

Anime

The resin of the amami-gum tree (*Hymenaea courbaril*). Its name comes from its heavily insect-infested natural state. It is used to make varnish and perfume.

Argan oil

The oil extracted from the kernels of the argan tree (*Argania spinosa*). The oil is used as food, and as an ingredient in cosmetics.

Arrowroot

This term is used for the edible starch obtained from the underground stems or rhizomes of a number of tropical plants. True arrowroot comes from the arrowroot plant (*Maranta arundinacea*). Arrowroot flour is an easily-digestible starch that is often used to feed infants and others with dietary issues. Due to its high viscosity, the starch is also used industrially in the manufacture of things like cosmetics and glue.

Atropine

A highly toxic tropane alkaloid that occurs in certain plants, especially in the nightshade (*Solanaceae*) family, such as belladonna and henbane. It has important medicinal uses and is on the World Health Organization's Model List of Essential Medicines.

Bagasse

The fibrous residue which remains when sugarcane or sugar beet has been crushed to extract its juice. It is usually burned as fuel in furnaces.

Balm of Gilead

A resin obtained from the Balm-of-Gilead tree (*C. gileadensis,* see entry for Commiphora). Since antiquity, it has been valued as a rare perfume with medicinal qualities.

Basil oil

The essential oil extracted from several species of basil, especially great basil (*Ocimum basilicum*), clove basil (*O. gratissimum*), and camphor basil (*O. kilimandscharicum*). It is used in perfumery and is also reported to have insect-repellent (including toxicity to mosquitoes) and anti-fungal properties.

Bay rum

A cologne local to the Caribbean, made from a mixture of rum and the inedible essential oil derived from the leaves of the bay rum tree (*Pimenta racemosa var. racemosa*).

Bdellium

Also known as bdellion, it is an oleo gum resin extracted from the trees *Commiphora wightii* and *C. Africana* (see entry for Commiphora). It is used in perfumery, as incense, and in traditional medicine. It is often used as an adulterant of the more expensive myrrh.

Beechmast, Beech oil

Also known as beech nuts, beechmast is the fruit of the European beech tree (*Fagus sylvatica var. sylvatica*). It is used as food for livestock such as pigs and poultry. Beech oil is derived from beechmast. It is suitable as lighting oil and for cooking, and is used as a substitute for butter in some parts of France.

Beeswax

A wax produced by bees for constructing the comb, which is used for honey storage and the protection of juvenile bees. The wax is composed of esters of fatty acids and various long-chain alcohols. It is indigestible by humans. Beeswax has many purposes, including the production of candles, cosmetics, and paints.

Benzoin

Also known as gum benjamin, it is a balsamic resin from primarily three species within the *Styrax* genus of flowering shrubs, which are known collectively as the benzoin tree. The resin has traditionally been used for incense, perfumery (as a scent and fixative), as a flavoring, and medicinally for its antibiotic properties. Most notably, it is the primary ingredient in Friar's Balsam, also known as tincture of benzoin.

Berberine

A compound derived from a class of alkaloids found in certain plants, especially common barberry (*Berberis vulgaris*), goldenseal (*Hydrastis canadensis*), and yellowroot (*Xanthorhiza simplicissima*), among others. It is used as a yellow dye, and also has a long history of use in traditional medicine. It is currently being investigated as an antibiotic, and for other pharmaceutical uses.

Betel nut

Also known as the areca nut, it is the seed of the areca palm (*Areca catechu*). It is widely chewed throughout the Pacific Islands, Melanesia, and other regions, for the alkaloids that produce a stimulant effect. However, the nut contains known carcinogens and carries other health risks.

Birch tar

A pitch (resin) rendered by dry distillation of certain species of birch tree bark. It is used as an adhesive and as an ingredient in pharmaceuticals.

Bistre

A pigment, usually used as ink, made from the soot of burned beech wood. It is a medium-brown with a yellowish cast.

Borage seed oil

Oil rendered from the seed of the borage plant (*Borago officinalis*). It has a long history of use in traditional medicine, and is currently being investigated for use in the treatment of inflammatory disorders.

Bort

Small, badly colored impure diamonds that are utilized mainly as abrasives.

Bran

The outer covering or husk of cereal grains. It is used as feed for livestock and for packing material. As human food it is ground into meal and used either alone or mixed with flour.

Brazilin

A red dye made from the heartwood of the sappanwood tree (*Biancaea sappan*), and the brazilwood tree (*Caesalpinia echinata*). It is used to dye fabric, and to make red paint and ink.

Butter

A product made from the fat from the milk of mammals, most often cows, but also sheep, goats, buffalo, and others. Butter that has been clarified to remove the protein solids is called *ghee*.

Cajuput oil

An essential oil extracted from the leaves of several species of tree in the *Melaleuca* genus, particularly *M. cajuputi* (cajuput, or paper-bark teatree). It is an extremely pungent oil that is used as an ingredient in liniments such as Tiger Balm, and topical decongestants such as Olbas Oil.

Calabash

The name refers to the hard rind of the fruit of at least two different species of plant, especially the calabash-tree (*Crescentia cujete*), and the calabash vine (*Lagenaria siceraria*). This hard rind is used to make utensils (such as bowls, and water carriers), which are also called calabashes.

Calamine

A pharmaceutical preparation of either: mostly zinc oxide (an astringent) and a small amount of ferric oxide (an antipruritic); or, a compound of zinc carbonate. It is a liquid suspension and is used topically as an anti-itch medication. It is on the World Health Organization's Model List of Essential Medicines.

Calcium

A metallic element that is the fifth most abundant element, but must be extracted from its compounds by electrolysis. Among its uses are: in the production of metal alloys; bleaches, pottery, paints, medicines and fertilizer. It is also a necessary mineral for human nutrition.

Camel hair

Camel hair is light, has low thermal conductivity, and high durability. It is used to manufacture warm clothing, tents, blankets, and rugs. Both dromedaries and Bactrian camels produce hair suitable for producing textiles; though Bactrian camels produce much more than dromedaries.

Camphor

A waxy, flammable, white or transparent solid terpenoid found in select tissues of certain trees and shrubs, especially the camphor tree (*Cinnamomum camphora*), rosemary (*Rosmarinus officinalis*), and ocotea (*Ocotea usambarensis*). Camphor has many uses, principally as medicine and as an insect repellent and preservative. It is edible, but is toxic in large quantities.

Canada balsam

Made from the resin of the balsam fir (*Abies balsamea*), it has unusual properties that have led to unique uses. Canada balsam does not crystallize with age, which has led to its use as an invisible-when-dry glue for glass. It is used in optics (for gluing lens elements together), as a mounting medium for making permanent microscope slides, and in the construction of a Nicol prism, which is used to produce polarized light.

Cane

The name given to the stems of many plants of the grass family, for example, rattan (genus *Calamus*). The stems vary in thickness from a fraction of an inch to several inches, and from a few feet to over 200 feet in length. The stems are used for a variety of purposes, from building furniture to constructing houses.

Cannabidiol

Cannabidiol (CBD) is the primary phytocannabinoid compound found in the *Cannabis sativa* plant (marijuana or hemp), making up 40% of the extract of the plant. It is non-psychoactive, and is used for medicinal purposes.

Canola oil

The edible oil pressed from the seeds of the canola cultivar of rape (*Brassica napus subsp. napus*). It is the third most common vegetable oil after soybean and palm oil.

Caoutchouc

A natural rubber also called India rubber (regardless of its source), it is the initially-processed form of the latex of certain trees and plants, particularly rubber tree (*Hevea brasiliensis*), the white rubber vine (*Landolphia* spp.), and the Ceara rubber tree (*Manihot carthagenesis*). It is distinguished from other varieties of natural rubber by the proteins it contains, which can cause allergic reactions in some people. Caoutchouc is used extensively in many applications, and is valued for its large stretch ratio, high resilience, and for being extremely waterproof.

Carap oil

Also known as crab oil, it is extracted from the almond (seed) of the andiroba tree (*Carapa guianensis*). The oil is rich in olein, palmitin and glycerin, which makes it useful in soap-making. It is also used as a insect repellent, as a wood protector and in traditional medicine of the Amazon region.

Carbonado

A very hard, dark, impure form of diamond, known also as "black diamond." It is used as an abrasive and for diamond set drills.

Carmine

Also known as cochineal extract, crimson lake, or Natural Red 4, it is a bright red pigment produced by an aluminum salt of carminic acid. Carminic acid is obtained from several species of scale insects, especially the cochineal. It is used as a pigment in paint, cosmetics, and other products; it is also used as a food dye.

Carnauba wax

A wax extracted from the leaves of the carnauba palm (*Copernicia prunifera*). It is highly valued as an ingredient in wax polishes used for floors, fruit, cars, musical instruments, shoes, and other items. It is also used in the manufacture of a variety of items such as soap, paper, candles, and wood finishes.

Carrageenan

A polysaccharide obtained from red algae, primarily carrageen or Irish moss (*Chondrus corpus*). It is used commercially as a thickening agent, mainly in the food industry.

Carrot seed oil

The oil extracted from the seeds of the carrot plant (*Daucus carota subsp. sativus*). It is used in perfumery and in food aromatization.

Carthamin

An orange-red pigment extracted from the flowers of the saffron plant (*Carthamus tinctorius*). Its use as a food, fabric, and cosmetic dye dates back to about 2000 BC in Egypt, and continues today.

Cashmere wool

The downy undercoat of the Cashmere goat (see entry for goat), which is used as a fine textile fiber.

Cassia gum

A thickening agent made from the dried and ground seed pods of the leguminous sicklepod plant (*Senna tora*).

Castor oil

The cold-pressed oil obtained from the seed of the castor bean tree (*Ricinus communis*). It has many uses, including as medicine, as a lubricant, a food additive, and others.

Catechu

Also known as black cutch, as opposed to white cutch, which comes from a different plant source. It is an extract of the heartwood of several species of acacia tree, most notably the catechu or black cutch (*Senegalia catechu*). It is used as a red dye, in tanning (due to the high tannin content), and medicinally as an astringent.

Cedarwood oil

An essential oil derived from various species of coniferous trees, usually in the pine or cypress families, and especially true cedar (*Cedrus* spp.). It has many uses in medicine, art, industry, and perfumery.

Celluloid

One of the first thermoplastic materials, it is a class of compounds made from nitrocellulose and camphor. It is easily moldable. It is also highly flammable, especially when being manufactured. It has largely fallen out of use except for select purposes, such as the coating on musical instruments.

Ceresine

A mineral wax refined from native ozokerite, which is used commercially as an adulterant of beeswax.

Charcoal

A lightweight residue derived by pyrolysis (slow heating in the absence of oxygen) of primarily wood or bone. The purpose is to remove water and other volatile components in order to make a fuel that burns cleaner and hotter. Charcoal is also used as a filter for purifying water, among other uses.

Cheese

A product made from milk curds (coagulated milk proteins); it is usually make from cow's milk, but can be made from the milk of other domestic mammals. There are several hundred varieties of cheese, with a wide variety of flavor, textures, and additives. Twenty percent of the world's milk production is used for cheese.

Chicle

A natural rubber product produced from the latex of certain trees in the genus *Manilkara*, especially the sapodilla tree (*Manilkara zapota*), native to Mesoamerica and the Caribbean. It has a high sugar content and was historically used as chewing gum.

Cinnamon

A spice made from the dried bark of five species of evergreen tree within the genus *Cinnamomum*. The one most commonly sold in the United States is Chinese cinnamon (*Cinnamomum cassia*), though the higher-quality is Ceylon cinnamon or true cinnamon (*Cinnamomum verum*).

Citronella oil

The essential oil extracted from the leaves and stems of some species of lemongrass (genus *Cymbopogon*), in particular, *C. nardus* and *C. winterianus*. It is valued for its insect repellent properties and antifungal properties. It is also used in perfumery, cosmetics, flavoring, soap, and candles.

Coal tar

A byproduct of the production of coke and gas from coal. It is a complex mixture of phenols, hydrocarbons, and other organic compounds. Since the 1800's it has been used medicinally to treat skin disorders; it has anti-inflammatory, anti-fungal, anti-itch, and anti-parasitic properties. It is on the World Health Organization's Model List of 100 Essential Medicines. Industrially, it is used as a wood preservative.

Cocaine

A psychoactive alkaloid found in the leaves of plants in the genus *Erythroxylum* (coca), which acts as a narcotic and a stimulant. It is considered an illegal drug in most parts of the world.

Coconut milk, coconut oil

Coconut milk is the liquid contained in the hollow of the seed of the coconut palm (*Cocos nucifera*). It is also called coconut water. Coconut oil is extracted from the white flesh inside the seed. Both products are consumed as food, and are also used in the manufacture of soap and cosmetics.

Cod liver oil

A dietary supplement derived from the liver of cod fish (genus *Gadus*). It contains the omega-3 fatty acids EPA and DHA, as well as vitamins A and D.

Coir

The thick outer layer of coarse fiber from the coconut, the seed of the coconut palm (*Cocos nucifera*). This fiber is used for making door mats, matting rope, bristles for brooms and brushes, and for upholstery.

Colza oil

A non-drying oil obtained from the seeds of oilseed rape (*Brassica napus subsp. oleifera*). It is considered non-edible due to the high levels of eruric acid. It is widely used as a machine lubricant, for the production of biodiesel, and as lamp oil.

Copal

The name can refer to the resin of specific trees, such as the copal tree (*Protium copal*), or the Zanzibar copal (*Hymenaea verrucosa*), or New Zealand's kauri tree (*Agathis australis*), among others. It also refers more generically to a class of resins in an intermediate stage of polymerization and hardening between gummy resins and amber. It is particularly valued as an ingredient in varnish, and as an incense.

Copra

When the white flesh inside the seed of the coconut palm (*Cocos nucifera*) is harvested and dried, it is called copra. It is in this form that it is shipped. Copra can be eaten, but it is more often used as the source of coconut oil, which makes up two-thirds of its weight. When the oil is extracted, the residue pulp is known as poonac and is used in making a rich cattle cake fodder.

Cork

The light, thick outer layer of bark of the cork oak (*Quercus suber*). The cork can be harvested about every ten years, and does kill the tree, as the cork will grow back. Cork is put to a variety of uses, including wine bottle stoppers, flooring, shoe soles, insulation, and others.

Corn syrup

A sugar syrup also known as glucose syrup, manufactured using the starch obtained from maize (*Zea mays*), also known as corn. The syrup is manufactured from the starch through a multi-step biological process involving both bacteria (genus *Bacillus*) and fungi (genus *Aspergillus*). Corn syrup is the second most common carbohydrate sweetener in the United States, behind cane sugar.

Crambe oil

An oil expressed from the seed of the crambe plant (Crambe *hispanica subsp. abyssinica*). It is inedible due to high levels of eruric acid, but (like colza oil) is useful for industrial purposes such as lubricant or fuel.

Cresol

A naturally-occurring class of organic compounds called methylphenols, they are a colorless oily liquid derived from wood or coal. The derivatives have many industrial uses, for example in the preparation of disinfectants and dyes. Cresol is an intense irritant to the skin and mucous membranes, and is toxic when ingested.

Crofelemer

An anti-diarrhea medication made from an extract of the dragon's -blood plant (*Croton lechleri*).

Dammar gum

A resin obtained from the *Dipterocarpaceae* family of trees, native to India and East Asia, for example the white dammar tree (*Vateria indica*) and the saltree (*Shorea robusta*). It is used to make varnish, and as incense. Some is collected fresh by tapping trees, and some is collected in fossilized or semi-fossilized form from the ground, much like copal.

Dhupa fat

An oil, also called Indian copal, rendered from the seed of the white dammar (*Vateria indica*) tree. The oil is high in saturated fatty acids and is solid at room temperature. It is edible, and is also used in soap and cosmetics.

Digoxin

An organic compound which is found in the leaves of many species of the plant genus *Digitalis*, commonly known as foxglove. It is an important heart medication, that is on the World Health Organization's Model List of Essential Medicines. It is also highly toxic in amounts only slightly above the therapeutic level.

Down

A layer of fine feathers found under the tough exterior feathers in birds. Down is used as an insulative material in clothing and bedding. Some species of birds, such as the eider duck, produce large quantities of highly insulative down that can be collected from nests without harming the bird. Some down, however, is gathered by live-plucking the birds, or as a by-product of raising the birds for meat.

Dragonfruit

A name used to refer to the fruit of several cactus species, but mainly to that of the night-blooming cereus *Hylocereus undatus* (pitahaya) and *Stenocereus gummosus* (pitaya).

Dragon's Blood

A bright red resin that is obtained from different species of a number of different plant genera: *Croton, Dracaena, Daemonorops, Calamus,* and *Pterocarpus.* The red resin has been in continuous use since ancient times as varnish, medicine, incense, and dye.

Emery

A granulation of the rock also called emery. It is composed largely of corundum (aluminum oxide), mixed with varying amounts of other minerals, such as spinels, magnetite, and rutile. It is used as an abrasive powder.

Esparto

A fiber produced from two species of grass (*Lygeum spartum* and *Stipa tenacissima*), both called esparto grass and both native to the regions surrounding the Mediterranean. The fiber has many uses in the countries to which it is native, mainly for weaving durable goods such as baskets, rugs, and rope. The shoes known as espadrilles were traditionally made from esparto rope. In Spain, there is a deep cultural tradition surrounding esparto weaving.

Ethanol

A biofuel alternative to gasoline that is produced as a byproduct of processing sugar from sugar cane. It can also be produced from corn (maize), sugar beets, and palm oil.

Eucalyptus oil

An essential oil steam-distilled from the leaves of many species of *Eucalyptus* tree, but primarily the blue gum, *E. globulus.* It is used as an industrial solvent, and antiseptic, insect repellent, and (in very small quantities) as a food additive in products like toothpaste and cough drops.

Excelsior

Also known as "wood wool," it is shredded wood (most notably from aspen trees) used as packing material.

Frankincense

A resin produced by four species of tree within the *Boswellia* genus, also known as the Frankincense tree. It has been used for several millennia in the regions of Africa, the Middle East, and Asia, in incense, perfumery, and medicinally.

Galangal

A name used to refer to the aromatic rhizome of four plant species within the *Zingiberaceae* (ginger) family, which are native to China and Southeast Asia. The rhizomes are used extensively as a spice and for medicinal purposes. The species are: greater galangal (*Alpinia galanga*); lesser galangal (*Alpinia officinarum*); fingerroot, or Chinese ginger (*Boesenbergia rotunda*); and kencur, black galanangal, or sand ginger (*Kaempferia galanga*).

Gambier

Also known as pale catechu, it is an extract of the leaves of the gambier shrub (*Uncaria gambier*). Gambier extract is used as a brown dye, a tanning agent, and a food flavoring.

Gamboge

A deep saffron-yellow pigment produced from the resin of several species of tree within the genus *Garcinia*, primarily the gamboge tree (*G. hanburyi* and *G. morella*). It is the pigment traditionally used to dye the robes of Buddhist monks.

Geranium oil

An essential oil distilled from the leaves of the rose geranium (*Pelargonium graveolens*), and other species in the genus. It is used in the perfume industry as its own scent, or as an adulterant of rose oil. It is also used as a flavoring in food and pipe tobacco.

Ghatti gum

A gum resin from the bark of the axlewood tree (*Anogeissus latifolia*). It is remarkable for its emulsification and thickening property, and has been widely used in food, pharmaceuticals, paper, and other items. It is often used as a substitute for gum arabic.

Glass

Glass is silicon dioxide that has been heated to its melting point, from which it can be poured or worked into a variety of useful forms such as sheets, vessels, and others. Though at ambient temperatures it has very low viscosity and is brittle, it is technically a liquid and not a solid. Pure glass is colorless and transparent, but many substances can be either be added or applied as a coating to impart color or other properties.

Guano

The accumulated excrement of seabirds and insect-eating bats. It is valued as a fertilizer, being rich in nitrogen, phosphate, and potassium. The best guano comes from arid climates, and the richest seabird deposits are found next to areas of rich oceanic food sources, such as those off the shores of South America.

Guar gum

Also called guaran, it is a starch extracted from the guar bean (*Cyamopsis tetragonoloba*). It has many applications, including: as a thickening agent in food, animal feed, toothpaste and other cosmetics; in the textile and paper industry; as a binder in the pharmaceutical industry; as a waterproofing agent in explosives.

Guayule

A natural rubber product produced from the latex of the guayule plant (*Parthenium argentatum*). It has many of the uses and characteristics of caoutchouc (the rubber latex taken from the rubber tree), but it is hypoallergenic, in that it does not contain the proteins that cause allergic reactions.

Guggelsterone

A compound obtained from the guggel tree (*Commiphora mukul*), used as a dietary supplement to reduce cholesterol levels in the liver. Its efficacy has not been systematically demonstrated.

Gum arabic

A gum that is the hardened sap of some species of acacia, especially the gum arabic tree (*Vachellia nilotica*) and the red acacia (*Vachellia seyal*). It is edible, with many uses, including: as a food stabilizer; a key ingredient in lithography, printing, and paint; as edible glue; and to control viscosity in a variety of products.

Gutta-percha

A natural rubber product made from the latex of the gutta-percha tree, a name that refers to certain species of the genus *Palaquium* that are native to Malaysia. It is distinguished from other natural rubbers by its rigidity, that it does not become brittle when it is hard, and that it is biologically inert. Its many uses include: as insulation for electrical wires and as tooth fillings in dentistry.

Halmaddi

The fragrant resin of the halmaddi tree (*Ailanthus triphysa*), used in India to make incense. Currently, extraction of the resin is highly restricted in an effort to protect the trees.

Hay

An animal fodder made from grass, clover, alfalfa, and other forage plants that is allowed to dry in the field before being cut and bundled for feed.

Hearts of palm

A vegetable harvested from the inner core and growing bud of certain species of palm tree, especially the acai palm, jucara, coconut, palmetto, and peach palm.

Helenalin

An organic compound found in several species of the *Arnica* genus, such as arnica (mountain tobacco). It is toxic to mammals, but has a history of use as a traditional medicine in Europe. It is currently being investigated for potential medical applications.

Hemp

A fiber obtained from the hemp plant (*Cannabis sativa var. sativa*); it was one of the first plant fibers to be spun into textile fiber almost 10,000 years ago. It is a very durable and flexible fiber that can be woven into textiles for clothing and other uses. The word "canvas" is derived from "cannabis."

Hemp seed, hemp oil

The seed of the hemp plant (*Cannabis sativa var. sativa*), is used as food for humans and animals, primarily as bird seed. The oil pressed from the seeds is also edible when raw. When oxidized, it becomes solid and can be used for a variety of purposes, including as an ingredient in cosmetic creams and plastic.

Henequen

A fiber produced from the leaves of the henequen plant (*Agave fourcroydes*). It is similar to sisal fiber, though not as high quality, and is used to make things like rope and twine.

Henna

A brownish-golden dye derived from the henna tree (*Lawsonia inermis*). It is used extensively as a cosmetic dye for the skin, hair, and fingernails, as well as a dye for silk, wool, and leather. Henna is used extensively in the form of body art known as mehndi, which originated in ancient India.

Honey

A viscous food product produced by honey bees that is composed mainly of simple sugars (glucose and fructose) and water. Some plants are particularly important as the source of nectar, which the bees collect and use to make the honey.

Hyoscine

Also known as scopolamine, it is a highly toxic compound found in certain plants of the nightshade (*Solanaceae*) family. It has many medicinal uses and is on the World Health Organization's Model List of Essential Medicines.

Hyoscyamine

A highly toxic compound found in certain plants of the nightshade (*Solanaceae*) family. It affects the central nervous system, and is used as a medication; is lethal in amounts that are only slightly above a therapeutic dose.

Indigo

A blue dye derived from a few species of plants, usually from the genus *Indigofera*, and especially from true indigo (*I. tinctoria*). However, it can also refer to the blue dye obtained from Chinese indigo (*Persicaria tinctoria*), among others.

Inulin

A polysaccharide produced by many plants, but is commercially extracted from chicory root (*Cichorium intybus*). It is added to foods as a source of dietary fiber, and has additional nutritional benefit. It is also used in medicine to measure kidney function.

Ipecac

A white powder obtained from the roots and rhizomes of the ipecacuanha plant (*Carapichea ipecacuanha*), used to make syrup of ipecac. It is a powerful emetic, previously used as an emergency treatment for the ingestion of poison. It has largely been replaced by safer, more effective treatments, such as activated charcoal.

Iron gall ink

A writing and drawing ink made by combining iron salts with tannic acid and gum arabic as a binder. It was the standard ink for many centuries, between about 500 AD to the 1900's, and is still in use today. The original source of the tannic acid was from oak galls, which gives the ink its name.

Isinglass

A thin edible gelatin that is used as a flocculant for clarifying wines, spirits, and beers; as an adhesive notable for its use in the repair of paintings; and for preserving fresh eggs. It is made from the swim bladder of large fish; in the past, it was made mainly from sturgeon, but now it is usually made from cod.

Ivory

The tooth or tusk material of large mammals, such as elephant, walrus, or hippopotamus. It is workable and durable and is used mainly decoratively for things such as small carvings, buttons, and jewelry. Vegetable ivory, used for similar purposes, comes from the seeds of ivory palm trees of the genus *Phytelephas*.

Jojoba oil

A liquid wax ester extracted from the seeds of the jojoba plant (*Simmondsia chinensis*). Its peculiar chemical composition gives it an extreme shelf-life stability and resistance to high temperature, when compared to true vegetable oils. Since the 1970's it has been used as a replacement for whale oil in perfumes and cosmetics. It is edible but non-nutritive, as it is indigestible by humans.

Jute

A bast fiber from plants of the genus *Corchorus*, primarily *C. capsularis* (white jute) and *C. olitorius* (tossa jute). It is a soft, shiny fiber that can be spun into coarse threads. It is the most affordable fiber, and the second most commonly produced, after cotton. It is used to make burlap, hessian, and gunny cloth.

Kapok

The fiber collected from the outer casing of the seeds of the kapok tree (*Ceiba pentandra*). Kapok fiber is light, buoyant, resilient, and resistant to moisture, but very flammable. The fibers are labor-intensive to harvest and difficult to spin, but they have been used extensively as a filler in mattresses, pillows, and in life jackets.

Kino

A red gum produced by various plants, especially in the genus Eucalyptus, in response to mechanical tissue damage. Kino is used in medicine, as a source of tannin, and as a dye.

Kohl

A cosmetic paste made from powdered stibnite (antimony trisulfide) mixed with fat. It has been used since ancient times in the Middle East, North Africa, and South Asia as an eyeliner and to darken the brows.

Kola nuts

The nuts of several species of evergreen trees in the genus *Cola*, especially *C. acuminata* and *C. nitida*. Like cacao, which is also in the mallow family, the nuts contain caffeine and theobromine. The nuts are either chewed, or used to flavor beverages.

Kukui nut

The seed of the candlenut tree (*Aleurites moluccanus*), which has a very high oil content. Most commercially-grown nuts are used to produce edible oil. Traditionally, the nut has many uses in addition to the oil: the nuts were burned as a light source, charred to make tattoo ink, and made into varnish and cordage preservative.

Lac

A resin secreted by the female lac bug (*Kerria lacca*), native to India and Asia. It is refined to make shellac, a type of varnish.

Lacquer

True lacquer is a varnish made from the resin of the lacquer tree (*Toxicodendron vernicifluum*). When liquid, the varnish contains the compound urushiol, which causes allergic contact dermatitis in some people; however, the urushiol evaporates as the varnish dries, making an allergic reaction much less likely.

Lignum vitae

The name refers to an extremely hard, dense, and resinous wood, particularly the wood of trees in the genus *Guaiacum* (especially *G. officinale* and *G. sanctum*). However, it is also used to refer to the wood of other trees with similar properties. Because it is extremely durable and self-lubricating, it is renowned for its use in shipbuilding, and as the gears in master clockmaker John Harrison's marine chronometers.

Lime

Lime is the common name for calcium oxide or calcium hydroxide. It is primarily obtained from limestone and has many uses, particularly in building (as the main ingredient in Portland cement) or as a soil conditioner. There are two main forms of lime: the highly caustic quicklime (calcium oxide); the less caustic slaked lime or hydrated lime (calcium hydroxide).

Linen

A textile made from the bast fibers of the flax plant (*Linum usitatissimum*). The fibers are soft and stronger than cotton, but less elastic. The best grades are used for things like clothing and bedding, while the coarser grades are used for cordage and canvas.

Linseed oil

The edible oil pressed from the seeds of the flax plant (*Linum usitatissimum*). It is used as food, a nutritional supplement, and as an ingredient in paint and varnishes.

Lithium salts

Lithium occurs in a number of compounds known as lithium salts. Lithium carbonate in particular is used as a treatment for mood disorders and is included in the World Health Organizations' Model List of Essential Medicines. It was the medicinal ingredient in the first formulation of the soft drink called 7Up.

Litmus

A dye obtained from certain lichens and used to make indicator paper, which is used to indicate whether a liquid's pH is acidic (paper turns red), alkaline (paper turns blue), or neutral (paper turns purple). The most common source lichens include archil (*Roccella tinctoria*), *Roccella montagnei*, and *Dendrographa leucophoea*.

Loofah

A sponge made from the dried skeleton of the mature fruit of the *Luffa aegyptiaca* gourd.

Mace

A spice made from the dried, ground seed coating (aril) of the nutmeg tree (*Myristica fragrans*).

Malt

Malt refers to cereal grains that have been through the malting process. This involves making the grains germinate, and then halting the germination by hot-air drying. This process increases the sugar content of the grain, and alters the protein content. Various cereals are malted, but barley is the most common.

Manna

A sugary sap extracted as a food source from a few species of trees and shrubs, particularly in the ash (*Fraxinus*) and *Eucalyptus* genera. The sugar mannose and sugar alcohol mannitol are both derived from manna.

Mastic

The gum resin of the mastic tree (*Pistacia lentiscus*). Mastic has been used medicinally for thousands of years, both externally as an antifungal and antibacterial; and internally. It is also used as a spice, a chewing gum, an ingredient in cosmetics, to make varnish, and in the preparation of the holy oil myron, used by the Greek Orthodox Church.

Millstone

Used in gristmills for grinding cereal grains, millstones are commonly large wheel-shaped stones cut from such material as burrstone, which provide a hard, sharp grinding surface.

Miraculin

A compound found in the berries of the miracle fruit plant (*Synsepalum dulcificum*), native to West Africa. It is a taste-modifier that has the effect of causing sour foods to taste sweet. In spite of its long history of use as a food flavoring, in the United States it is classified as an unapproved sweetener and has been banned from import or sale since the 1970's.

Modal

A type of rayon, or semi-synthetic fiber spun almost wholly from reconstituted cellulose, usually from beech trees. As a fiber it is stronger and more stable when wet than rayon.

Mohair

The long, silky fibers of the coat of the Angora goat. Mohair is known as the "diamond fiber" and is notable for its durability and luster.

Molasses

The edible thick, brown syrup drained from raw sugarcane.

Monkey bread

The edible pulp of the fruit of the baobab tree (*Adansonia* spp.). It is eaten fresh, or dried and made into a flour, or used as a beverage base.

Monoi oil

A scented oil made by soaking the leaves of the Tiare flower (or Tahitian gardenia, *Gardenia taitensis*) in coconut oil. It is used as a perfume, and also has use in traditional medicine to treat a variety of illnesses including inflammation and ghost sickness.

Montan wax

Also known as lignite wax or OP wax, it is a hard wax obtained from lignite coal via solvent extraction. It is used for making car and shoe polishes, paints, (at one time) phonograph records, and as a lubricant for molds.

Musk

An organic compound used as a fixative and scent in perfumery. The original source was the musk deer, but alternative synthetic and plant sources have largely replaced the original.

Myrrh

An aromatic oleo resin produced by several species within the *Commiphora* genus, most notably the myrrh tree, *C. myrrha*. It has been used since antiquity in incense, perfumery, and medicine.

Nacre

Also known as mother-of-pearl, it is an organic-inorganic material made by certain mollusks to line the inner part of their shells. It has iridescent quality that has made it a popular ornamental material for thousands of years over a wide range of cultures throughout the world.

Neatsfoot oil

An oil rendered from the shin and foot bones (but not the hooves) of cattle. It is most often used as a treatment for leather.

Nicotine

An alkaloid found to varying degrees in species of the nightshade (*Solanaceae*) family of plants, most notably the domesticated tobacco plant (*Nicotiana tabacum*). It acts as a stimulant and has medicinal and recreational use; it is a toxin, and produces a variety of adverse effects at moderate to large doses. In the past, it was used as an insecticide.

Okonite

A material made by combining rubber with the hard black waxy substance that remains after the distillation of the mineral ozokerite. It is used mainly as an electrical insulator.

Olive oil

An edible oil expressed from the fruit of the olive tree (*Olea europaea*). Ninety percent of cultivated olive fruit is used to produce the oil. Archaeological evidence suggests that olive oil production dates back to about 6000 BC in the eastern Mediterranean. Today, olive oil is one of the most common vegetable oils and is produced and consumed in many regions of the world.

Opium

A product of the latex of the unripe seed pod of the opium poppy (*Papaver somniferum subsp. somniferum*). It is the source of a class of alkaloids known as the opiates, which include morphine, codeine, noscapine, papaverine, and thebaine. From these compounds, many narcotic painkillers (such as codeine and oxycodone) and recreational narcotics (such as heroin) are made.

Opopanax

Also known as opobalsam and bisabol, the name refers to a variety of oleo gum resins produced by several species of plant. Most commercial opoponax is produced by the species *Commiphora erythraea* and *C. kataf*. It is used in perfumery, traditional medicine, and as pest control for livestock.

Orcinol

A substance extracted from several species of lichen known as orchella weeds, the most common of which is archil (*Rocella tinctoria*). Orcinol is used in the manufacture of several dyes whose color varies according to process, but are generally in the reddish-brown to blue-purple spectrum. These dyes include orcein, archil (or cudbear), orchil, lacmus, C.I. Natural Red 28, and litmus.

Orris root

Made from the rhizome of two species of iris (*Iris x germanica* and *Iris pallida*), it was previously used medicinally, but is now mainly used as a scent and fixative in perfumery and potpourri. Both the dried, ground root and the essential oil are used. It takes approximately one ton of the root to produce five pounds of essential oil.

Paclitaxel

Also known as Taxol, it is a chemotherapy medication originally derived from the Pacific yew tree (*Taxus brevifolia*). It is on the World Health Organization's Model List of Essential Medicines.

Palm oil

An edible oil derived from the fruit of several species of palm tree, primarily the African oil palm (*Elaeis guineensis*), but also the American oil palm (*Elaeis oleifera*) and the maripa palm (*Attalea maripa*). It is one of the most commonly produced and consumed vegetable oils in the world.

Papain

An enzyme present in the fruit and latex of the papaya (*Carica papaya*) and mountain papaya (*Vasconcellea cundinamarcensis*). It has a long history of use as a meat tenderizer, and is still an ingredient in many commercial meat tenderizers. It also has medical applications; most notably, it is the prime ingredient in the medication Accuzyme, which is used for wound debridement.

Paraffin wax

A wax derived from petroleum, coal, or oil shale. It is relatively chemically inert, but is flammable. It has many commercial uses, including: candles, lubrication, electrical insulation, food coating (it is edible, but indigestible), and making crayons.

Pearl

Pearls are made when certain invertebrates, particularly oysters in the genus *Pinctada*, deposit nacre (an organic-inorganic substance composed of calcium carbonate) around an irritant in concentric layers. Pearls have been valued as gemstones for centuries. They can be natural or cultured.

Pemou oil

An essential oil derived mainly from the roots of the Fujian cypress (*Fokienia hodginsii*), native to Southern China and Vietnam. It is used in perfumery and aromatherapy.

Peppercorn

The fruit of the pepper plant (*Piper nigrum*), which is dried and ground to make the spice known simply as pepper, or black pepper. It is one of the oldest, and still the most widely traded spice in the world.

Pilocarpine

An alkaloid used to make the glaucoma medication Pilocarpine, originally extracted from several species of plant in the genus *Pilocarpus*, especially the jaborandi (*P. microphylla*). It is on the World Health Organization's Model List of Essential Medicines.

Plaunotol

An anti-ulcer medication made from an extract of the croton plant (*Croton stellatopilosus*).

Poppyseed

The tiny edible seeds produced by the ripened seed pod of the opium (or breadseed) poppy (*Papaver somniferum*). They are used as food, and to produce the edible poppyseed oil.

Propolis

Propolis or bee glue is a resinous mixture that honey bees produce by mixing saliva and beeswax with exudate gathered from tree buds, sap flows, or other botanical sources. It has several uses, including: as an ingredient in varnish and in chewing gum; and as a catalyst in automobile wax.

Pyrethrum

An insecticide made from the dried, powdered flowerheads of the pyrethrum flower (*Tanacetum cinerariifolium* and *T. coccineum*) and tansy (*T. vulgare*). It is one of the few insecticides approved for use in organic gardening. It is also used as an insect repellent.

Quassin

Quassin is an organic compound extracted from the wood and bark of the bitterwood tree (*Quassia amara*). It is one of the most bitter compounds found in nature. It is used as an insecticide in organic farming, and to kill mosquito larvae in ponds. It is used medicinally as an anti-malarial drug and against lice and fleas. It is also used as a food flavoring.

Quillaia

Also known as Murillo bark extract, Panama bark extract, Quillay bark extract, and soapbark extract, it is the powdered inner bark of the soapbark tree (*Quillaja saponaria*). It has many uses as a food additive, particularly as a humectant in baked goods and a foaming agent in soft drinks; it is used in pharmaceuticals as an adjuvant with vaccines to increase their effectiveness. It is also used as an adjuvant for spray repellents in agriculture.

Quinine

A organic compound present in the bark of several species within the genus *Cinchona*, especially the cinchona tree (*C. calisaya*). It is primarily known as an anti-malarial drug, but it is also used as a bitter flavoring agent in beverages, most famously in tonic water and bitter lemon.

Raffia

A coarse fiber made from the leaf veins of the raffia palm (*Raphia taedigera*). It is used for cordage, as well as basketry, shoes, hats, and mats.

Rice paper

A paper made from the pith of the rice-paper plant (*Tetrapanax papyrifer*), used mainly to make artificial flowers, and as a medium for watercolor paintings.

Rosin

Also called colophony, or Greek pitch, it is turpentine (a resin from pines and other conifers), that has been heated to evaporate the volatile elements, leaving behind a brittle solid that is composed mainly of resin acids. Rosin has many industrial uses, including: as an ingredient in printing inks, varnishes, soap, paper, and soldering fluxes; it is used as an emulsifier in food and medicine; powdered rosin is used as a friction-increasing material in many applications.

Rotenone

A naturally-occurring chemical compound found in the leaves, seeds, and roots of some plants, especially members of the *Fabaceae* family (for example, in the genus *Derris*). It is widely used as an organic pesticide and fish poison.

Royal jelly

A substance secreted by honeybees and fed to their larvae, especially queen larvae. It is used as a dietary supplement and an ingredient in cosmetics, though the claimed health benefits have not been supported by systematic studies.

Saffron

A spice made from the filaments that grow inside the flower of the saffron crocus (*Crocus sativus*). It is also used as a yellow dye. It is the most expensive spice in the world by weight.

Sago

A starch product extracted from the pith of the trunk of the sago palm (*Metroxylon sagu*). It is a staple food in the region of Indonesia and Melanesia.

Salicylic acid

A compound derived from salicin, which is found in the bark of most species in the willow (*Salix*) genus of plants. Salicylic acid has many medical applications, including: for the treatment of skin conditions such as acne and psoriasis; as the key starting material for acetylsalicylic acid (aspirin); bismuth subsalicylate is the key ingredient in the digestive relief aids Pepto-Bismol and Kaopectate. It is on the World Health Organization's Model List of Essential Medicines.

Sandarac

A resin obtained from a few species of cypress-like conifers, especially the sandarac cypress (*Tetraclinis articulata*), but also some species of *Callitris* (the cypress-pine tree). It is used to make varnish and incense.

Saponin

A chemical compound found in many plant species, like soapwort (*Saponaria officinalis*) and yucca (*Yucca* spp.). It is potentially toxic, but is used as a soap, and as an emulsifier and foaming agent in food. It is also used as a fish poison.

Senna

Senna, or senna glycoside, is a compound derived from the plant Indian senna (*Senna alexandrina*). It is on the World Health Organization's Model List of Essential Medicines and is the key ingredient in many laxatives, such as Senokot and Ex-Lax.

Sepia

A rich brown pigment obtained from the ink sac of the common cuttlefish in the genus Sepia. It has been used as a writing and drawing ink since Greco-Roman times. In modern times, it is more commonly used as a food dye and flavoring.

Shea butter

An oil rendered from the seed of the shea tree (*Vitellaria paradoxa*); its component fatty acids give it the consistency of butter at room temperature. It is widely used as a cosmetic ingredient, and in some parts of Africa it is a food source.

Shellac

Shellac is made by melting the resin called lac, produced by the lac bug (*Karria lacca*), and dissolving it in ethanol. It is a useful, high-gloss varnish that is a tough primer, sanding sealant, odor blocker, tannin blocker, and wood stain.

Shikimic acid

An organic compound extracted primarily from the fruit of the Chinese star anise tree (*Illicium verum*) although it can also be extracted from the seeds of the American sweetgum tree (*Liquidambar styraciflua*). It is used to make the anti-influenza medication Tamiflu (oseltamivir).

Silk

A natural protein fiber harvested from the cocoons made by the larvae (caterpillars) of certain species of moth; notably, the Tussar silk moth (*Antheraea mylitta*), the Ailanthus silk moth (*Samia cynthia ricini*) and the domestic silk moth (*Bombyx mori*).

Sisal

A fiber produced from the leaves of the sisal plant (*Agave sisalana*). It is noted for its strength and durability, and is widely used for rope, twine, mats, and other products.

Sorbs

The edible fruit of the service tree (*Sorbus domestica*), which is made into jams, jellies, and an alcoholic drink resembling cider.

Spermaceti

A wax obtained from the head of the sperm whale and used for candles, cosmetics, and textile manufacture. Sperm whales are endangered, and the hunting of whales is illegal in most countries, so spermaceti has been replaced in all of its former uses.

Steel

The utility of iron increased exponentially with the discovery around 1000 BC, of combining iron with carbon to form steel, which is many times harder than iron. Steel is now by far the most commonly used metal, with a large number of applications. There are many types of steel, alloyed with a variety other metals to achieve the desired properties.

Stevia

A non-nutritive sweetener made from the leaf extracts of the stevia plant (*Stevia rebaudiana*), comprised mainly of steviol glycosides, which taste like sugar but are not metabolized by the body.

Storax

Also known as styrax, it is a balsamic resin obtained from the sweetgum trees *Liquidambar styraciflua* (American sweetgum) and *Liquidambar orientalis* (Levant sweetgum). Storax is used as a flavoring, fragrance, and in pharmaceuticals (most notably, as an ingredient in Friar's Balsam). It is also chewed like gum, to freshen breath and clean teeth. The chemical compound styrene, which is the precursor to polystyrene, was originally derived from storax.

Straw

A term used to describe the dried stalks of various cereal plants, commonly used for bedding and animal fodder. It is also used to make strawboard, to weave items such as hats and baskets, and for roof thatching.

Strychnine

An extremely toxic alkaloid found in the tissues of several members of the *Loganiaceae* family, most notably the nux-vomica tree (*Strychnos nux-vomica*). Its most common use is as a pesticide, being used to kill small feral animals like rats, birds, and others. It has a history of use in the traditional medicine of India and China, but its use is extremely hazardous, with no clinical evidence to support any therapeutic benefit.

Sugar

An nutritious organic compound found in the sap of many plants. Commercially, most pure sugar for human use comes from sugarcane (*Saccharum* spp.) and sugar beet (*Beta vulgaris*). Sugar is used either as food or to produce ethanol, a biofuel alternative to petroleum-based fuels.

Tallow

Tallow is a rendered form of beef and mutton (sheep) fat, which is solid at room temperature. It has many uses in addition to food, including soap-making, candles, and fuel.

Tannin

Tannin is a compound produced in the tissues of many plants. It is an astringent with the property of being able to bind to and precipitate proteins and various other organic compounds, including alkaloids and amino acids. There are classes of tannins, each having particular useful properties. Not all plants have all classes of tannins. Some examples of the properties and uses of tannins are: tanning hides into leather, making ink, as a component in the production of wood adhesives, as a component of anti -corrosive primer.

Tapa cloth

A bark cloth made from the inner bark of the branches of the paper mulberry tree (*Broussonetia papyrifera*). The inner bark is soaked in water and beaten to remove unwanted substances and to render the bark supple enough to work. The cloth is used to make clothing, and is almost always decorated by stamping or stenciling dye or paint made from a variety of plant sources, into elaborate and highly symbolic patterns.

Tapioca

The dried, granular extract of the tuberous root of the cassava (manioc) plant (*Manihot esculenta*). It is an important source of food starch, particularly in the tropical regions.

Taspine

A neurotoxin derived from the dragon's-blood plant (*Croton lechleri*), which has many industrial and medical applications.

Tea

The term usually refers to a beverage made from the leaves of the tea plant (*Camellia sinensis*). It is the second most widely consumed beverage in the world, after water. The teas known as black, green, and white are all made from the tea plant. Tea contains the compound caffeine, which acts as a stimulant.

Tea oil

An edible oil produced primarily from cold-pressing the seeds of the tea oil plant (*Camellia oleifera*), though other species are used to a lesser extent. It is an important cooking oil in South Asia.

Tea tree oil

Also known as melaleuca oil, it is an essential oil extracted from the leaves of the narrow-leaved tea tree (*Melaleuca alternifolia*), a small tree or shrub native to northern Australia. The oil is used medicinally, and is considered to have anti-microbial properties.

Thymol

A compound that comprises up to 50% of the essential oil extracted from the thyme plant (*Thymus vulgaris*), and crimson beebalm (*Monarda didyma*). It has a long history of use as an antiseptic, and is currently used mainly as an ingredient in mouthwashes.

Toddy

The sap obtained by incising the flower clusters of the coconut palm (*Cocos nucifera*). It can be boiled to produce palm sugar, or fermented to produce palm wine, among other uses.

Tonka bean

The seed of the cumaru tree (*Dipteryx odorata*), which is used as a spice similar to vanilla. The essential oil is used in perfumery. It contains the organic compound coumarin, from which is derived the chemical that forms the basis of anticoagulant drugs such as warfarin and coumadin. Coumarin itself is not an anticoagulant, though in large doses it can have a toxic effect.

Tortoiseshell

A material harvested primarily from the shell of the hawksbill sea turtle, which can be cut and highly polished and used as ornamentation. The hawksbill is a critically endangered animal and it is illegal in many countries to hunt it.

Tragacanth

A gum resin obtained from several species of tree or shrub in the genus *Astralagus* (milkvetch). It is also known as Shiraz gum, Shiraz, gum elect, or gum dragon. Its traditional uses include: as an emulsifier, thickener, and stabilizer in food and pharmaceuticals; in incense; as a binder in artist's pastels; as mucilage, it is used as a burn treatment; it is used in the printing of cotton cloth; and as a binder in confectionery.

Tsubaki oil

A fragrant oil cold-pressed from the seeds of the common camellia (*Camellia japonica*), which is used as a hair care product.

Tung oil

Also known as Chinese wood oil, it is pressed from the seed of the Tung oil tree (*Vernicia fordii*). The oil hardens on exposure to air, making it a drying oil that is popular as a wood finish.

Turpentine

A distillation of the resin of certain species of mostly pines and other conifers. It can be separated into resin and spirit of turpentine, which is used as a solvent. The resin can be used medicinally as an antiseptic.

Upas

A deadly poison derived from the latex of the upas tree (*Antiaris toxicaria*). In the past it was used to tip poison arrows, and was known in China as "Seven Up Eight Down Nine Dead" to denote the number of steps a poisoned man would take before he died.

Vanilla, Vanilla Extract

The spice vanilla is an essential oil steam distilled from the dried fruit pod (or "bean") of several species of vanilla orchid (most commonly, *Vanilla planifolia*, but also *V. tahitensis* and *V. pompona*). It is the second most expensive spice in the world, after saffron. Vanilla extract, on the other hand, is a solution made by macerating the dried fruit pod and then percolating it in ethanol and water. It is a less expensive version, used as a food flavoring.

Vetiver oil

The essential oil distilled from the roots of khuskhus grass (*Chrysopogon zizanioides*, also known as vetiver). The oil is aromatic and is used in perfumery, cosmetics, as a food flavoring (especially to make khus syrup), and as a termite repellent.

Wine

Generically, the term can refer to an alcoholic beverage made by fermenting high-sugar-content fruit or other parts of a plant. Most often, it refers to the beverage made from the wine grape (*Vitis vinifera*).

Wintergreen oil

Wintergreen oil (methyl salicylate) is an organic compound derived from several species of plants and trees, especially sweet birch (*Betula lenta*). It is used medicinally as a topical analgesic, and as a flavoring. The body metabolizes the oil into salicylic acid, the main ingredient in aspirin. Salicylic acid is toxic and potentially deadly in higher doses, especially in children.

Withy

A strong, flexible willow stem that is used for thatching, basketry, and gardening (for fencing and support).

Wool

Although the term is used to describe fibers obtained from several animals, most often "wool" refers to the fiber obtained from the coat of the domestic sheep (*Ovis aries*). It is the most commonly used animal fiber in the world. It is known for its strength, durability, elasticity, and insulative properties. Sheep's wool is also a source of lanolin, a waxy substance that makes the fibers water repellent, but is also used in cosmetics as an emollient.

Xanthan gum

A polysaccharide with many industrial uses, it is most commonly used as a food additive and in cosmetics, as a thickener and stabilizer. It is the result of the fermentation of natural sugars by the species of bacteria *Xanthomonas campestris*, which is the same species responsible for producing black rot on broccoli, cauliflower, and other leafy vegetables.

Ylang-ylang oil

An essential oil derived from the flowers of the cananga tree (*Cananga odorata*) and climbing ylang-ylang (*Artabotrys hexapetalus*) which is used in perfumery.

RESOURCES LISTED
BY TAXONOMIC FAMILY

Acoraceae
(Acorus)
Sweet flag
Adoxaceae
(Moschatel)
Elder
Altingiaceae
Sweetgum tree
Amaranthaceae
(Amaranth)
Beet
Epazote
Glasswort
Quinoa
Spinach
Amaryllidaceae
(Amaryllis)
Chives
Garlic
Leek
Onion
Anacardiaceae
(Sumac, cashew)
Cashew
Gandaria
Lacquer tree
Mango
Marula
Mastic tree
Pistachio tree
Sumac
Terebinth

Anatidae
Eider duck
Goose
Mallard duck
Muscovy duck
Anguillidae
(Eel)
Eel
Annonaceae
(Custard apple, soursop)
Cananga tree
Cherimoya
Grains of Selim
Pawpaw
Sweetsop
Apiaceae
(Parsley, carrot, celery)
Ajowan
Alexanders
Angelica
Anise
Arracacha
Asafoetida
Caraway
Carrot
Celery
Chervil
Cicely
Coriander
Cumin

Dill
Fennel
Parsley
Parsnip
Samphire
Apidae
Honey bee
Apocynaceae
(Dogbane)
Dogbane
Frangipani
Milkweed
White rubber vine
Aquifoliaceae
(Holly)
Holly
Yerba mate
Araceae
(Arum)
Elephant yam
Taro
Araliaceae
Ginseng
Rice-paper plant
Araucariaceae
(Araucarians)
Kauri
Arecaceae
(Palm)
Acai palm
African oil palm
Babassu palm
Betel palm
Carnauba palm
Coco de mer
Coconut tree
Date palm
Ivory palm

Peach palm
Raffia palm
Rattan
Sago palm
Asparagaceae
(Asparagus)
Agave
Asparagus
Henequen
Sisal
Yucca
Asphodelaceae
Aloe
New Zealand flax
Asteraceae
(Sunflower, daisy, aster)
Arnica
Artichoke
Black salsify
Chamomile
Chicory
Dandelion
Endive
Guayule
Lettuce
Marigold
Pyrethrum
Safflower
Sagebrush
Salsify
Stevia
Sunflower
Sunroot
Tarragon

Wormwood

Yacon

Bangiaceae

Laver

Nori

Berberidaceae

(Barberry)

Barberry

Betulaceae

(Birch)

Birch tree

Hazel

Hornbeam

Sweet birch

Bignoniaceae

(Bignonia)

Calabash tree

Chica

Ipe

Bixaceae

(Achiote)

Achiote tree

Boraginaceae

(Borage, forget-me-not)

Alkanet

Borage

Bovidae

Cattle

Chamois

Goat

Sheep

Water buffalo

Yak

Brassicaceae

(Cabbage, mustard, crucifer)

Abyssinian cabbage

Arugula

Cabbage

Crambe

Garden cress

Garlic mustard

Horseradish

Mustard

Radish

Rape

Rutabaga

Sea kale

Turnip

Wasabi

Watercress

Woad

Bromeliaceae

(Bromeliads)

Pineapple

Burseraceae

(Torchwood)

Commiphora

Copal tree

Elemi

Frankincense tree

Kenari nut

Myrrh tree

Buxaceae

(Box)

Boxwood

Cactaceae

(Cactus)

Pitahaya

Pitaya

Prickly pear

Calophyllaceae

Mammee

Camelidae
  (Camel)
  Alpaca
  Bactrian camel
  Dromedary
  Llama
Canellaceae
  Canella tree
Cannabaceae
  (Cannabis)
  Hackberry
  Hemp
  Hop plant
  Marijuana
Capparaceae
  (Caper)
  Caper bush
Caprifoliaceae
  (Honeysuckle)
  Valerian
Caricaceae
  Papaya
Caryophyllaceae
  (Pink, carnation)
  Soapwort
Celastraceae
  (Staff vine, bittersweet)
  Spindle tree
Cheloniidae
  (Marine turtles)
  Hawksbill sea turtle
Cichlidae
  (Cichlids)
  Tilapia
Clupeidae
  (Herring)
  Herring
  Menhaden

Sardine
Shad
Sprat
Clusiaceae
  Gamboge tree
  Mangosteen
Colchicaceae
  Autumn crocus
Combretaceae
  Arjuna tree
  Axlewood
Convolvulaceae
  (Morning glory)
  Jalap
  Sweet potato
Cornaceae
  Dogwood tree
Cucurbitaceae
  (Gourd)
  Calabash vine
  Colocynth
  Cucumber
  Jabilla
  Loofa
  Melon
  Squash
  Watermelon
  Wax gourd
Cupressaceae
  (Cypress)
  Coast redwood
  Cypress-pine
  Fujian cypress
  Giant sequoia
  Incense cedar
  Japanese red cedar
  Juniper
  Sandarac cypress

Cyclanthaceae
Panama hat palm
Cyperaceae
(Sedge)
Papyrus
Water chestnut
Cyprinidae
Carp
Dactylopiidae
Cochineal
Dioscoreaceae
(Yam)
Yam
Dipterocarpaceae
Kapur tree
Saltree
White dammar
Ebenaceae
(Ebony)
Ebony tree
Persimmon
Elaeagnaceae
(Oleaster)
Sea buckthorn
Silverberry
Engraulidae
Anchovy
Equidae
Donkey
Horse
Mule
Ericaceae
(Heather, heath)
Bilberry
Blueberry
Cranberry
Heather
Huckleberry

Erythroxylacea
(Coca)
Coca
Euphorbiaceae
(Spurge)
Candlenut tree
Cassava
Castor bean
Chinese tallowtree
Croton
Rubber tree
Tung oil tree
Fabaceae
(Pea, bean, legume)
Acacia
Adzuki bean
Alfalfa
Amami-gum
Amboyna wood
Araroba
Bambara groundnut
Barwood tree
Bean
Bitter vetch
Brazilwood
Calabar bean
Carob tree
Catechu
Chickpea
Clover
Copaiba
Cowpea
Cumaru
Dividivi
Fava bean

Fenugreek
Flame of the Forest
Gorse
Grass pea
Guar
Gum arabic tree
Hyacinth bean
Ibope
Indian senna
Indigo
Jandi
Jicama
Lentil
Licorice
Lima bean
Logwood
Mesquite
Milkvetch
Monkeypod
Mung bean
Pea
Peanut
Rooibos
Rosewood
Runner bean
Sicklepod
Soybean
Sunn hemp
Tamarind
Wisteria
Zanzibar copal

Fagaceae
(Oak, beech)
Beech tree
Chestnut tree

Cork oak
Oak
Tanbark oak
Valonia oak
Gadidae
(Cod)
Cod
Haddock
Pollock
Whiting
Gentianaceae
Gentian
Geraniaceae
Rose geranium
Gigartinaceae
Carrageen
Ginkgoaceae
Ginkgo tree
Grossulariaceae
(Gooseberry, currant)
Currant bush
Gryllidae
(Crickets)
Cricket
Hamamelidaceae
(Witch hazel)
Witch hazel
Iridaceae
(Iris)
Freesia
Orris
Saffron crocus
Irvingiaceae
Dika
Juglandaceae
(Walnut)
Hickory tree
Pecan tree
Walnut tree

Kerridae
(Lac insects)
Lac insect

Lamiaceae
(Mint, deadnettle)
Basil
Beebalm
Betony
Catnip
Crosne
Hausa potato
Hyssop
Lavender
Marjoram
Mexican mint
Mint
Oregano
Patchouli
Perilla
Rosemary
Sage
Savory
Teak
Thyme

Laminariaceae
Giant kelp

Lauraceae
(Laurel)
Avocado
Bay laurel
Camphortree
Chinese cassia
Oregon myrtle
Sassafras

Lecythidaceae
Brazilnut tree

Leporidae
Rabbit

Linaceae
Flax

Loganiaceae
Nux vomica

Lythraceae
(Loosestrife)
Henna tree
Pomegranate
Water caltrop

Magnoliaceae
(Magnolia)
Champak
Tuliptree

Malvaceae
(Mallow)
Balsa tree
Baobab tree
Cocoa tree
Corchorus
Cotton
Durian
Kapok
Kola tree
Linden
Marsh mallow
Musk mallow
Okra

Marantaceae
(Arrowroot)
Arrowroot
Leren

Margarodidae

(Ground pearls)

Polish cochineal

Meliaceae

(Mahogany)

Andiroba

Mahogany

Merlucciidae

Hake

Monimiaceae

Boldo

Moraceae

(Mulberry, fig, breadfruit)

Banyan tree

Breadfruit

Fig

Jackfruit

Mulberry

Old fustic

Osage orange

Paper mulberry

Upas tree

White mulberry

Moschidae

Musk deer

Musaceae

(Banana)

Abaca

Banana

Myricaceae

Sweetfern

Sweetgale

Wax myrtle

Myristicaceae

(Nutmeg)

Nutmeg

Myrtaceae

(Myrtle)

Allspice

Bay rum tree

Blue gum tree

Cajuput

Cider gum tree

Clove

Eucalyptus

Feijoa

Guava tree

Jambolan

Jarrah

Karri

Manuka

Marri tree

Mindanao gum

Myrtle

Nephropidae

Lobster

Oleaceae

(Olive)

Jasmine

Manna ash

Olive tree

Orchidaceae

Vanilla orchid

Ostreidae

Oyster (true)

Pandanaceae

(Pandanus)

Pandan

Papaveraceae

(Poppy)

Opium poppy

Parastacidae
(Freshwater crayfish)
Marron
Passifloraceae
Passion fruit
Pedaliaceae
(Sesame, pedalium)
Sesame
Phasianidae
(Ground fowl)
Chicken
Turkey
Pinaceae
(Pine)
Balsam fir
Cedar
Deodar cedar
Douglas fir
Fir tree
Hemlock tree
Larch
Pine tree
Silver fir
Spruce
Piperaceae
(Pepper)
Black pepper
Cubeb
Kava
Plantaginaceae
(Plantain)
Foxglove
Platanaceae
(Plane tree)
Sycamore

Pleuronectidae
(Right-eye flounders)
Halibut
Plaice
Poaceae
(Grass)
Bamboo
Barley
Esparto grass
Fescue grass
Khuskhus
Lemongrass
Maize
Marram grass
Millet
Oat
Reed
Rice
Rye
Sorghum
Sugarcane
Wheat
Podocarpaceae
Yellowwood
Polygonaceae
(Buckwheat, knotweed)
Buckwheat
Chinese indigo
Rhubarb
Sorrel
Portulacaceae
(Purslane)
Purslane
Proteaceae
(Protea)
Chilean hazelnut
Macadamia nut

Pteriidae

(Feather oysters)

Oyster (pearl)

Quillajaceae

Soapbark

Ranunculaceae

(Buttercup, crowfoot)

Marsh marigold

Rhamnaceae

(Buckthorn)

Buckthorn

Cascara buckthorn

Jujube

Rosaceae

(Rose)

Almond

Apple

Apricot

Bramble

Cherry

Chinese quince

Hawthorn

Loquat

Medlar

Peach

Pear

Plum

Quince

Rose

Servicetree

Strawberry

Rubiaceae

(Madder, coffee, breadstraw)

Cinchona

Coffee tree

Gambier

Ipecac

Madder

Noni

Tiare

Woodruff

Rutaceae

(Citrus, rue)

Baeltree

Bergamot orange

Citron tree

Clementine

Jaborandi

Kumquat

Lemon

Limeberry

Orange

Sichuan pepper

Sweet boronia

White sapote

Yuzu

Salicaceae

(Willow)

Aspen

Osier

Poplar

Willow

Salmonidae

Salmon

Santalaceae

(Sandalwood)

Sandalwood

Sapindaceae

(Soapberry)

Ackee

Genip

Guarana

Horse chestnut
Longan
Lychee
Maple tree
Sapotaceae
(Zapote, gutta-percha)
Argan tree
Balata
Canistel
Gutta-percha tree
Mamey sapote
Miracle fruit
Sapodilla tree
Shea tree
Star apple
Saturniidae
(Emperor moth, silkmoth)
Ailanthus silkmoth
Mopanie
Silkmoth
Tussar moth
Schisandraceae
Star anise
Scombridae
(Mackerel)
Bonito
Mackerel
Tuna
Simaroubaceae
Halmaddi
Quassia
Simmondsiaceae
(Jojoba)
Jojoba

Smilacaceae
(Greenbrier)
Sarsaparilla
Solanaceae
(Nightshade)
Belladonna
Chili pepper
Eggplant
Henbane
Jimsonweed
Kutjera
Mandrake
Potato
Tobacco
Tomatillo
Tomato
Soleidae
Sole
Styracaceae
Benzoin tree
Suidae
Pig
Taxaceae
(Yew)
Yew tree
Theaceae
(Tea)
Camellia
Tea plant
Thymelaeaceae
(Mezereon)
Lign aloes
Ramin
Tropaeolaceae
(Nasturtium)
Nasturtium

Ulmaceae
(Elm)
Elm
Slippery elm
Urticaceae
(Nettle)
Nettles
Ramie
Verbenaceae
(Verbena, vervain)
Lemon verbena
Verbena
Vitaceae
Grape
Muscadine grape
Winteraceae
Mountain pepper
Winter's bark
Zingiberaceae
(Ginger)
Awapuhi
Cardamom (false)
Cardamom (true)
East Indian arrowroot
Ginger
Grains of paradise
Korarima
Turmeric
Zedoary
Zosteraceae
Eelgrass
Zygophyllaceae
(Caltrop)
Lignum-vitae
Verawood

Resources and Products
Listed by Product Type

(Products are listed in bold type, followed in italics by the resource or resources from which they are derived)

*Note that the broad category of "food" has been omitted from the list. This is because the majority of plant and animal resources included in the dictionary are used for food.

Abrasive

Bort *Diamond*
Carbonado *Diamond*
Corundum
Diatomaceous earth
Emery *Corundum*
Garnet
Ilmenite
Pumice
Sand
Walnut
Zirconium

Adhesive

Potato

Alloy

Antimony
Beryllium
Bismuth
Cadmium
Chromium
Cobalt
Copper
Gallium
Iridium
Lead
Lithium
Manganese
Molybdenum
Neodymium
Nickel
Niobium
Platinum
Pyrolusite
Rhodium
Silicon
Steel *Iron*
Tellurium
Tin
Titanium
Tungsten
Witherite
Zinc

Beverage

Agave
Chamomile
Chicory
Cocoa tree
Coffee tree
Elder
Guarana
Kava
Myrtle
Passion fruit

Rice (Asian)
Rooibos
Servicetree
Sweetfern
Tea   *Tea plant*
Terebinth
Toddy   *Coconut tree*
Wine   *Grape, Muscadine grape*
Yerba mate

BUILDING MATERIAL

Alabaster
Chalk
Cane   *Bamboo, Reed, Rattan*
Clay
Cork   *Cork oak*
Diatomaceous earth
Dolomite
Eelgrass
Fire clay
Ganister
Glass   *Sand, silica*
Granite
Gypsum
Lime   *Limestone*
Limestone
Magnesite
Marble
Marl
Pitaya
Pumice
Quartz
Reed (common)
Sand
Sandstone
Silica
Slate
Sorghum
Travertine

CLEANING AGENT

Borax
Fuller's earth
Potassium
Quinoa
Saponin   *Soapwort, Yucca*

COSMETIC

Aloe vera   *Aloe*
Awapuhi
Coconut milk *Coconut tree*
Henna   *Henna tree*
Kohl   *Stibnite*
Oat

DYE

Acacia
Alizarin   *Madder*
Anatto   *Achiote tree*
Apatite
Berberine *Barberry*
Bilberry
Brazilin   *Brazilwood*
Buckthorn
Catechu   *Catechu*
Chica
Flame of the Forest tree
Galls
Gambier
Henna   *Henna tree*
Hornbeam
Iceland moss
Indigo   *Indigo*
Kino   *Eucalyptus*
               Barwood tree
               Marri tree
               Flame of the Forest
Lac insect
Litmus   *Archil*
Logwood

Marigold

Noni

Orcinol   *Archil*

Old fustic

Rhubarb

Safflower

Saffron   *Saffron crocus*

Sorrel

Sumac

Turmeric

Valonia oak

Woad

Essential Oil

Acacia

Ajowan

Angelica

Anise

Baeltree

Balsam fir

Basil oil   *Basil*

Bay laurel

Bay rum   *Bay rum tree*

Beebalm

Bergamot orange

Birch tree

Blue gum tree

Cajuput

Carrot seed   *Carrot*

Cedarwood   *Cedar*

Celery

Chamomile

Champak

Chinese cassia

Citron tree

Citronella oil   *Lemongrass*

Clementine

Coriander

Deodar cedar

Dill

Elder

Elemi

Eucalyptus

Fennel

Fenugreek

Frangipani

Freesia

Geranium oil   *Rose geranium*

Ginger

Hazel

Hyssop

Jasmine

Juniper

Kumquat

Lavender

Lemon

Lemon verbena

Lemongrass

Lign aloes

Manuka

Marjoram

Marri tree

Mexican mint

Mint

Monoi oil   *Tiare*

Mustard

Myrtle

Nasturtium

Nutmeg

Orange tree

Oregano

Orris root   *Orris*

Parsley

Patchouli

Pemou oil   *Fujian cypress*

Rose

Rosewood

Sage

Sandalwood

Sassafras

Silver fir
Star anise
Sweet boronia
Sweetgale
Tarragon
Thyme
Thymol   *Beebalm, thyme*
Tonka bean *Cumaru*
Vanilla   *Vanilla orchid*
Valerian
Verbena
Vetiver oil *Khuskhus*
Wintergreen *Sweet birch*
Wisteria
Ylang-ylang *Cananga tree*

FEATHERS

Down   *Eider duck, goose*

FERTILIZER

Anhydrite
Apatite
Buckwheat
Chalk
Clover
Dolomite
Epsom salt
Gorse
Gypsum
Hyacinth bean
Indigo
Kainite
Lentil
Lime   *Limestone*
Marl
Menhaden
Nitrate
Phosphates
Potassium
Rye
Sea buckthorn

FIBER

Abaca
Agave
Alpaca
Angora wool *Rabbit*
Babassu palm
Baobab tree
Betel palm
Birch tree
Camel hair   *Bactrian camel*
                 Dromedary
Carnauba palm
Cashmere wool *Goat*
Coir   *Coconut tree*
Cotton
Date palm
Dogbane
Eelgrass
Esparto   *Esparto grass*
Hemp   *Hemp*
Henequen   *Henequen*
Jute   *Corchorus*
Kapok   *Kapok*
Khuskhus
Linden
Linen   *Flax*
Llama
Milkweed
Mohair   *Goat*
New Zealand flax
Okra
Panama hat palm
Pandan
Paper mulberry
Papyrus
Pawpaw
Peach palm
Peanut
Pineapple
Raffia   *Raffia palm*

Ramie
Reed
Silk   *Ailanthus silkmoth*
                 Silkmoth
                 Tussar moth
Sisal   *Sisal*
Sunn hemp
Upas tree
Willow
Wool   *Sheep*
Yak
Yucca

FLAVORING

Angelica
Awapuhi
Basil
Bay laurel
Bay rum tree
Benzoin   *Benzoin tree*
Boldo
Chervil
Chives
Cicely
Dill
Elder
Epazote
Gambier
Garlic mustard
Gentian
Ginseng
Hop plant
Hyssop
Jasmine
Kola tree
Lemongrass
Licorice
Marigold
Marjoram
Mexican mint

Mint
Musk mallow
Oregano
Quinine   *Cinchona*
Rosemary
Sage
Sarsaparilla
Savory
Stevia   *Stevia*
Sweet flag
Tarragon
Thyme
Vanilla extract *Vanilla orchid*
Woodruff
Wormwood

FODDER

Abyssinian cabbage
Alfalfa
Argan tree
Arugula
Axlewood
Barley
Barwood tree
Bean
Beechmast   *Beech tree*
Beet
Bitter vetch
Breadfruit
Buckwheat
Carob tree
Carrot
Cassava
Chickpea
Clover
Copra   *Coconut tree*
Cotton
Cowpea
Crambe
Cricket

Date palm
Dika
Fava bean
Fenugreek
Fescue grass
Flax
Glasswort
Gorse
Grape
Grass pea
Guar
Heather
Hemp seed   *Hemp*
Holly
Hornbeam
Horse chestnut
Hyacinth bean
Ibope
Jandi
Lentil
Maize
Menhaden
Millet
Mustard
Oak
Oat
Old fustic
Pea
Peach palm
Peanut
Potato
Prickly pear
Purslane
Rape
Rice (Wild)
Rutabaga
Rye
Sea buckthorn
Sorghum
Soybean

Sunflower
Sunn hemp
Sunroot
Turnip
Water chestnut
White mulberry

Fuel

Bagasse   *Beet, sugarcane*
Beet
Chinese tallowtree
Coal
Ethanol   *Maize, sugarcane*
Gorse
Hazel
Maize
Manure   *Cattle, yak*
Methane
Peat
Petroleum
Phosphates
Plutonium
Poplar
Reed
Sorghum
Sugar   *Beet, sugarcane*
Sunn hemp
Sunroot
Uranium

Gemstone

Agate
Amber
Amethyst
Beryl
Chalcedony
Corundum
Diamond
Elbaite
Feldspar
Garnet

Hematite
Jet
Lapis lazuli
Malachite
Opal
Pearl   *Oyster (pearl)*
Peridot
Silica
Spinel
Topaz
Tourmaline
Turquoise
Zircon

INK

Carbon black *Petroleum*
Sepia   *Cuttlefish*
Squid
Walnut

INSECT REPELLENT

Bean
Catnip
Chives
Citronella oil   *Lemongrass*
Clove
Epazote
Pawpaw

LATEX

Balata
Breadfruit
Canistel
Caoutchouc   *Rubber tree*
                   White rubber vine
Cassava
Chicle   *Sapodilla tree*
Dandelion
Guayule   *Guayule*
Gutta-percha   *Gutta-percha tree*
Upas   *Upas tree*

LEATHER

Cattle
Chamois
Goat

MASTICATORY

Betel nut   *Betel palm*
Chicle   *Sapodilla tree*
Kola tree

MEDICINE

Aloin   *Aloe*
Alum   *Alunite*
Amboyna wood
Angelica
Atropine   *Belladonna*
                   Jimsonweed
                   Henbane

Autumn crocus
Awapuhi
Beebalm
Berberine   *Barberry*
Betony
Bismuth
Boldo
Borage seed oil   *Borage*
Borax
Calabar bean
Calamine   *Calamine*
Cannabidiol   *Marijuana*
                   Hemp
Carap oil   *Andiroba*
Cascara buckthorn
Catechu   *Catechu*
Chili pepper
Coal tar   *Coal*
Colocynth
Crofelemer   *Croton*
Cubeb
Digoxin   *Foxglove*
Elm

Epsom salt
Garlic
Gentian
Ginkgo tree
Ginseng
Gold
Hawthorn
Helenalin *Arnica*
Horse chestnut
Horseradish
Hyoscine *Mandrake*
Jimsonweed
Henbane
Belladonna
Hyoscyamine *Henbane*
Jimsonweed
Belladonna
Iodine
Ipecac *Ipecac*
Jabilla
Jalap
Kino *Barwood tree*
Marri tree
Eucalyptus
Flame of the Forest
Linden
Lithium salts *Lepidolite, Lithium*
Marigold
Marsh mallow
Milkweed
Nicotine *Tobacco*
Noni
Opium *Opium poppy*
Oregon myrtle
Paclitaxel *Yew tree*
Papain *Papaya*
Paper mulberry
Papyrus
Pilocarpine *Jaborandi*
Platinum

Plaunotol *Croton*
Pyrolusite
Quassin *Quassia*
Quillaia *Soapbark*
Quinine *Cinchona*
Sagebrush
Salicylic acid *Willow*
Senna *Indian senna*
Shikimic acid *Sweetgum tree*
Star anise
Slippery elm
Tannin *(numerous species contain tannin)*
Taspine *Croton*
Tragacanth *Milkvetch*
Wax myrtle
White sapote
Willow
Winter's bark
Witch hazel
Wormwood
Yam
Zinc

MUCILAGE

Musk mallow
Okra
Prickly pear

OIL

Abyssinian cabbage
Acai palm
Almond
Amber Oil *Amber*
Argan oil *Argan tree*
Babassu palm
Beech oil *Beech tree*
Buckthorn
Canola oil *Rape*
Carap oil *Andiroba*
Castor oil *Castor bean*

Chilean hazelnut
Coconut oil *Coconut tree*
Colza oil *Rape*
Copra *Coconut tree*
Cotton
Crambe oil *Crambe*
Dhupa fat *White dammar*
Dika
Glasswort
Guava tree
Hemp oil *Hemp*
Hickory tree
Jabilla
Kapok
Kukui nut *Candlenut tree*
Lettuce
Linseed oil *Flax*
Mamey sapote
Marula
Milkweed
Musk *Angelica, Musk deer*
Musk mallow
Mustard
Nutmeg
Olive oil *Olive tree*
Palm oil *African oil palm*
Peanut
Petroleum
Poppyseed *Opium poppy*
Radish
Safflower
Saltree
Sea buckthorn
Sesame
Shea butter *Shea tree*
Soybean
Sunflower
Sweet flag
Tamarind
Tea oil *Camellia*

Tsubaki oil *Camellia*
Tung oil *Tung oil tree*

ORNAMENT
Alabaster
Cobaltite
Coco de mer
Corals
Gold
Ivory *Ivory palm*
Jade
Magnesite
Marble
Niobium
Obsidian
Poultry
Quartz
Rhodochrosite
Rhodonite
Serpentine

PAPER
Papyrus
Rice paper *Rice-paper plant*
Tapa cloth *Paper mulberry*

PESTICIDE
Betony
Croton
Diatomaceous earth
Mammee
Nicotine *Tobacco*
Pyrethrum
Quassin *Quassia*
Strychnine *Nux vomica*

PIGMENT
Alkanet *Alkanet*
Bismuth
Bistre *Beech tree*
Brazilin *Brazilwood*
Carmine *Cochineal*

Carthamin *Safflower*

Chromium

Cobalt

Galls

Hematite

Ilmenite

Lapis lazuli

Neodymium

Ochre

Pyrolusite

Realgar

Selenium

Sepia *Cuttlefish*

PLASTIC

Celluloid

Maize

Okonite *Ozokerite*

Petroleum

POTTERY

Clay

Feldspar

Fire clay

Kaolin

Microcline

Quartz

Sand

Silicon

Sillimanite

Witherite

RESIN

Amboyna wood

Agarwood *Lign aloes*

Anime *Amami-gum*

Baeltree

Balm of Gilead *Commiphora*

Bdellium *Commiphora*

Benzoin *Benzoin tree*

Birch tar *Birch tree*

Blue gum tree

Cajuput

Camphor *Camphor tree*

Kapur tree

Canada balsam *Balsam fir*

Cashew

Copaiba

Copal *Zanzibar copal*

Kauri

Copal tree

Dammar gum *Saltree*

White dammar

Dogbane

Douglas fir

Dragon's Blood *Rattan*

Elemi

Frankincense tree

Galls

Gamboge *Gamboge tree*

Ghatti gum *Axlewood*

Gum arabic *Gum arabic tree*

Halmaddi *Halmaddi*

Juniper

Lac *Lac insect*

Lacquer *Lacquer tree*

Larch

Lignum-vitae

Mammee

Mastic *Mastic tree*

Myrrh *Myrrh tree*

Oakmoss

Opopanax *Commiphora*

Propolis *Honey bee*

Pyrethrum *Pyrethrum*

Rosin *Pine tree*

Sandarac *Cypress-pine*

Sandarac cypress

Spruce

Storax *Sweetgum tree*

Tragacanth *Milkvetch*

Turpentine *Terebinth*

Fir tree, Pine tree

SHELL

Cuttlefish
Nacre *Oyster (pearl)*
Tortoiseshell *Hawksbill sea turtle*

SPICE

Ajowan
Allspice
Anise
Canella tree
Caraway
Cardamom
Celery
Chili pepper
Cinnamon *Cinnamomum*
Clove
Coriander
Cubeb
Cumin
Fennel
Ginger
Grains of paradise
Grains of Selim
Korarima
Mace *Nutmeg*
Mountain pepper
Mustard
Nutmeg
Papaya
Peppercorn *Black pepper*
Saffron *Saffron crocus*
Star anise
Sumac
Tonka bean *Cumaru*
Turmeric
Vanilla *Vanilla orchid*
Wasabi
Winter's bark
Zedoary

THICKENING AGENT

Alginate *Giant kelp*
Corn starch *Maize*
Guar gum *Guar bean*

TOOL

Agate
Flint
Jade
Metals
Millstone *Burrstone*
Obsidian
Wood

UTENSIL

Calabash *Calabash tree*
Calabash vine

Coco de mer
Clay
Loofah *Loofa*
Meerschaum
Metals
Papyrus
Reed (common)
Sponge
Wood

WATER PURIFIER

Activated carbon
Alum *Alunite*
Aragonite
Charcoal *Wood*
Diatomaceous earth
Montan wax *Coal*
Reed (common)

WAX

Beeswax *Honey bee*
Candelilla wax *Candelilla*
Carnauba wax *Carnauba palm*
Ceresine *Ozokerite*
Chinese tallowtree

Lac insect
Wax myrtle
Jojoba oil   *Jojoba*

WOOD

Acacia
Agarwood   *Lign aloes*
Amami-gum
Amboyna wood *Amboyna tree*
Andiroba
Apple
Ash tree
Aspen
Axlewood
Baeltree
Balata
Balsa tree
Balsam fir
Banyan tree
Barwood tree
Beech tree
Birch tree
Blue gum tree
Boxwood
Brazilnut tree
Brazilwood
Breadfruit
Cajuput
Camphortree
Candlenut tree
Canella tree
Catechu
Cedar
Champak
Cherry tree
Chestnut tree
Chilean hazelnut
Coast redwood
Cork   *Cork oak*
Cumaru

Cypress-pine
Deodar cedar
Dogwood tree
Douglas fir
Ebony tree
Elm
Eucalyptus
Excelsior   *Aspen*
Flame of the Forest tree
Fujian cypress
Giant sequoia
Hackberry
Hawthorn
Hazel
Heather
Hemlock tree
Hickory tree
Holly
Hornbeam
Horse chestnut
Ibope
Incense cedar
Ipe
Jackfruit
Jandi
Japanese red cedar
Jarrah
Jujube
Juniper
Kapur tree
Karri
Lignum vitae   *Lignum-vitae*
                    Verawood
Linden
Mahogany
Maple tree
Marri tree
Mesquite
Mindanao gum
Monkeypod

271

Oak
Olive tree
Oregon myrtle
Osage orange
Pear
Pecan tree
Persimmon
Pine tree
Poplar
Quebracho
Ramin
Rosewood
Saltree
Sandalwood
Sandarac cypress
Sassafras
Silver fir
Spindle tree
Spruce
Sweetgum tree
Sycamore
Tamarind
Teak
Tuliptree
Upas tree
Walnut
Willow
Winter's bark
Withy *Osier*
Yellowwood
Yew tree